Home
Automation

FOR

DUMMIES®

A Wiley Brand

Home Automation

FOR

DUMMIES®

A Wiley Brand

by Dwight Spivey

Home Automation For Dummies®

Published by: **John Wiley & Sons, Inc.,** 111 River Street, Hoboken, NJ 07030-5774, www.wiley.com

Copyright © 2015 by John Wiley & Sons, Inc., Hoboken, New Jersey

Published simultaneously in Canada

For general information on our other products and services, please contact our Customer Care Department within the U.S. at 877-762-2974, outside the U.S. at 317-572-3993, or fax 317-572-4002. For technical support, please visit www.wiley.com/techsupport.

Wiley publishes in a variety of print and electronic formats and by print-on-demand. Some material included with standard print versions of this book may not be included in e-books or in print-on-demand. If this book refers to media such as a CD or DVD that is not included in the version you purchased, you may download this material at http://booksupport.wiley.com. For more information about Wiley products, visit www.wiley.com.

Library of Congress Control Number: 2014946669

ISBN: 978-1-118-94926-9

ISBN 978-1-118-94926-9 (pbk); ISBN 978-1-118-94927-6 (ebk); ISBN 978-1-118-94964-1 (ebk)

Manufactured in the United States of America

10 9 8 7 6 5 4 3 2 1

Contents at a Glance

Introduction 1

Part I: Introducing Home Automation 5
Chapter 1: Home Automation 101..7
Chapter 2: What You Need to Get Started 23
Chapter 3: Determining Your Home Automation Needs (and Wants) 37

Part II: Automating Inside Your Home 49
Chapter 4: Keeping Your Cool or Turning Up the Heat 51
Chapter 5: Nice and Tidy Does It! 75
Chapter 6: I'm in the Mood for . . . Anything: Automated Lighting..........89
Chapter 7: Safe, Sound, and Hunkered Down................................109
Chapter 8: Home, Home on the Automatic Range:
   The Automated Kitchen 135
Chapter 9: Monitoring Water Use and Detecting Leaks....................155
Chapter 10: Smart Home Entertainment 165

Part III: Automating Outside Your Home..................... 189
Chapter 11: Checking the Weather...191
Chapter 12: Your Grandfather's Dream, Your Reality:
   Automating Lawn Care 205

Part IV: Taking Command of Your Home
Automation Systems 225
Chapter 13: Working with Mobile Devices and Computers..................227
Chapter 14: Controlling Your Home from One Platform....................249

Part V: The Part of Tens 265
Chapter 15: Ten Easy Ways to Begin Automating Your Home...............267
Chapter 16: Ten Great Websites for Home Automation 285
Chapter 17: Ten Other Options for Automating Your Life 301

Index 319

Table of Contents

Introduction *1*

About This Book 2
Foolish Assumptions 2
Icons Used in This Book 3
Beyond the Book 4
Where to Go from Here 4

Part I: Introducing Home Automation *5*

Chapter 1: Home Automation 101 .... **7**

Defining Home Automation 8
   Doing it the old-fashioned way 8
   Automating homes today 10
Benefitting from Home Automation 11
   Convenience is key! 11
   S-E-C-U-R-I-T-Y 13
   The bottom line: $ 15
Understanding the Tech Involved in Home Automation 16
   The technical state of home automation today 16
   Current home networking protocols 17
   The future of home automation technology 22

Chapter 2: What You Need to Get Started **23**

Happiness Is a Wireless Network 24
   Preparing your network for the extra load 24
   Being cautious when adding new devices to your network 27
Having the Right Tools for the Job 30
   Actual tools you'll need 31
   Computers and smartphones and tablets, oh my! 31
   Power to get the job done 33

**Chapter 3: Determining Your Home Automation Needs
(and Wants)** **37**

Considering Factors Before You Buy 38
   Identifying your automation goals 38
   Assess your needs 43
Deciding How Much You Want to Automate 46
   Starting small 46
   Going LARGE 47

Part II: Automating Inside Your Home 49

Chapter 4: Keeping Your Cool or Turning Up the Heat 51

Controlling Your Thermostat from Afar 52
How setting temps remotely benefits you 52
The tech behind the thermostat 53
Introducing the Big Players in the Thermostat Arena 54
Honeywell 54
Nest 58
Belkin 61
ecobee 63
Lennox 67
Trane 70
Venstar 73

Chapter 5: Nice and Tidy Does It! 75

Cleaning Up While You're Away 76
Keeping clean while on the go 76
Automating cleaning chores..76
Understanding how it all works 77
Introducing a Who's Who of the Remote Cleaning World......................77
iRobot 77
LG 82
RoboMop...82
Neato Robotics 84
Grillbot 85
RoboSnail 87

Chapter 6: I'm in the Mood for . . . Anything: Automated Lighting 89

Lighting Your Life Automatically 90
Reasons for automatic lighting 90
Auto-lighting technology...91
Illuminating the Kings of Automatic Lighting 92
Philips 93
INSTEON..97
TCP 102
SmartThings 104
Belkin 107

Chapter 7: Safe, Sound, and Hunkered Down 109

Establishing Security in the Automatic Age......................................110
Keeping your eyes homeward...111
Locking things down 111

Staking Out the Wardens of Home Security 112
    SmartThings 112
    Belkin 114
    Alarm.com 115
    ADT 117
    Vivint 118
    Schlage 120
    August 123
    Yale 125
    Lockitron 126
    Kwikset 129
    Piper 132

Chapter 8: Home, Home on the Automatic Range: The Automated Kitchen 135
    Cooking Without Being in the Kitchen, and Other Kitchen Awesomeness 136
    Checking Out the Top Home Automation Chefs..........................137
        Crock-Pot with WeMo 137
        LG 139
        Whirlpool 141
        GE 143
        iDevices 145
        Quirky 152

Chapter 9: Monitoring Water Use and Detecting Leaks 155
    Watching Your Water Usage 156
        The why's of monitoring water 156
        The how's of monitoring water 157
    Assessing the Water Monitoring Mavens 157
        Wally 158
        Driblet 160
        INSTEON 162

Chapter 10: Smart Home Entertainment 165
    Modernizing Home Entertainment 166
        Home entertainment today..166
        Smart home entertainment technology 167
    Introducing the Smart Home Entertainment Gurus 168
        Roomie 168
        Blumoo 172
        Logitech 173
        Apple 176
        Roku 178
        Google...181
        Bose 185
        Sonos 186

Part III: Automating Outside Your Home 189

Chapter 11: Checking the Weather 191
Keeping Tabs on the Weather 191
Checking the Weather Automatically 192
   Netatmo 193
   ARCHOS 197
   AcuRite 199

Chapter 12: Your Grandfather's Dream, Your Reality: Automating Lawn Care 205
Caring for Your Lawn Doesn't Have to Break Your Back 206
   Reasons for automating lawn care 206
   Lawn care tasks that you can automate 207
Getting to Know the Top Companies in Lawn Automation 207
   Robomow 208
   Husqvarna 211
   LawnBott 214
   Robotic mowers around the world 216
Watering Your Lawn Automatically 220
   Cyber Rain 220
   Rachio 222

Part IV: Taking Command of Your Home Automation Systems 225

Chapter 13: Working with Mobile Devices and Computers 227
Discovering Devices Commonly Used for Smart Home Automation 228
   Smartphones 228
   Tablets 235
   Computers 239
Keeping Apps Up-to-Date 245
   iOS 245
   Android 247
   OS X 247
   Windows 248

Chapter 14: Controlling Your Home from One Platform 249
Examining the Lack of Unity 250
   Recognizing the "higgledy-piggledy" state of home automation 250
   Seeing ways to achieve platform unity 251

Choosing the Single-Platform Path 251
    Peeling Apple's HomeKit 252
    Wink-ing at Home Depot 255
Opting for Multi-Protocol Solutions 257
    Revolv-ing around a hub 257
    Building your CastleOS 259
    Link(sys)ing with Staples Connect 262

Part V: The Part of Tens 265

Chapter 15: Ten Easy Ways to Begin Automating Your Home 267

Wink 268
    Philips Hue products 269
    Dropcam 271
    Nest Protect 272
    Quirky Spotter 274
    Quirky+GE Pivot Power Genius 275
    Leviton Dimming Plug-In Lamp Module 276
    Quirky Tripper 277
WeMo 279
    Insight Switch 279
    NetCam 280
    LED Lighting 282

Chapter 16: Ten Great Websites for Home Automation 285

Smarthome 285
CNET 287
CEA 288
SmartThings 289
Amazon 290
Home Controls 292
Z-Wave.com 294
ZigBee Alliance 295
Lowes 296
Home Depot 297

Chapter 17: Ten Other Options for Automating Your Life 301

Cleaning Your Home's Gutters 302
Making a Robot Part of Your Family 303
Feeding Pets While You're Away 305

Cleaning Up Kitty Litter 307
    Using standard litter...307
    A kitty toilet? Why, yes, indeed!..308
Cleaning Your Pool the Robotic Way.......................................308
Waking Up to a Fresh Cup of Joe...310
Starting Your Vehicle Remotely...311
Flushing Your Troubles Away Automatically 312
Pulling the Shades from Across the Room..............................314
Controlling Your Home's Humidity...316

Index *319*

Introduction

*F*lying was a pleasure meant only for birds or for fools jumping off a cliff with homemade wings. The stuff of fancy and fantastical tales. In 1903, a couple of brothers put that kind of talk to rest with the first flights of their Flyer in North Carolina.

Computers in the home was something only seen in science-fiction films until a few kids got together in one of their parents' garage and created a little thing they called the Apple I. According to Forrest Gump, that little "fruit company" has done quite well since those days.

Staying on that theme, folks used to think that teleportation was only possible in *Star Trek,* but just yesterday I was beamed from my local transporter to our secret moon base in no time flat! It was really — uh oh! I'm not supposed to talk about that yet . . . just forget you read that last paragraph, please.

Nothing to see here. Moving on.

The point is that when it comes to technology, fiction can often become reality. The fiction of being able to automate our homes became a reality a few decades ago, but it was something only the very (and I do mean *very*) well-heeled could afford. Since the advent of the smartphone (there's that "fruit company" again) and the proliferation of cellular networks, we have had greater access to each other and our world than we've ever dreamed. As smartphones and apps have grown in popularity, so has the need to use them in ways many of us couldn't have conceived of before. Today we not only can make calls and send texts, but we also use our smartphones (and tablets) for watching movies, catching up on the news, checking weather forecasts, viewing live sporting events, listening to our favorite music, and many more tasks that Isaac Asimov couldn't have thought of.

Wi-Fi networks and the Internet have also opened the door (in some cases literally) to a whole new level of home accessibility: using our smart devices and apps with our home's Wi-Fi network to remotely control and automate tasks in our home. You can use your iOS or Android device to adjust the temperature, set the mood with customized lighting schemes, preheat the oven so you can cook your meal the moment you walk in the door, and even tell your lawn mower to start cutting your grass. That's just scratching the surface of what you can do with today's smart home automation technology — and in this book, I happily tackle the subject with you.

About This Book

This book introduces you to the smart home revolution, which is today's way of automating and/or remotely controlling common, everyday tasks via your smartphone or tablet (and in some cases, your computer), your home's Wi-Fi network, and the Internet. My aim throughout the tome is to explain why you want to automate, how you can do so, and just what you can accomplish with it. This book also shows you a multitude of the aforementioned tasks that you can accomplish using automation and/or remote control, and how to go about the process of automating those tasks. I discuss not only tasks and the technologies, but also the companies that are the major players in today's emerging smart home market.

The *For Dummies* series of books has been helping folks (like me) make the most of technology and other things that enhance our lives when we are properly taught how to utilize them, and I've written this book using those wonderful time-tested methods. The organization of this series is stuff of legend, and I've made sure not to deviate from them. Feel free to jump around as you like, or follow along in exact page order — whatever suits your needs. After all, this book is for you to learn about smart home automation, and it's designed to help folks at various levels learn as they see fit.

Some items in the book, such as sidebars and Technical Stuff, are simply there because I thought they were neat. Don't get me wrong, they do contain helpful information, but feel free to skip them if you like.

You'll find this book is absolutely chock-full of URLs (otherwise known as webpage addresses) that you can use to check out the products I discuss. All of them were functional at the time of this writing, but trust me when I say that URLs can — and do — change often.

While reading this book, you may notice that some web addresses break across two lines of text. If you're reading this book in print and want to visit one of these webpages, simply key in the web address exactly as it's noted in the text, pretending as though the line break doesn't exist (this might be hard for some English majors, but give it a try anyway). If you're reading this as an e-book, you've got it easy — just click the web address to go directly to the webpage.

Foolish Assumptions

Dear reader, you assume a certain amount of knowledge and expertise from me as the author of this book. I, too, have certain expectations of you, my audience, when it comes to your ability to put the information contained herein to good use.

I assume that you are familiar with the Internet, and have at least a cursory knowledge of your home's Wi-Fi network (which I also naturally assume you have). If you don't know diddly about either of these things, you'll definitely want to bone up on the subjects before delving into this tome too deeply. I don't expect you to know how to create a website, how to run Ethernet cable throughout your home, or how to set up a network that even the federal government couldn't crack into. However, you should at least know how to surf the web and how to successfully connect to and use your computer and smart devices, like phones and tablets, with your Wi-Fi network.

If at this point you're wondering what all this talk is about computers and smart devices, my advice to you is to immediately put this book down after completing this paragraph. Next, peruse your local bookstore (I'm safely assuming you're not reading this book's introduction on Amazon.com) for other *For Dummies* titles that will catch you up to the rest of the world in those subjects of interest. When you're ready, I'll be here waiting to guide you on into the wonderful world of the smart home.

I do not assume that you have any clue about how to rewire your home's electrical system or network cabling. For the record, neither is required to perform any of the tasks in this book.

Icons Used in This Book

Throughout this book I highlight items that I think deserve your attention just slightly outside of what I discuss in the primary material, or maybe I expand on a topic. I use the following icons to accomplish this:

Give close attention to items beside this icon. They generally will help you achieve results being covered more easily, or may help you avoid pratfalls in the process. Tips also may point you in a different direction entirely.

I know folks who use anything from reminders on their smartphones to writing notes on their hands with Sharpies to make sure they don't forget important goings-on. The Remember icon is the *For Dummies* way of doing something along those lines, helping you to remember important things relevant to the topic at hand.

When you see this icon, watch out! There's something here that I really want to alert you to regarding the current topic of discussion. An example would be if a certain home automation protocol would conflict with other protocols in your current home automation setup, I would certainly make you privy to that knowledge in a Warning icon.

Geeks rejoice! This icon alerts you to items that may be of interest to you in your quest for home automation. Topics featured with this icon may or may not be exactly relevant to the one being discussed in the chapter, or may be something pertaining to topical trivialities. I just couldn't help myself and thought you might be interested in them, so there.

Beyond the Book

I've put a ton of information between the covers of this book, but there's even more information that you can access on www.dummies.com, such as

- ✔ I provide you with a Cheat Sheet at www.dummies.com/cheatsheet/ homeautomation that lists the following:

  - The best home lighting devices

  - The top smart thermostats

  - Wi-Fi routers to use with your smart home automation system

- ✔ You also will find extra helpful online articles at www.dummies.com/ extras/homeautomation that discuss

  - The best smartphones and tablets

  - Streaming media providers

  - Ten top whole-home automation companies (they do all the work for you, in other words)

  - A list of links to all the outdoor home automation products I mention in Chapters 11 and 12

Where to Go from Here

I wrote *Home Automation For Dummies* with the idea in mind that you, dear reader, would be able to tackle the subject either in the order that it's written or in bits and bites as you desire. In other words, there is no one way in which you must read this book. I will say, however, that if you're a complete newbie at this whole smart home thing, you'll be best served to start at Part I; from there you'll have enough of a frame of reference to understand the subjects in the other four parts.

Congratulations on automating and remotely controlling your home. Ain't technology great? I guarantee you'll think so when you're enjoying a nice evening on the town with a loved one and you receive a text from your robotic lawn mower letting you know the mowing has been finished.

Part I
Introducing Home Automation

getting started

with

Home Automation

In this part . . .

- ✔ Discover the "smart" way to automate your home with Wi-Fi and smart devices.

- ✔ Understand the benefits of automating your home.

- ✔ Know what you'll need to get started with smart home automation.

- ✔ Determine what tasks in the home you want to automate.

Chapter 1

Home Automation 101

● ●

In This Chapter

▶ Examining changes in home automation over the years

▶ Benefitting from automating your home

▶ Understanding home automation technology

● ●

"*H*ow do we make life better?"

"How do we make more time for what really matters?"

"Why can't television commercials for technology companies incorporate music that doesn't involve finger snaps, hand claps, xylophones, and ukuleles?"

Those three questions haunt me every day, as I'm sure they do you, gentle reader. However, only the first two issues are ones that I think mankind will actually be able to do anything about in the near future. That said, I concentrate on those in this book.

People have always had to work, and we've always tried to find ways to make that work easier, whether by developing better tools and technologies to do the work or by making other folks or things do the work for us. Sick of digging up dirt with your bare hands to plant seeds? Let's invent the plow and make our cattle do the heavy lifting. No longer want to beat your clothes with a rock in the nearest creek? We'll invent the washing machine, then. Don't want to carry ten jugs with you to the river to gather water? By George, I think aqueducts and plumbing might be a good idea. We are always on the lookout for ways to do tasks better or shirk them altogether — and that's a good thing, if you ask me.

Home automation is yet another step in this struggle for making life better. Some folks may scoff at the idea that automation means life is better, but I'll bet those same folks don't mind using a gas or electric mower when it comes time to cut the lawn. I'll wager a pretty penny that they really appreciate their automatic dishwashers and their refrigerators, too. Time marches on — and so does technology.

Defining Home Automation

Let's see . . . if I were to give my own definition of what home automation is, I'd first look at the definitions for each of the two words that make up the phrase. For that task, I consult the *Merriam-Webster* website (www.merriam-webster.com):

- ✔ **home (noun):** the place (such as house or apartment) where a person lives
- ✔ **automation (noun):** automatically controlled operation of an apparatus, process, or system by mechanical or electronic devices that take the place of human labor

Combining the two definitions, I initially conclude that home automation is the act of automatically controlling tasks within the home that are normally performed through an act of human labor. While this sounds neat and orderly, it actually isn't so (but it's getting there, and quickly). Home automation has been around for a long time, but it's beginning to really take off for consumers at all price points in this Internet age.

That said, and before I get too far ahead of myself, let's take a brief look at how home automation has been achieved in the past and how it's getting done these days.

Doing it the old-fashioned way

"Is there an old-fashioned way of doing home automation?" you ask. My reply: "Yes, indeed."

Before I get too far afield, allow me to define what I mean by "old-fashioned" in terms of home automation: spending thousands (and sometimes tens of thousands) of dollars to implement customized automation solutions within a section of your home (such as the entertainment room seen in Figure 1-1) or throughout the entire space.

Home automation has been around for quite a while, but some of its technology tended to be available primarily for folks with fat bank accounts. Why? Glad you asked.

- ✔ Home automation used to be a specialty premium service, requiring a great deal of money to manufacture.
- ✔ Installing a home automation system often required extensive rewiring and other electrical work.

✔ Ongoing support and maintenance of a customized home automation solution was (and in some cases, still is) expensive by nature.

✔ Systems were truly customized to the individual home, creating higher costs.

These are just some of the reasons for the super-high cost of past systems, and for the still-high costs of similar comprehensive home automation solutions today. Controlling your entire home's lighting just wasn't something that most of the housing market was doing until recently. Also, old-fashioned home automation was something you did within the confines of your home; rarely were you able to handle tasks remotely. Some home automation technologies, such as intercoms and garage door openers, were never as expensive as others to implement, and therefore more prevalent in homes. However, they were the exception rather than the rule.

Before I finish this section, I want to make it understood that I see nothing wrong with whole-home, customized automation, and many companies today excel at it (and bully for you if you have the moola to do it!).

Figure 1-1: This entertainment room is fantastic, fun, beautiful, and by no means inexpensive.

Image courtesy of Home Entertainment, Inc.

Self-installing a home automation system

I'm certain some of you handier folks reading this book (for which I humbly thank you, by the way) are thinking about implementing the type of whole-home system I just described yourself, and that's certainly a possibility. However, depending on the extent you want to automate your home, the time needed will be great, the work involved will be monumental, and the cost will still be up there a bit. I'm not trying to discourage do-it-yourselfers at all, if that's truly what you want to do, but if you think you might be even the slightest bit concerned about my earlier caveats, either let companies that specialize in these kinds of installations handle it for you, or please do read on with an expectation that you can learn how to automate your home without tremendous headaches and hassles.

If you are interested in this particular type of home automation, by all means, visit the websites for these wonderful companies that are more than capable of helping you make your home automation dreams come to life:

- Home Entertainment, Inc.: www.homeentertainmentinc.com
- Crestron: www.crestron.com
- Savant: www.savant.com
- Control4: www.control4.com

Automating homes today

I don't know about you, but most people would jump at the chance to automate more things in their lives if doing so were affordable and could be achieved with reasonably minimal effort. Well, you're in luck. Most of us are able to automate at least certain aspects of home life today because they don't cost an arm or a leg, and they aren't difficult to install.

Home Automation For Dummies focuses on how you can simply and relatively inexpensively control many of your daily tasks. Not only that, most of what I cover can be handled remotely, meaning you don't even have to be at home to do this awesome stuff.

Today, all you need to implement a home automation system is an Internet connection and (in some cases, but not all) a device to control it, such as a smartphone, table, or computer. Of course, you have to purchase a system or appliances, but many of them that utilize your Wi-Fi network (or even your home's power lines) are inexpensive. Another bonus with today's home automation technology is that you can start as small as you like and build up to as large as you like. For example, with a kit such as the WeMo Switch + Motion kit from Belkin (see Figure 1-2), you can begin with just a smart wall outlet and a motion detector, but can add more and more WeMo devices to your heart's content.

Figure 1-2:
Starting with a beginner's kit, like this one from Belkin, you can start small with home automation and work your way up.

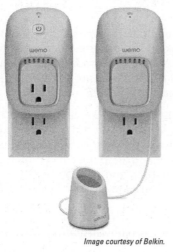

Image courtesy of Belkin.

Benefitting from Home Automation

The idea of home automation is really cool and futuristic, but if that's your only motivation to automate the things in your home, you just might be missing the forest for the trees. Sure, you can impress friends by turning on your fireplace with a tap of your iPhone, but benefits of home automation go way beyond bragging rights.

Convenience is key!

Convenience is indeed the key; otherwise, what's truly the point? The words "home" and "automation" fit together perfectly to describe how to get things done easier, better, and faster than ever before, which equates to convenience.

Want a few examples of how today's home automation is convenient? Okay, here you go:

- Your teenage son calls from a friend's cellphone and tells you he's locked his keys and everything else he owns in the car you let him borrow. This kid is 30 minutes away — not good. Suddenly you remember you had installed a device in your car that enables you to unlock it (and even start it) from a million miles away with your smartphone. A few taps and swipes on your phone, and your son is back in the car. Convenience.

- The lawn needs mowing before company arrives this weekend, but you've been in meetings all week on the other side of the country, and now you're stuck in the airport. Whip out your Android phone, open your robotic lawn mower's app, and tell it to get to work. The lawn's done before your plane even lands. Convenience.

- You and the family are singing "Let It Go" of *Frozen* fame for the 100th time on your road trip to Disney World when it dawns on you (three hours away from home) that you left the lights on and an electric heater running in the bathroom. You calmly fire up your iOS tablet, open the app for your home automation system, and turn off the lights and the outlet the heater is plugged in to. Dare I use the "C" word again? You bet I do. Convenience.

Here are a few other things you can do conveniently *from anywhere* with today's home automation:

- Adjust your home's thermostat.

- Control your sprinkler system.

- Preheat your oven from anywhere, with an app like GE's Brillion (along with supported appliances, of course), seen in Figure 1-3.

- Unlock or lock your front door.

- Raise or lower the window shades.

- Change the schedule of your coffee pot.

- Initiate a washing or drying cycle.

- Clean your aquarium.

- Control how much television your kids watch.

- Keep tabs on how much electricity you're using.

- Be alerted to a water leak in your bathroom.

- Find out if someone enters your home unannounced.

- Clean your cat's kitty litter.

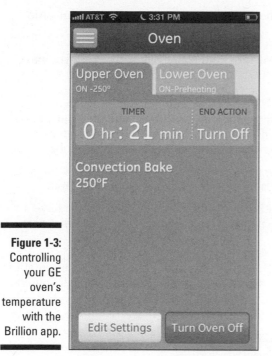

Figure 1-3:
Controlling
your GE
oven's
temperature
with the
Brillion app.

I'm sure things are starting to click for you when I say that remotely controlled home automation affords a level of convenience that most people have not yet experienced. And that list just scratches the surface!

S·E·C·U·R·I·T·y

Fewer things in life are more appreciated than security — in this case, knowing (or at least feeling) that you're more safe doing things a certain way or using certain devices. Today's Internet-based home automation technology gives one just that kind of security.

Sure, home security companies have been in existence for decades now, and they are great at what they do. People also have had personal means of protection that usually work as intended, provided they're used properly. Security cameras have also been providing more home security for some time, although they typically were expensive to install. With today's tech,

however, you can secure your home in myriad ways you never were able
to before:

- ✔ Wi-Fi cameras provide a look into your home from anywhere you have
  an Internet connection.

- ✔ Motion detectors keep you privy to any activity in your home.

- ✔ Smart locks and security apps, such as the one from alarm.com shown
  in Figure 1-4, allow you to lock and unlock your doors, no matter
  whether you're home or visiting family halfway around the globe.

- ✔ When coupled with the use of door and window sensors, apps can alert
  you via text or email when someone enters your home uninvited.

- ✔ You can control lighting within your home from anywhere you have a
  connection to the Internet, making it appear to folks outside that someone is home.

And these are just some of the things that Internet-enabled home automation
systems and devices can do to help raise your level of personal and family
security.

Figure 1-4:
Apps and
smart
locks work
together to
keep your
home safe
and secure,
and alert
you to any
problems.

Image courtesy of Alarm.com.

The bottom line: $

Sooner or later, I have to delve into the bottom line: money. Now is as good a time as any.

Today's Internet and network-based home automation technologies are much more wallet-friendly than whole-home options. The savings between the two home automation routes is astronomical: I'm talking low hundreds for the former and well into the thousands for the latter. Of course, the amount you spend on either totally depends on what you want to do, but the gap is still significant no matter how high-powered you go with Internet and network-based solutions. Attaining an equal amount of control with a whole-home solution will run your initial costs sky high due to the labor and technology involved.

Here's how today's home automation technology can help you save your precious and hard-earned cash:

✔ Probably the most obvious money savings can be achieved by a reduction in lighting costs. With today's solutions, you can remotely control lighting to the *nth* degree:

  • Turn lights on or off with a touch of your smartphone or tablet's screen.

  • Create lighting schedules so that lights come on and go off at designated times.

  • Tie your lights into motion sensors so that lights come on when you enter a room and go off when you leave it.

  • Dim lights automatically based on other lighting conditions in the room, such as sunlight directly coming through windows or skylights during certain hours of the day.

  • Smart, low-wattage LED bulbs, like INSTEON's 2672-222 (see Figure 1-5), can provide nearly or the same amount of light as standard bulbs running at much higher wattages.

  • Smart LED bulbs don't need replacing nearly as frequently as standard bulbs, saving you tons in bulb costs over the life span of the LED.

  • Smart LED bulbs put off much less heat, so cooling and heating costs are affected.

✔ Water leak detection can prevent a high water bill, and also the some- times enormous costs of water damage.

✔ Keeping home temperatures level saves a chunk of change over fluc- tuating temps. Also, turning thermostats on or off remotely can save a bundle, too.

✔ You save fuel when you don't have to turn around and go home because you did something like forget to lock the front door when you ran out. Just use the app on your smartphone to lock the deadbolt while motoring along on your merry way.

✔ Robotic mowers save money on gas because they use electricity. With prices like they are at the pump, this can translate into big savings.

As long as you use your home automation technology in an intelligent way, you will save money compared to operating things status quo. There's no way around it.

Figure 1-5:
Smart LED bulbs save you lots of coin.

Image courtesy of INSTEON.

Understanding the Tech Involved in Home Automation

As with everything else in the world of computers and electronic devices, home automation only gets better as it moves forward. Technology in modern computers has jumped light-years over the decades, as has tech used in how people make and listen to music. In the same way, home automation tech has moved from the Stone Age to something most of us are totally at home with: the Internet.

The technical state of home automation today

Home automation technology has changed a great deal over the decades. Certain communication protocols (more on those as you continue to read) used for home automation have been around for a long time and, unfortunately, some are getting rather long in the tooth. Others, though, have retained their popularity and are still in widespread use.

The way that home automation worked in whole-home solutions of the past was that a central controller was placed in the home and the user controlled it through wall-mounted keypads and remote control boxes.

These days, whole-home solutions are much improved and incorporate Internet and network-based technologies to connect you to your home. You can also remotely control your home using smartphones and tablets. The operating systems are typically customized for their clients, though, as is everything in a whole-home system.

Modular Internet and network-based solutions that utilize apps and the web are taking the market by storm, due to affordability, convenience, and the capability to be added on to.

Another factor in their growth is that folks are familiar with their modes of usage. Lots and lots of people have smartphones and tablets today, and most of those devices are running on iOS or Android operating systems. The modular home automation solutions allow you to buy products that you interact with through other products (your smart devices and home network) that you're already familiar with. You know how to tap and swipe touchscreens, right? Most apps work the same, or at least similarly, to other apps, so the learning curve isn't steep.

Current home networking protocols

A protocol is a set of rules, or standards, that a technology employs to ensure stability. For example, networking utilizes protocols to keep communications consistent across devices, and those protocols are adhered to across the various platforms they are running within. This same concept applies to home networking technologies, too, with the aim of making sure that various types of automation devices can be controlled by a central device.

Many companies today use more than one home automation protocol in their controller systems, ensuring compatibility with a greater number of devices.

Let's take a look at the most common protocols used in home automation today.

X10

Image courtesy of X10.com.

X10 has been around for as long as I have, since the 1970s, and that can be taken either in a good way or a bad way (much like me, too, I guess). Here's what you need to know about X10:

- ✔ X10 originally was intended solely to use your existing home wiring to communicate with devices.

- ✔ X10 does now have a wireless communication component, but it isn't as robust as others on the market.

- ✔ X10 wasn't originally designed to be used in environments with competing signals and communication protocols, so it doesn't have the same security measures that other protocols do.

Go to `www.x10.org` to find out more about the protocol and devices that support it.

Because power lines are more complex than they used to be, and since X10 is a much older protocol, its speeds aren't all that good. As a matter of fact, if you're new to the home automation game and don't already have an existing X10 environment, it's best to skip X10 and move on to one of the newer protocols.

UPB

Image courtesy of Powerline Control Systems, Inc.

Universal Powerline Bus (UPB) was created by PCS Powerline Control Systems in 1999. Like X10, UPB is designed to work over your home's existing power lines, but unlike X10, it does appear to be fairly stable when it comes to transmitting information. UPB is dissimilar in still another way to X10, but this time, it isn't necessarily a good thing: UPB doesn't support any form of wireless communication. Needless to say, insofar as your search for the right home automation protocol for your needs, UPB shouldn't be too high on the list. (In fact, I don't even discuss it any further.)

Z-Wave

Image courtesy of Z-Wave Alliance.

Z-Wave is one of the most popular protocols in use today; it was developed in 2007 specifically for home automation devices. Well more than 200 companies around the world use Z-Wave. I'd say it's a big deal (as far as home automation goes). More about Z-Wave:

- Products that support Z-Wave work with each other seamlessly, regardless of manufacturer, which makes Z-Wave an even bigger deal.

- Z-Wave devices use very little power, so if they're battery-powered they'll last longer than you might expect. Some products list battery lives in terms of years.

- Z-Wave utilizes a mesh network for communication, meaning that one device passes along information to the next device, and so on down the line.

A really nice website dedicated to all things Z-Wave is www.z-wave.com. If you're considering going with Z-Wave products during your home automation investigation, you'll certainly want to visit the site more than once.

Z-Wave is owned by the Z-Wave Alliance, which has done a great job in getting developers the help they need to create products using the Z-Wave standard. If you're a developer looking to jump into Z-Wave, check out http://z-wave.sigmadesigns.com/.

ZigBee

Image courtesy of ZigBee Alliance.

Like Z-Wave, ZigBee is another relatively new protocol for home automation, and it is also enjoying a certain amount of popularity right now. A few interesting tidbits about ZigBee:

- ✔ ZigBee was developed by the Institute of Electrical and Electronics Engineers (IEEE), the same folks who brought you the networking protocols used by your computers and smart devices.

- ✔ The ZigBee Alliance is tasked with getting the word out about the ZigBee protocol. The Alliance is comprised of a team of businesses, universities, and government agencies interested in pushing the ZigBee message to the masses.

- ✔ ZigBee uses a mesh network to communicate among devices running the protocol, meaning its range and power increase with every device you add to your home automation network.

Intrigued? Visit `www.zigbee.org` for a smorgasbord of information on the protocol.

ZigBee is quite popular, but you must be careful to purchase all your ZigBee-enabled devices from the same manufacturer. Reliability between ZigBee devices made by different companies is suspect, at best, since companies are not forced to deploy ZigBee in the same manner.

INSTEON

I N S T E O N ®

Image courtesy of INSTEON.

The good people at SmartLabs, Inc., came up with INSTEON in 2005, so it is also a relative newcomer to the home automation market. Here are some important things to know about INSTEON:

- ✓ Since INSTEON is owned by SmartLabs, it is able to run a tight ship, as all its devices work together with ease.
- ✓ INSTEON boasts over 200 products that run the home automation gamut:
  - Light bulbs
  - Light switches and dimmers
  - Motion sensors
  - Thermostats
  - Wi-Fi cameras
  - Sprinkler controls

And so much more, I promise!

INSTEON uses dual-band communication in many of its devices, which means it can communicate over both your home's existing power lines and via RF (radio frequency), doubling its effectiveness.

Wi-Fi

Image courtesy of Wi-Fi Alliance.

The newest protocol, at least in terms of its use in home automation, is (are you ready?) Wi-Fi. Obviously, Wi-Fi has been around for quite a while and most of us have used it with laptops and smartphones and tablets for years.

However, only fairly recently have manufacturers begun to develop home automation devices that use it. A bit about Wi-Fi as it pertains to home automation (the good and the bad, by the way):

- Many people already have a Wi-Fi network in their homes, so there's no need to purchase a separate hub to control home automation devices that use Wi-Fi.

- Wi-Fi is fast — maybe. I say maybe because your Wi-Fi network only has so much bandwidth to go around. If your home automation devices are sharing bandwidth with every other conceivable Wi-Fi gadget you own on the market (smartphones, tablets, laptops, game consoles, televisions, you name it), you may experience disruptions and slowdowns in controlling your home auto devices.

- Wi-Fi is a power hog, so you can't use it reliably with devices that need battery power to work. It drains batteries much too quickly.

The Wi-Fi Alliance is a worldwide organization of companies that develop and support Wi-Fi. They're also the folks who came up with the famous Wi-Fi logo you all see whenever you go to Starbucks and your favorite bookstores. To learn more about the Alliance, as well as Wi-Fi itself, check out www.wi-fi.org.

The future of home automation technology

All these aforementioned protocols have their pluses and minuses. By themselves, they don't play very nicely with one another. Other companies, such as Apple and Revolv, have seen this problem coming and are tackling it head on by creating environments that can control several, if not all, of the home automation protocols, tying all your devices together and eliminating the need for you to stick with just one manufacturer. For more in-depth information, read Chapter 14, which covers what I call "home automation oneness."

Chapter 2

What You Need to Get Started

In This Chapter

▶ Assessing your home network's capability to work with home automation

▶ Making sure your network is safe from intruders

▶ Understanding which items you'll need to begin automating your home

*P*reparation is key to most things we do: There's no getting around it, unless you're one of those folks who just "wings it."

Your girlfriend has just accepted your invitation to marriage. What do you think happens next? Now, there may be that infinitesimally small faction out there who did just "wing it," finding the local parson and getting hitched right away. But for the most part, the newly minted fiancée (with the help of every other female she's ever met) immediately sets about the tasks that any bride-to-be should: finding a dress, caterer, reception hall, baker, flowers, invitations, music, and on and on the list goes. By the time she's ready to walk down the aisle, everything imaginable has been checked, double-checked, triple-checked, and checked once more for good measure. Your fiancée's hard work may look like nothing more than a big hoopla at the time, but it will be the reason you have beautiful memories of that day 30 years from now.

How about kids and school? More than a little preparation goes into the first day of school, especially if you have more than one child. Your school makes a list, seemingly as long as your arm, and off you go to the store. You dive into the sea of other parents, which resembles a mosh pit of sorts, searching for the items on your list. Of course, your child's teacher has listed the rarest birds in school supplies, such as the three-subject winged college-ruled hot pink notebook with built-in cup holder. Regardless, once you're home with your hard-won supplies and get everything for that glorious first day, something just feels good about it — really good. Of course, if you're smart like my wife, you skip the stores and do your shopping online, but I digress.

If "winging it" is your cup of tea, this chapter might not be, but I still encourage you to read on. You might discover a nugget or two tucked away in here that will spark you to at least be kinda sorta prepared for setting up your home automation system.

Happiness Is a Wireless Network

Are you old enough to recall a day when you had to sit with your computer, whether it was a laptop or not, at a dedicated location where you could connect it to a network cable? Of course you are; it wasn't that long ago that Wi-Fi came into the main. While the capabilities to quickly transfer files to servers, email your buddies, and surf the web were awesome, you still were tethered to that one spot.

While Wi-Fi was slowly gaining more steam thanks to better and less expensive laptops, it wasn't until the advent of the smartphone that Wi-Fi began to proliferate. Once Steve Jobs first introduced the world to the iPhone, and the only way to connect it to the Internet was wirelessly, you immediately knew the world and the way you communicated in it were about to change. Even though the full ramifications of a truly wireless world hadn't quite yet hit home for most of us, you couldn't help but know that life was better without the tether.

Nowadays most people with Internet access in their homes run a Wi-Fi network of some kind using a wireless router (like the two shown in Figure 2-1). We can now walk around the house as we listen to streaming music on our smartphones without a wire visible (save for the headphones' wires, unless they're Bluetooth).

Preparing your network for the extra load

A wireless network is like any other in that it can efficiently handle only so much workload. Thankfully, routers can handle pretty hefty workloads due to high bandwidth support. *Bandwidth,* for those who don't know, is the measure of the amount of information a network device can pass through at any one time.

In today's homes, wireless networks are being put to the test. A single home wireless network may be doing all the heavy lifting for a plethora of devices:

- Multiple smartphones are common in homes today, and more often than not, those folks who don't have unlimited data plans with their cell provider will want to use their Wi-Fi network for surfing the web and conducting other Internet-based tasks.

- Multiple tablets in a home translate into a heavier load on a wireless network; there's no other way to connect them to the Internet.

- Multiple laptops in a home also cause a drag on your wireless network.

✔ Other devices, such as streaming media players like Roku devices (shown in Figure 2-2), Apple TV, and Google's Chromecast, place a high demand on your wireless router. Your kids may be streaming a Disney movie in one room, your spouse may be checking out the latest season of *Downton Abbey,* and you might be streaming the big game in your man cave. That kind of activity would make most wireless networks struggle to catch their breath.

Recognizing network problems

All the preceding examples were to say that your wireless network already may be working very hard to keep up with your needs, and adding more to the load with a home automation system could cause enough extra strain that the whole thing comes to a crawl. Please understand, I'm not saying this is the case for all: You may never need to change anything on your network. You may be able to incorporate all the home automation devices you can get your hands on without noticing so much as a hiccup in your network's performance. On the flip side of that argument, though, you might add a single device to your system and find it unusable (doubtful, but never say never).

Figure 2-1: Wireless routers, like Apple's Airport Extreme (top) and the Linksys WRT1900AC (bottom), help provide Internet connectivity wherever you may be in your home.

Top: Image courtesy of Apple, Inc.
Bottom: Image courtesy of Linksys, Inc.

Image courtesy of Roku, Inc.

Figure 2-2:
Streaming devices, like the Roku 3, can cause a wireless router to struggle.

How can you recognize that your network is having problems due to overload? Here are a few telltale signs to look for:

✔ Simply enough, you can't seem to browse the Internet and load web pages as fast as you have before.

✔ Things start to get wonky, such as a streaming video begins to get choppy with a noticeable degradation in quality, or transferring files from your computer to another takes dramatically much more time than it has before.

✔ You lose your Internet connection altogether.

Before adding devices to your network, test your network speed by communicating with other devices and browsing the web. Run the exact same tests after you add a device to your network. If everything is more or less the same, your network is running well, even with the additional device. If everything comes to a near-halt, the newly added device is most likely the culprit. Remove the device and see if everything instantly returns to normal. If so, you will need to do something to increase your network's bandwidth in order to use the device.

Another issue you may run into with your home automation devices is that your network's range may not be sufficient. For example, you might place a device in a room that doesn't get a good signal from your router. In this case, the device may not get enough signal to communicate reliably, if at all.

Speeding up and extending your network

How to resolve this network issue, especially if you're bent on getting this home automation thing off the ground? Here are a few ways to get the job done:

- ✔ **Upgrade your wireless router.** If your current router is made of wood or has "Moses wuz here" carved on the bottom of it, it's probably a good idea to do so anyway.

- ✔ **Relocate your router, or at least place it higher than it may be.** It currently may be located in an area that isn't conducive to sending a strong signal. Finding a different place for it to reside, preferably a central location, could alleviate the problem.

- ✔ **Get a second router (or access point).** If getting a new router or relocating your current one isn't something you can or want to do, getting a second router (or access point) is the way to go. Connect the two via Ethernet cable, and your woes will be history.

- ✔ **Purchase a wireless range extender.** Wireless range extenders, like that seen in Figure 2-3, do just what their name implies: They extend the range of your current router by picking up the signal and rebroadcasting it at greater strength. Strategically placing one or more of these may instantly make your problems disappear. Be aware that these little guys don't always work as well as you'd like, since they are receiving and sending signals using the same channel.

Being cautious when adding new devices to your network

In case you didn't know, the Internet isn't the most secure place in the world. Many folks think they're anonymous on the web, or that their home network is privy to them and them alone. Well, I'm sorry, but nothing could be further from the truth. There are folks out there — bad folks, I don't mind saying — who are out to exploit the Internet for their gain and your loss. They have ways of getting into your life that you may not be aware of.

Did you know that folks can access your Wi-Fi from outside your home? Depending on your network's signal strength, they could even be sitting in a car on the street outside your home, using your Wi-Fi signal to do all kinds of nefarious things.

They don't necessarily have to get into your network directly through your router itself; they can use devices that are connected to your Wi-Fi to get inside. Folks, these people can even view what you see on your webcams or monitors. Did you hear about the couple in Texas who discovered that hackers had been spying on their baby using the camera they installed in the baby's room? Scary, scary stuff.

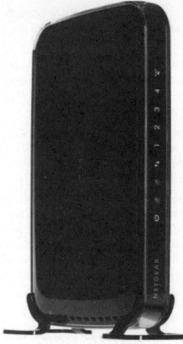

Figure 2-3:
Wireless
range
extenders,
like the
Netgear
N600, help
your Wi-Fi
signal reach
beyond
its normal
capacities.

Image courtesy of Netgear.

Securing networked devices

This is a book about home automation, not about setting up secure networks. Plenty of great tomes on the market cover the topic, and there are also a slew of websites that can tell you how to lock down your home network. I humbly advise you to look into some of these resources. My aim with this section of the book is to make you aware that your privacy is at risk and that adding devices that I discuss in this book to your network can further expose you if you don't take precautions.

Here are a few tips for securing your network from prying eyes:

  ✔ Many devices come with default usernames and passwords that you're supposed to change, but lots of folks don't bother to do so. Leaving these default usernames and passwords on your devices is like leaving your front door wide open.

✔ Use a firewall between your Internet connection and the devices on your network as a first defense against intruders. The firewall can typically be enabled on your router, but that isn't the only one you can enable. Computers usually have firewalls on them, too; consult your operating system's Help sources for more information.

✔ Enable security protocols on your router when setting up your Wi-Fi. Be sure to use a robust password for connecting to the network, too.

✔ Many home automation devices that connect to your Wi-Fi network may not have any security features at all, which is problematic, to be sure. Be sure to ask vendors about security features included in their devices, as well as how to best set them up for your network.

✔ Turn on whatever network security and privacy functions your smartphones or tablets may feature, such as those in iOS (shown in Figure 2-4).

If you aren't familiar with home network security, I highly suggest getting up to speed on the subject or bringing in a professional who is.

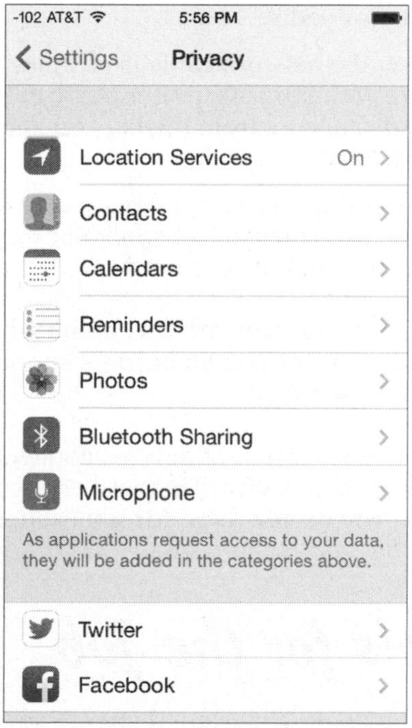

Figure 2-4:
Privacy settings on your smartphone or tablet are key components in securing devices on your network.

Monitoring your network for intrusions

It's creepy to think that someone could be on your network without your knowledge. Who knows what he's doing on it or what he may be accessing?

Knowing if anyone is on your network unauthorized is actually not all that complicated:

1. **Log in to your router.**

   If you don't know how, consult the documentation that came with it or contact the manufacturer.

2. **Go to the section within the router software that shows what devices are connected to it.**

   Some devices in the list may look familiar and others may not. However, just because something doesn't look familiar to you doesn't mean it isn't one of your devices. Here's how to determine what the devices connected to your network are:

   • One at a time, turn off the Wi-Fi connection on wireless devices you're using. When a device disappears from the list, you know it was the device you just disabled Wi-Fi on.

   • One at a time, disconnect the network cable from computers or other devices that are wired to your router. As with wireless devices, when a device disappears from the list you know it was the one you just disconnected.

   • Once you've performed this inventory, if there are any devices in the list you can't account for, you can feel confident that someone with bad intentions is connected to your network.

Should you find devices connected to your network that aren't authorized, consult your router's documentation, or the manufacturer's support team, for ways to block those devices from gaining access.

It's a good idea when performing this inventory of devices connected to your network to write down the names of each device. That way you won't have to go through this routine every time you decide to perform this check.

Having the Right Tools for the Job

Tools are items you use to get a job done. That said, there are several manners of tools that you will need to set up and operate your home automation system, and that's exactly the function of this section of the chapter.

Actual tools you'll need

When the word "tool" is bandied about, most folks automatically think of hammers and nails and such. Well, indeed, you may need some actual tools when getting your home automation equipment up and running. Some items, such as webcams and light bulbs, don't need tools at all. Webcams simply sit somewhere and light bulbs just screw into your light sockets. Other devices, like thermostats and locks, require tools — tools that most folks have in their toolbox.

Here's a basic list of tools you need for some jobs related to installing your home automation system:

- A screwdriver set that includes several sizes of both flathead and Phillips head screwdrivers
- Pliers, including those of the needle-nose variety
- Wire cutters
- A voltmeter for measuring voltages in wires
- A sledgehammer for taking out your frustrations on a tree stump outside if everything doesn't go as planned (better to pound a tree stump than toss a $300 home automation device off the balcony)

Computers and smartphones and tablets, oh my!

Yes, computers, smartphones, and tablets are indeed tools. Most of us use them every day for anything from getting our jobs done to talking with Mom 1,000 miles away to playing games. They are tools, and as such, are up next in the discussion of home automation tools.

The majority of home automation devices in this book connect with one or all of the aforementioned tools, and even more, they are controlled by them to varying degrees:

- Most home automation devices supply their own apps for smartphones and tablets.
- Others work with third-party apps and controllers, like the Wink hub and app shown in Figure 2-5, to ensure success on such devices.

✔ Some manufacturers, though very few, provide computer operating system-specific applications to control their devices. (I don't understand why they would waste the resources to develop such a tool, especially in light of the next point, but that's just me.)

✔ Still others incorporate web pages (like that shown in Figure 2-6) that users can connect to and control devices via the Internet from any device (computer, smartphone, or tablet) that is connected to the web.

Figure 2-5: Wink's hub and app combine to control lots of third-party home automation devices.

Images courtesy of Wink, Inc.

Home automation companies support these operating systems:

✔ **iOS:** The operating system that controls Apple's iPhone and iPad devices

✔ **Android:** Controls a large segment of non-Apple smartphones and tablets

✔ **OS X:** Operating system that runs Apple's line of personal computers

✔ **Windows:** Microsoft's operating system that runs a majority of non-Apple personal computers

✔ **Linux:** The most popular free operating system that comes in many different forms

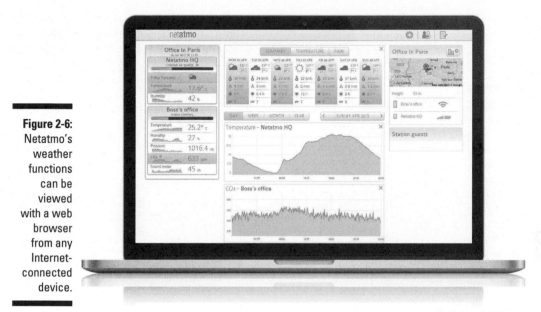

Image courtesy of Netatmo.

Figure 2-6: Netatmo's weather functions can be viewed with a web browser from any Internet-connected device.

See Chapter 13 for much more detailed coverage about these devices, their operating systems, and how to keep them up and running so your home automation system is at peak performance.

Power to get the job done

Home automation devices require power from some source, whether it be

- Directly wired (like a thermostat)
- Plugged into an outlet (like WeMo's Smart Switch, shown in Figure 2-7)
- From batteries (water detection sensors, for instance)

Today's home automation devices are designed to jump right into your home as it is, with little to no wiring of any kind needed. However, that doesn't mean that you might not need electrical work of some type performed in certain cases. Here are some examples:

- You need more outlets to take full advantage of new home automation devices.
- Your present wiring is faulty or dangerous. If you have frequent electrical issues, make sure that your home's electrical system can handle the extra load.

✔ You live in an older home that retains most of its original wiring. Upgrading wiring might be necessary if you want to install some devices, like the INSTEON thermostat in Figure 2-8, which requires low-voltage wiring and won't work with older high-voltage wiring.

Figure 2-7:
Some home automation devices allow standard devices to plug into them, thereby controlling the standard device with very little effort and no new wiring.

Image courtesy of Belkin.

Figure 2-8:
Some devices will require updated electrical rewiring if your current wiring is too old to work with them, like today's crop of smart thermostats.

Image courtesy of INSTEON.

Should you find that you need wiring, if you don't know what you're doing, seek the help of a licensed electrician. While you may not relish the expense involved in obtaining the services of an electrician, it sure beats paying a doctor to correct your body's electrical system (assuming you don't fry it, that is). Am I correct? I should also mention that you need to be absolutely certain that doing your own wiring is even something you can legally do in your neck of the woods. Many areas require certified electricians to do any electrical work needed, so be sure to check with local authorities before you do anything.

This will not come as an epiphany to those of you who know what you're doing when it comes to electrical work, but will be a good reminder for those who don't do this sort of thing regularly: Be absolutely certain to cut the power at the main electrical panel in your home! If you aren't sure what I'm talking about in this case, in the name of all that is good, do not attempt any electrical work on your own.

Chapter 3

Determining Your Home Automation Needs (and Wants)

In This Chapter

▶ Considering which factors are important to your home automation needs

▶ Determining what you want to automate in your home

To be prepared is half the victory.

— Miguel de Cervantes

*I*t's all about the preparation, friend.

Do you think General George S. Patton was prepared when his troops went into battle? Can you imagine one of the greatest leaders in United States military history just showing up with a few guys he picked up at the bar on the way to the front lines? No, I don't think so. Patton knew his troops and they knew him, and as such they were prepared for whatever was thrown their way.

If you ever saw the late Steve Jobs at an Apple event launching a new product, like the iPhone, I doubt the word "unprepared" comes to mind. The man was a master showman and salesman, and every pitch had been made to perfection. I'll bet Jobs knew where every crease and wrinkle in his turtleneck was.

Julia Child could cook, I'll have you know. As one of the world's premiere chefs in her day, she was also an international celebrity with her own cooking show. When she cooked on her show, every single ingredient was already measured and prepared, and all she had to do was reach for everything she needed, keeping the show running smoothly and allowing her to use her fantastic wit and charm to quickly whip up a bit of this and a bit of that.

The three preceding examples illustrate that you must be prepared for whatever comes your way when you undertake any task. Patton never could know what his adversaries were going to do, but he had to be prepared to face and combat whatever it may be. Steve Jobs handled hiccups during his presentation with a cool head and his professionalism. Julia Child handled any and every issue that came about while making her show and during interviews with her usual humor and grace, just like I'm sure you'll do when running into minor bumps on the road to home automation.

Considering Factors Before You Buy

Being prepared is the only way to avoid the monkey wrenches life likes to throw our way, and even when you're prepared as best you can be, life will still find a crazy way to toss one more curve ball at you. This is especially true when it comes to home projects. Luckily, the home automation I discuss in *Home Automation For Dummies* doesn't involve needing to wire a home while it's being built from the ground up (although that's easier than wiring after the house is built), so you don't have to worry too much about construction issues. However, there's still a lot to think about.

Identifying your automation goals

It's good to have goals in life, for sure, and a big part of preparation is defining those goals. What are your home automation goals? Only you can answer that question, but in the next sections, I provide you with a few things to think about to help you narrow them down.

A little at a time or all in

Are you planning to do everything at once or a bit at a time? I discuss this in depth later in this chapter, but you may want to begin thinking about it now.

Multiple manufacturers

Do you mind buying multiple products from multiple manufacturers? Some folks like to stay with the same brand (such as buying your computer, smartphone, and tablet from the same company), while others don't mind mixing it up a bit. The best approach when it comes to home automation is to only buy products from one manufacturer. It may not be possible to do so, based on what you want to automate in your home, but if it is possible you'll do well to heed my advice.

Definitely stick with one manufacturer when it comes to devices running the ZigBee protocol. ZigBee is a bit loose when it comes to making manufacturers stick to their standards, so there is a possibility of incompatibility if purchasing from different makers.

Committed versus tinkering

Are you automating for novelty or functionality? Be honest with yourself: Do you really want to automate your home and simplify your life, or are you more into tinkering with the latest and greatest technology? This is important for you to determine because it will affect how you search for devices.

If you want to make your life better through home automation, then your search will certainly encompass the more practical devices, such as lighting controls, security devices, thermostats, and the like. An example of a practical device for someone who is serious about saving money and controlling her home's temperature, but she doesn't have central heat and air, is the Quirky Aros smart window air-conditioner, shown in Figure 3-1. The Aros can be controlled remotely via your smartphone or tablet using the Wink app, which you can download from the iOS or Android App Store. (See Chapter 4 for more on controlling the heat and air-conditioning in your home.)

Figure 3-1: Home-owners without central heat and air can still control their home's temp remotely with the Quirky Aros.

Image courtesy of Quirky Incorporated.

If you're a tinkerer, then you can afford to be more adventurous in your quest for home automation quirkiness. For example, how about a self-cleaning kitty litter box, like the Classic Self-Cleaning Litter Box from LitterMaid (shown in Figure 3-2)?

Figure 3-2:
Kitty litter cleanup is automated and stink-free these days.

Image courtesy of Spectrum Brands, Inc.

Or how about the Pivot Power Genius from Quirky (see Figure 3-3), which is a power strip unlike any you've used before: It bends at each outlet to accommodate differing plug sizes and to fit into odd spaces. Another cool feature is that you can control it, and by extension, the devices plugged into it, through the use of an app on your smartphone or tablet.

More than one key master

Will more than one person be controlling your devices? Most home automation devices can be controlled by more than one smartphone or tablet (or computer), but some can't. If you plan to allow multiple people to have control over your home automation devices, be certain to verify with the manufacturers that they support this capability.

Most companies require you to create an account with them. These accounts allow you to log in to their systems and register your home automation devices with them. Once your device is registered with the account, you can then log into the account via an app on your smartphone or tablet, or from a web browser on your computer. Logging in to the account gives you control over your devices, whether you're in the home or not. To allow more than one user to control your home automation devices remotely, you can use the account on each of their smart devices. Of course, each account user must know the username and password of each account.

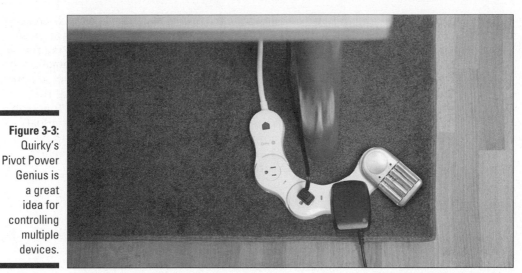

Figure 3-3:
Quirky's
Pivot Power
Genius is
a great
idea for
controlling
multiple
devices.

Image courtesy of Quirky Incorporated.

Keep in mind, too, that although you may have more than one person who can control your devices, you will most likely want someone to be the primary user. Some manufacturers do allow this kind of control; be sure to check with them if this is an important feature for you.

As you can imagine, if you have several different devices from different manufacturers you're going to end up with a ton of usernames and passwords. Be sure to jot down information about each account so you don't forget it, and keep that info in a safe location.

One app to rule them all, or not

How much space do you have available on your iOS or Android device? Go ahead and check. I'll wait.

Whistling . . . twiddling of thumbs . . .

Okay! How much do you have? Whatever the number, I just wanted you to have a look so that you would know exactly how much capacity you have. You see, once you wade into the home automation pool, you might drown in a sea of apps, and whatever storage space you may have had at the start of your home automation adventure will significantly decrease afterward.

Having made you aware of the space hit your smartphone and/or tablet will take, you should also know that there's an alternative. First, ask yourself, "Self, do I mind multiple apps on my *(insert type of smart device you have here)* controlling my home automation stuff, or do I want to minimize the number of apps I'm tied to?" Only you can answer that to your satisfaction.

If you decided that having an app for each and every thing is okay, then keep on truckin', partner. However, if you determined that having as few apps as necessary is a better idea, then you'll be glad to know that minimizing the number of apps you have is actually easy to do. Several home automation companies develop solutions for you. Chapter 14 covers this subject in detail, but I wanted to give you a heads up here so that you wouldn't sweat the "one app per device" horror. Understand, though, that most of the "one-app" solutions out there depend on another device to help keep the individual devices in line: a hub. This is not a bad thing at all. I just want you to be aware of that. Here are a few companies that offer a one-app solution for your home automation endeavors:

- ✔ **INSTEON (hub and app):** www.insteon.com
- ✔ **Revolv (hub and app):** www.revolv.com
- ✔ **CastleOS (hub and app):** www.castleos.com
- ✔ **Apple's HomeKit (app only):** www.apple.com
- ✔ **Wink (app only and hub/app solutions, shown in Figure 3-4, are available, depending on the devices you want to control):** www.winkapp.com

Figure 3-4:
Wink's app and hub work hand-in-hand, and also trim your home automation apps down to one.

More and more solutions seem to pop up every day, so keep your eyes peeled for more app-only and app/hub solutions for your home automation needs. In my opinion, having one of these options beats the heck out of having to flip through your smartphone trying to find the app that controls your lights, and then flip to another app for your thermostat, then flip back to your lights to turn one on or off . . . what a hassle.

Assess your needs

Once you have a handle on how you want to go about managing your home automation devices, you need to figure out what your needs are before incorporating a home automation system into your abode. Following are several things to consider, and I'm sure that you'll probably think of a few more yourself.

Your home's size

What is the size of your home? This is a really important question when it comes to figuring out how many devices you'll need to cover the bases in your home.

If you have a really large home, you're going to need many more devices than someone with a smaller home. You'll naturally have more needs:

- More lights to control
- Possibly multiple floors with multiple thermostats
- More area to cover, so you'll need to make sure you have sufficient signal strength throughout your home for your Wi-Fi (if your home auto system uses Wi-Fi for its primary means of communication)
- More locks due to more doors
- More motion sensors and door sensors, if you're beefing up security in your home automation system

There's plenty more I don't list here, but you get the drift.

Yard duty

Do you have a yard to care for? Do you plan on automating any of your lawn care? You know, you may say you enjoy cutting the grass, but why not let a robot do the job for you, like you see in Figure 3-5? (I devote all of Chapter 12 to automating yard work.)

Image courtesy of RobomowUSA.com.

Figure 3-5:
This gent
has it
figured out:
Let the robot
handle it!

Outlets and switches

Do you need extra outlets and switches installed? During the course of your home automation assessment, you may find that you want to place devices or your system's hub in a location that doesn't already have an outlet or a wall switch. If you do need them and know what you're doing, by all means go for it. If, however, you are someone who asks your nephew to come over and plug up your new appliances, you most definitely will want to contact a professional electrician to handle the job.

Wi-Fi concerns

Do you need to beef up your Wi-Fi network before you begin to install your home automation system? How can you tell?

Chapter 2 discusses network issues, but here are a few reminders:

- ✔ Most home automation systems use hubs that connect to your Wi-Fi router so that you can communicate with the system remotely. In many situations, your hub should be located centrally in the home so that its range extends to the point that it can communicate with as many devices as possible.

- ✔ Anything can block Wi-Fi signals, but some materials are much worse than others. Wood, plaster, glass, and cinder blocks aren't too bad on your signal, but brick, concrete, ceramic and metal are deal breakers. You may need to strengthen your network signals using range extenders — or adding a second router in some cases.

- ✔ Does your current router support the networking standards your home automation system needs? You need to contact both the router manu-facturer and the home automation system manufacturer to find out. Consulting their support websites should provide sufficient information, but if not, don't hesitate to call them.

Existing home automation systems

Do you have an existing home automation system already installed? I know this sounds like a silly question, but the reality is that if you do already have a system in place, you want to make sure that any new devices you get will work with that system. That is, unless you plan on scrapping the old system totally in favor of something new.

Now, when I say that you want to make sure new devices work with your current system, I don't mean that they necessarily have to be from the same manufacturer as that of the current system. I do mean, though, that they should mesh with the current system, or at least work independently of it. New devices also shouldn't hinder the current system's operation.

Current operating systems in use

What computers and smart devices do you currently have? Which operating system(s) does your new home automation stuff need to support?

These are definite considerations you need to make, in spite of the fact that most home automation devices today support both the iOS and Android operating systems for smartphones and tablets. You will find the occasional vendor that doesn't support Android, but you'll rarely find one that doesn't support iOS. That is not a slam on Android devices, by the way — it's just the truth of the matter.

On the flipside, you'll find few vendors that support native apps for OS X, but several (although still relatively few) do support native applications for their products on Windows. Virtually no vendors support Linux, as shameful as that may be.

If a home automation vendor provides a web interface for you to interact with its devices (which most do), the operating system your computer runs bears little consequence. As long as you can open a web browser on your computer, you should have no problem accessing the web interface for your home automation device.

Chapter 13 has more information on using your smartphones, tablets, and computers with your home automation goodies.

Deciding How Much You Want to Automate

Before you can begin getting prepared, you need to understand what you're preparing for. It's decision time, folks: Exactly how much do you want to automate in your home?

Do you want to just start off with a simple smart outlet that controls whatever device you see fit to plug into it? Or are you ready to go whole hog into home automation, decking out every room of your home with every bit of home automation technology you can scrounge up?

Starting small

Starting small simply means you're just getting your feet wet in home automation, not that you're somehow not putting sufficient effort into it. If you're at all hesitant about home automation, I suggest going the small route, anyway.

If you decide to start small, I recommend going a more universal route, rather than tying yourself to one specific automated task. An example would be starting with something like the WeMo Switch, seen in Figure 3-6. This device is simply an outlet that you can control with your smartphone or tablet using the WeMo app.

This kind of universal product enables you to see how home automation works at its most basic level, while pairing control with a simple, but powerful, app.

Figure 3-6:
A smart outlet, like the WeMo Switch, is a good way to get started with home automation.

Image courtesy of Belkin.

There are other smart outlets out there, and plenty of other devices of this general type, that will help you get an idea of what home automation can do for you.

Going LARGE

So, you're thinking about just diving right in with both fins, eh? That's what I'm talking about! Going for the gusto is how you roll.

In this scenario, I suggest you confine your home automation products to as few manufacturers as possible, such as going with INSTEON products throughout your home. The object of sticking with one manufacturer is to avoid any pitfalls that may occur due to incompatibility between products of various makers. Figure 3-7 shows the INSTEON Hub Home Automation Starter Kit (you can find it at `www.smarthome.com/insteon-hub-home-automation-starter-kit-premium.html`), which contains everything you need to get going:

- One INSTEON Hub (allows you to control all your devices from a central one)
- Two remote control dimmer switches
- Two on/off modules
- Two LED bulbs
- Two wireless motion sensors

    ✔ Two mini remotes (includes visor clips and tabletop stands)

    ✔ Two plug-in lamp dimmer modules

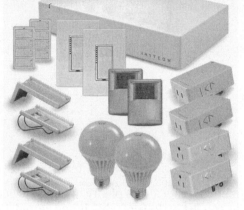

Figure 3-7:
A starter kit from the home automation manufac-turer of your choice is a great way to start big.

Image courtesy of INSTEON.

Other home automation companies provide starter kits of their own products, too, so find the kit that best suits what you're looking for before committing to one. Other starter kits to consider:

    ✔ **Iris Smart Kit:** Search for it at www.lowes.com.

    ✔ **SmartThings:** Go to shop.smartthings.com and click the Kits tab to find several starter kits.

    ✔ **Viper Starter Kit:** Visit www.viper.com/Home and click the Starter Kit tab.

    ✔ **INSTEON:** Visit http://www.insteon.com/retail-starter-kits.html to check out its selection of starter kits.

Many others are available, too. Just search for *home automation starter kit* in your favorite search engine and investigate the results.

Read the Chapter 2 section on home automation protocols. It's a good idea to find a protocol you like and stick to devices that run that protocol (as best you can, of course).

Part II
Automating Inside Your Home

In this part . . .

- Keep your home's temperature under control remotely.
- Clean up your home even when you're not there.
- Set up lighting scenes for each room in your home.
- Lock down your home and keep tabs on it while you're away.
- Discover kitchen gadgets and appliances you can use with your smart devices.
- Make sure you're notified immediately of any water leaks.
- Entertain your guests and yourself with today's smart home media tools.

Chapter 4

Keeping Your Cool or Turning Up the Heat

In This Chapter

▶ Controlling your home's temperature remotely

▶ Discovering products for automating your home's temperature

▶ Working with apps to make temperature adjustments and set schedules

*I*t's a million degrees outside (literally, a million degrees!) and you're on your way home after a ridiculously tough day at work. The AC in your car is on the fritz, and even with the windows rolled down it feels like you're peering over the lip of a volcano's crater. You can't wait to get home, where you can finally kick up your feet and cool off. You unlock the door, open it just a crack, and a rush of steamy, scorching air greets you instead of the cool, polar breeze you were expecting. Your husband turned off the thermostat before he left for work, and now you have to come home to a boiler room!

On the flipside of that scenario, it's a million degrees below zero outside (literally!) and you're again on your way home. You know that once you pull in your driveway, you'll only have a few seconds to dash from your car to the front door before your body is flash-frozen and you become a statue until the spring thaw. The thought of the warmth on the other side of your front door is what propels you from car to doorstep before the ice can begin to set on you. You unlock the door, bust open the front door, and are greeted by a wintry blast. Your husband (I'm picking on us guys because only we do these kinds of things) turned off the thermostat before he left the house this morning, leaving you to cope with subzero temperatures as you help the kids with homework.

Wouldn't it be great if you could just whip out your smartphone on the way home and check the temperature in your home from ten miles away? You could then set the temp from your device so your home will be waiting to cool you down or warm you up once you pull in the driveway. While that wasn't an option a few years ago, the advent of the smartphone and the proliferation of Wi-Fi has pushed us into the future, making such dreams a reality.

Controlling Your Thermostat from Afar

Temperature has long been a bone of contention in most households, as almost any couple can attest. One wants the temp at 85 in the winter and 55 in the summer. The other loves a happy medium of 72 degrees all the time. One believes the air-conditioning or heating should be cranking at all hours of the day and night, while the other would rather melt or freeze, depending on the season. Today's smart thermostats will benefit all involved, as you'll discover in the remainder of this chapter.

How setting temps remotely benefits you

I know what some of you are saying: "What's the big deal? Just set your thermostat to a reasonable temperature and when you get home all is well." To that I would refer you to the husband in the examples at the beginning of this chapter who can't stomach the thought of the thermostat running all day when no one's home. And what about those of us who don't have central heat and air?

The smart thermostats and other smart temperature devices on the market today will help ensure that when you need your heating or cooling on, you can take care of it with no problem from wherever you may be — provided you have an Internet connection of some kind. Let's talk about some of the benefits of controlling your home's temp smartly and remotely.

Saving money

Can you really save money with a smart thermostat? The answer may seem to be an obvious yes, but it actually depends a great deal on how you already control your home's temp.

If your thermostat is the old manual kind where you slide a switch marked C or one marked H to a certain temperature marking, then the answer is an emphatic "yes!" Smart thermostats don't require you to frequently bother with them to set your home's temp, and they're much more accurate when it comes to actually maintaining the temp you set. The smart thermostat will quickly pay for itself once you begin realizing the savings to your heating and cooling bills.

If you already own a standard programmable thermostat, then the answer may be "maybe." If you've diligently programmed your thermostat to turn on and go off at certain times of the day, and you maintain a reasonable temperature setting in the home when the thermostat is running, then your money savings using a smart thermostat over a programmable one probably won't be substantial (unless your programmable thermostat is faulty, of course). However, the capability to turn off your heating and cooling systems remotely could save you money if you aren't concerned about maintaining a constant temp in the home. For example, if you forgot to turn off the thermostat when you left your home, or if you later decide that you wish you had turned it off for the weekend instead of it running with its current programmed settings, you could easily handle the issue with a few taps on your smartphone. Money saved.

Another advantage of a smart thermostat over a programmable one is that many of the models give you real-time views of your energy usage, and provide other monitoring and reporting tools to keep you on top of your energy bills.

Saving time

Remotely controlling your smart thermostat, and simply employing a smart thermostat, will indeed save you time.

Sure, there's the initial installation and setup, but that's required of any thermostat. After your smart thermostat is up and running, though, you rarely will have to make changes unless you simply want to. But here's where the time saving comes in: You don't have to be in front of your smart thermostat to make those changes. There's no need to panic in the airport because you forgot to turn the thermostat off; just do it on your smartphone. No need to waste time calling neighbors or family members so they can adjust your thermostat; just whip out your trusty smartphone and get it done. If your mother is in town visiting, you won't need to give her instructions on running the thermostat; you'll be able to keep her warm and toasty from work using your smartphone. I could go on with example after example, but I think you get the drift by now.

The tech behind the thermostat

Thermostats have long been a staple in most households, but the technology has certainly improved over the decades.

Back in the day, the only thermostat one had at his or her disposal was what I call the "wake up and jerk back the covers test." Thankfully, over the last century or so we've graduated beyond that to more sophisticated methods.

Mechanical thermostats have long used purely mechanical means (hence their name) to determine the temperature of a room:

- ✔ Wax pellets
- ✔ Bulbs filled with gas or air
- ✔ Bulbs filled with mercury
- ✔ Bimetallic strips

Since those devices of Stone Age days, today's digital thermostats employ much more reliable electronic sensors to detect temperature with far greater accuracy. This increased accuracy can actually save you money in the long run by keeping temps in your home more consistent. These electronic sensors are also used by today's smart thermostats, which account for their excellent performance.

Introducing the Big Players in the Thermostat Arena

The smart thermostat arena is getting crowded with technical gladiators all vying for the emperor's attention (or yours, as the case may be). You now are going to explore the ever-expanding world of smart thermostats, visiting some of the well-known and not-so-well-known players in the market.

Honeywell

Some of you may be surprised that I'm not starting this section with Nest — considered to be the pioneer in smart thermostats. Instead, I thought we'd start off with the folks who gave us the iconic round thermostat (actually called "The Round") so many of us grew up with. Honeywell makes more than thermostats, to be sure, but the company will forever be synonymous with those little round gadgets.

Honeywell has certainly not been sitting idly by in this new age of smart doodads. They very much have their game on regarding this new phase of keeping up with room temps, as is evidenced by their newest little round thermostat, the Lyric.

While Honeywell has produced Wi-Fi–capable and digital/smart thermostats for a while now, Lyric, shown in Figure 4-1, is its first real dive into the new world of thermostats controlled by smart devices. Honeywell gets that many folks today are just as comfortable controlling their home technologies remotely from their smartphones as they are standing in front of the control itself: Thus, Lyric was born.

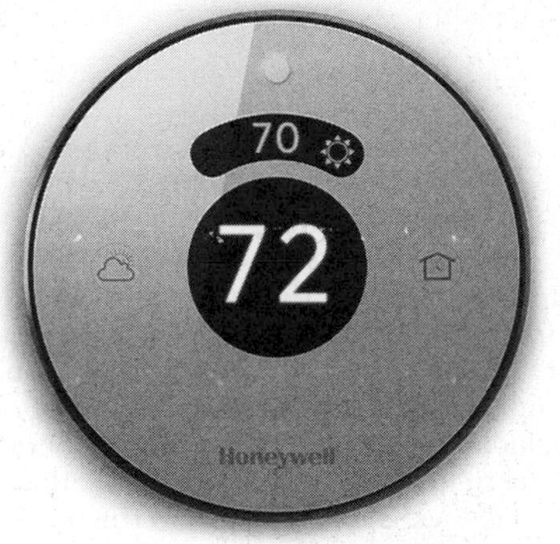

Figure 4-1:
Honeywell introduced another round thermostat into the market, the supersmart Lyric.

Image courtesy of Honeywell.

Lyric is designed to replace your current thermostat. In fact, Honeywell claims that 97 percent of existing thermostats can be replaced with the Lyric with little effort (in other words, complete rewiring not required). Another plus is that no power wire is needed for Lyric, so that's one less thing.

To be sure about Lyric's compatibility with your current wiring, your network, and your smart device, visit `http://lyric.honeywell.com/get-started/` and check out the great information provided by Honeywell. It does a great job of making you aware of whether the Lyric will truly be a good fit for you and your home.

Lyric installation

When you first get your Lyric and open the box, you might be surprised at how little information is actually contained therein. That's because installation instructions don't come in the box, but are instead part of the Lyric app (for iOS and Android devices), which is necessary to use your Lyric anyway. It's a good idea to go ahead and download the Lyric app from the iOS or Android App Stores before you get too far along with installation.

Honeywell claims you need a remarkably short list of tools to install your Lyric:

- ✔ Philips screwdriver
- ✔ Ballpoint pen
- ✔ Pencil
- ✔ Lyric app
- ✔ Your Wi-Fi password

That's a short list! However, if you're like me, your current thermostat has had so many coats of paint applied around its wall plate over the years that you'll also need a hammer and chisel to remove it from the wall.

Once you've downloaded the Lyric app, create an account with Honeywell by following the on-screen instructions. Once you're done, tap Install on the app (see Figure 4-2) and just follow along step by step until the job's complete. There are also instructions on the `http://lyric.honeywell.com/ get-started/` website, including some helpful videos. Of course, Honeywell has folks standing at the ready to help you with your installation questions, too: Just visit the aforementioned website and scroll to the bottom of the page to see all the ways you can contact the support team.

Setting up and using your Lyric

After you install the Lyric, you need to connect it to your smartphone or tablet and configure it for day-to-day use.

To connect and configure your Lyric:

1. **Connect your smart device to the Lyric network.**

   Find the Lyric's network using your iOS or Android device's network connection settings.

2. **Lyric will walk you through several questions regarding your heating and cooling system, your desired temperatures for when you are home or away, and more.**

3. **Connect the Lyric to your home's Wi-Fi network using the options within the app.**

   Be sure to have your network password on hand. Patience is recommended during this process; it may take a few minutes for the Lyric to connect to your network and sync with Honeywell's servers.

4. **Register your thermostat with Honeywell, which ties the device to the account you created when you first installed and opened the Lyric app.**

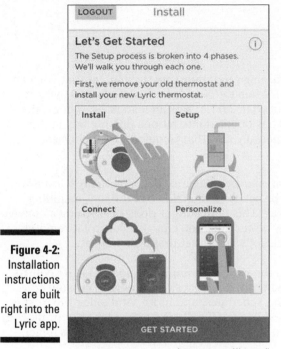

Figure 4-2:
Installation
instructions
are built
right into the
Lyric app.

Image courtesy of Honeywell.

Your Lyric is now ready to roll! Now all you have to do is sit back and relax as your Lyric controls the temperature in your home, whether you're there or not.

A great feature of Lyric is its Geofencing feature, which allows the Lyric to adjust the temperature in your home based on your proximity to it. If you're away from home, Lyric will know it because it's tracking your smart device's location. At that time, Lyric will heat or cool your home depending on the temperature presets you make on it. When the Lyric detects that you're within a certain distance from your home (again, this distance is something you preset), it will then begin cooling or heating your home to your specifications.

While I would consider the Lyric to be Honeywell's best competitor in this field, the company does have a range of other Wi-Fi–compatible thermostats that you can control via your smart device. Visit `http://wifithermostat.com/` for more information about those devices. You can also get more information on Lyric by going to `http://lyric.honeywell.com`.

Nest

Onward to Nest!

Nest is the best-known self-learning programmable thermostat that you can control via your smart device. When the Nest thermostat (owned by Nest Labs, by the way) was introduced in 2011, it was an instant hit. Today, the company that started in 2010 has boomed into a bona fide big boy in the home automation market (especially now that Google has bought Nest Labs for a few jillion dollars).

The Nest Learning Thermostat, shown in Figure 4-3, can actually learn how you like your temperature to be set at various times of the day, including whether you are home or away. This cool gadget does everything a conventional thermostat can do, only better. And you can also control it remotely via your iOS or Android device; let's not forget that little nugget.

A user directly interacts with the Nest Learning Thermostat via its control wheel, which can be spun and tapped to access heating and cooling controls, make device settings, set schedules, and more. And since the Nest is connected to the Internet, Nest can push software upgrades to your device automatically, keeping you up-to-date without so much as lifting a finger.

Installing your Nest

Before you get all giddy on me and rush out to purchase a Nest, I recommend that you visit `https://widgets.nest.com/compatibility/` to make sure your current heating and cooling systems will work with the device.

Figure 4-3:
The Nest Learning Thermostat doing what it does best: keeping your temps just right automatically.

Image courtesy of Nest Labs.

Once you have your Nest in hand, installing it is much like installing other thermostats:

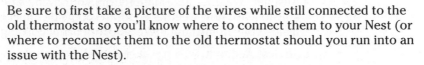

1. **Remove the old thermostat.**

   Be sure to first take a picture of the wires while still connected to the old thermostat so you'll know where to connect them to your Nest (or where to reconnect them to the old thermostat should you run into an issue with the Nest).

2. **Install the base for your Nest Learning Thermostat.**

   Nest provides a level built into the base itself to make sure it's properly leveled before attaching the base to your wall.

3. **Connect the wires as instructed for your wiring setup.**

4. **Connect the display to the base.**

   Just push the display onto the base until it clicks.

By the way, if you have problems when installing your Nest, or if you would simply like to have a professional install your Nest for you, go to `https://nest.com/thermostat/installation/` to find a local Nest guru.

Nest features

Nest is loaded with features that you're going to love. I mention a few of them here for you, but to get the full understanding of just how good the Nest Learning Thermostat is, check it out at the aforementioned website.

Nest includes these features:

- The Nest programs itself in about a week, based on your preferences and input.
- Auto-Away automatically turns off heating and cooling when you're away from home.
- Nest can learn how long it takes to heat or cool your home, and it will even display the time it takes to do so.
- While you can indeed control your Nest directly, you will love the Nest apps for your iOS and Android devices. The app helps you make adjustments to your thermostat and also view energy statistics for your home (illustrated in Figure 4-4). You can even control your Nest from your computer.
- The Nest Learning Thermostat uses sensors and Internet information to help keep you comfortable:

  - Temperature sensors detect how warm or cool your home is (as if I needed to tell you that!).

- • Humidity sensors help you see the humidity in your home.

- • Activity sensors detect when someone is in the home. When Nest detects that no one is present, it will activate its Auto-Away mode.

- • Nest gets weather information from your home's network, so it's able to learn how weather conditions outside affect the temperature inside your home, and make adjustments accordingly.

✔ A single Nest Account, which you create when setting up your Nest, can control up to ten thermostats.

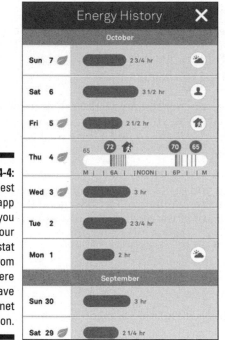

Figure 4-4:
The Nest Mobile app lets you control your thermostat from anywhere you have an Internet connection.

Image courtesy of Nest Labs.

There's so much more to know about the Nest Learning Thermostat that I simply cannot go into within the pages of this tome. I highly encourage you to check out everything Nest at www.nest.com to find out all the ways Nest can help keep your home comfy and cozy.

When you see Nest's famous Leaf logo on the thermostat's display, it means that you're currently saving energy. It's Nest's way of giving you a virtual pat on the back for saving energy and to give you a heads up on times that your wallet should feel a little heavier.

Belkin

You now have the scoop on two of the best thermostats around, but what if you're someone who doesn't have a thermostat? What if your preferred (or not) methods of heating and cooling your home are through electric heaters and window unit air-conditioners that don't use thermostats to make everything all nice and automatic? Don't worry, folks, Belkin's got your back!

Belkin has come up with an ingenious little device called the WeMo Switch, which is part of the broader WeMo line of awesome products. Here, I focus on the switch (see Figure 4-5) because it will help you control your non-Internet-friendly devices remotely.

The WeMo Switch (I call it the switch from here on) plugs into any standard 120-volt outlet. You can then connect any electrical device to the switch and control it from anywhere you have an Internet connection. What a cool idea!

When I say any electrical device (up to 120 volts, that is), I do mean it: From irons to televisions to heaters, you can turn them on or off, and even monitor their usage, using the free WeMo app for iOS or Android devices. If it can plug into an outlet, it can plug into your switch, and as long as your Wi-Fi is up and running, you have full control wherever you happen to be.

Here's how simple it is to get your switch up and running with your smartphone or tablet and your network:

1. **Plug your switch into any outlet, and then plug the electrical device it will be controlling into it.**

2. **Download the WeMo app on your smart device.**

3. **Go to your network settings on your smart device and connect to the WeMo network.**

4. **Open the WeMo app on your smart device and select your home's Wi-Fi network (enter the password, if necessary).**

   This connects your switch to your home's network.

5. **Give your Switch a descriptive name so you know which electrical device it controls in your home (for example, Heater in My Room or Living Room AC), select an icon for the switch to use, and tap Done.**

   Your switch will appear in your list of controlled electrical devices.

6. **Tap the power switch button next to your electrical device in the list to turn it on or off.**

   Green indicates the device is on, as illustrated in Figure 4-6.

Figure 4-5:
The WeMo Switch allows you to control and monitor any electrical device from anywhere you like (as long as you can connect to the Internet, that is).

Image courtesy of Belkin.

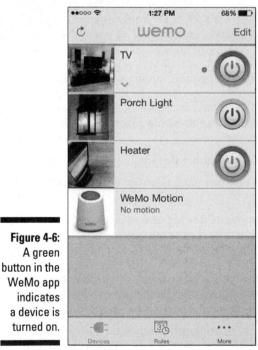

Figure 4-6:
A green button in the WeMo app indicates a device is turned on.

Image courtesy of Belkin.

That's all there is to it! You can now turn your electric heater or your AC unit on or off remotely without any other devices. I implore you to visit `www.wemothat.com` to see the entire lineup of WeMo devices, access WeMo support, and more.

WeMo devices can utilize the IFTTT (If This Then That) service to automate tasks with your Switch. IFTTT connects your devices to each other and to other websites to make things work together using "recipes." For example, you could connect your switch to the IFTTT Weather Channel so that it is alerted when the sun sets, and your switch can automatically turn on a hall light that's connected to it. For more information on what IFTTT is and how to use it with your WeMo Switch, check out `www.belkin.com/us/support-article?articleNum=8039`.

ecobee

Stuart Lombard and his company, ecobee, introduced the world to smart thermostats in 2007. Ever since, it has become one of the companies to watch in today's home automation market, but its market share has dwindled over the last few years because of its competitor, Nest. However, with the introduction of the ecobee3, ecobee has ratcheted up its offerings to compete with Nest. To be honest, it is more than an answer: The ecobee3, shown in Figure 4-7, is a veritable shout from the rooftops!

Figure 4-7: The sleek new ecobee3 does its job well.

Image courtesy of ecobee.

The ecobee3 takes the concept of thermostats like the Nest and Honeywell's Lyric to the next level. Don't get me wrong: Those are great devices, as are those I've yet to discuss, but in my humble opinion, the ecobee3 goes one level better because of its remote sensors, which I touch on in a bit.

Like its competitors, the ecobee3 is a learning thermostat and is compatible with the heating and cooling systems in most houses. Go to www.ecobee.com/compatibility/ to walk through a couple of simple steps to find out if your system is compatible.

Installation and setup

Installation of the ecobee3 is very much like the other smart thermostats:

1. **Remove the old thermostat, making sure to label the wires.**

   Better yet, take a picture of the wiring before you remove the thermostat.

2. **Insert the wires into the ecobee3 base according to the appropriately marked terminals.**

3. **Snap the faceplate onto the base and you're ready for action.**

Of course, things may need to be adjusted for whatever wiring you may have in your walls, and ecobee has you covered with much more detailed installation instructions should they be warranted.

Once you power on your ecobee3, you should be greeted by the ecobee "bee" logo, which is a good sign. If you don't see the bee, the wire connections may have issues.

If the wires behind your thermostat are connected to a high-voltage system, your system won't be compatible with ecobee3 (or the Nest or Lyric, for that matter). You can easily tell if your system is high-voltage by looking for a sticker somewhere on or inside it that indicates it's 110 volts or higher. Another simple way to tell is if the wires are tied together with wire nuts, which look like plastic caps. If so, again, the system won't be compatible.

The ecobee3 walks you through the process, making sure it has detected your wiring correctly, helps you set up other devices you may have connected (such as a humidifier), and learns what equipment your system uses.

The touchscreen on the ecobee3's front panel is great; it looks and feels like the touchscreen on your smartphone or tablet. The screen is clean and simple to understand, as well, so you won't be searching all over the place or pushing knobs or rings to find the settings you need. What makes it even better is that the interface on the thermostat is almost identical to the interface of the ecobee3 app (see Figure 4-8), so no matter which interface you're using, you still know how to get around.

Figure 4-8:
The
ecobee3
interface
looks and
behaves
almost
identically
on both the
thermostat
and the app.

The interface is simple, yet fully functional:

✔ The current temp is seen in the middle.

✔ An icon above the current temp shows whether the system is heating or cooling.

✔ The slider on the right side can be adjusted by tapping and scrolling up or down on the touchscreen.

✔ Tap the menu in the lower left of the screen to see the full menu. Some items on the thermostat menu pertain to the actual hardware itself and don't appear in the menu of the app, for good reason.

✔ Tap the cloud icon at the lower middle to see current weather in your area, including a forecast.

✔ Tap the Quick Changes button in the lower right (it looks like a gear) to make fast settings changes, such as instantly putting the thermostat into Home or Away mode.

The ecobee3 also has a web interface that you can use to control your thermostat. All you need to use it is a web browser and an Internet connection, and you're golden. The web interface is not identical to the thermostat and app interface, but it really can't be since the user interacts with it in such a different manner. Regardless of that, it's still a nice interface and does everything you need it to.

ecobee3's remote sensors

What sets the ecobee3 apart from its competitors is its implementation of remote sensors, which you can see in Figure 4-9.

Figure 4-9:
Remote
sensors
allow the
ecobee3
to detect
temperature
in rooms
other than
the one
where the
thermostat
is located.

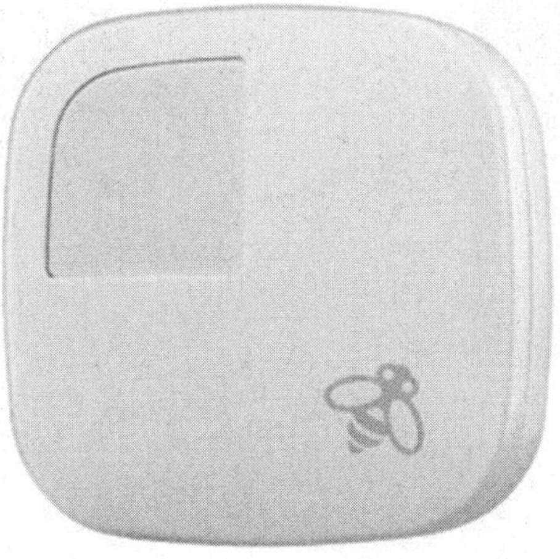

Image courtesy of ecobee.

These sensors can be placed anywhere in the house, and you can use up to 32 of the little fellows. These sensors are used by the ecobee3 to determine the temp in other rooms so that it can make adjustments to make the house as comfortable as possible for all involved. The sensors not only detect temperature, but they also detect when a room is occupied. Here's how the sensors work with the thermostat:

You're in the living room and your spouse is in the kitchen. Each room has a remote sensor, and the thermostat is in the hall. The thermostat is set to 72 degrees. Problem is that the living room is typically a bit cooler than in the hall, but the kitchen is characteristically warmer than both areas. The ecobee3 senses the differences in room temps and that both the kitchen and living room are occupied, so it takes an average of the temps and works to make sure that both rooms are as close as they can be to the desired whole-house temperature you've set. Your spouse then leaves the kitchen to join you in the living room, leaving the kitchen unoccupied. The sensor in the kitchen detects that the person has left and reports it to the thermostat. The thermostat then makes adjustments to how it cools or warms the house based on no longer needing to concentrate so much on the typically warmer kitchen. Nifty, huh?

Visit www.ecobee.com to see the ecobee3, as well as the company's other fine thermostats for both home and office. You can also purchase more remote sensors on the site. It's worth a view just for ecobee's claim to save up to 23 percent on your energy bills, don't you think?

Lennox

Until now, you haven't read about any of the major HVAC hardware manufacturers. However, Lennox has a really great smart thermostat itself, called iComfort.

iComfort, shown in Figure 4-10, is a touchscreen unit like the ecobee3, but the interface is much different. The touchscreen is wider than the ecobee3, and looks almost like an iPad mini or similar tablet.

Figure 4-10:
The iComfort is Lennox's offering in the smart thermostat market.

Image courtesy of Lennox International, Inc.

iComfort features

iComfort is packed full of features:

- ✔ Remotely control your home's temperature using the iComfort app for iOS or Android (see Figure 4-11), or log onto www.myicomfort.com and make settings adjustments via the web.

- ✔ One-Touch Away mode puts your system into a deep sleep, so no energy is needlessly spent heating or cooling your home while you aren't there.

- ✔ The touchscreen interface works very much like your iOS or Android device.

- ✔ Weather-on-Demand gives you a five-day forecast right on the thermostat.

- ✔ Whenever there's a problem, your iComfort will alert you via email, text, or through your mobile app. It can even contact your local Lennox dealer directly if you allow it to.

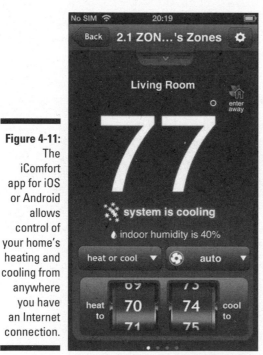

Figure 4-11:
The iComfort app for iOS or Android allows control of your home's heating and cooling from anywhere you have an Internet connection.

Image courtesy of Lennox International, Inc.

While Lennox would prefer you only use its thermostat with its HVAC units, have no fear that your non-Lennox system won't work with the iComfort. Lennox does say that you'll have a better experience with the overall system if you use only its premium products, but I leave that decision up to you, dear reader.

Don't think the default look of the Lennox will do it for you? Rest easy, gentle reader, Lennox has your back. Nuvango covers are available for your iComfort, and they give you the customizable look you want. The Nuvango covers fit around the outside edges of your iComfort and meet at the edges of your touchscreen. When the screen saver kicks in on the iComfort, it matches the pattern of your edge cover, as illustrated in Figure 4-12.

iComfort installation

I have to say that to me there is one major chink in the armor of the iComfort, and that's its installation. Actually, it's the fact that Lennox doesn't give you the option to install it yourself; the iComfort is installable only by a Lennox dealer. Even if you just want to check compatibility of your current HVAC units with iComfort, Lennox still pushes you to a dealer.

Don't get me wrong; I understand that the iComfort is Lennox's baby and the company wants to be sure installation is done right, but I still think it should offer the option to do-it-yourselfers who have the know-how to get the job done themselves.

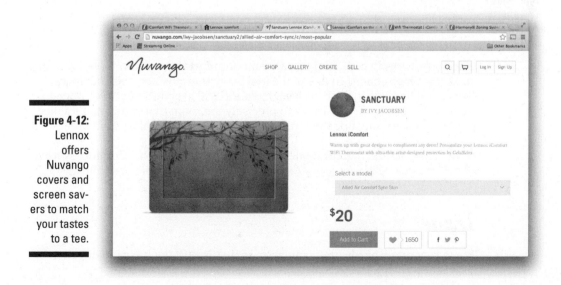

Figure 4-12: Lennox offers Nuvango covers and screen savers to match your tastes to a tee.

iHarmony zoning

I just finished giving Lennox a bit of a hard time for the dealer-only installation, but I'm about to balance that with a hearty pat on the back for its iHarmony Zoning System.

The iHarmony Zoning System is a great option for your home's HVAC system that allows you to heat or cool specific rooms or areas of your home by zoning off certain areas with their own thermostats, shown in Figure 4-13. These separate thermostats enable you to set custom temps for zoned areas: That's right, these areas are heated or cooled strictly to your specifications.

Figure 4-13: iHarmony thermostats can customize temps in individual areas or rooms of a home, working with iComfort to control your energy costs.

Image courtesy of Lennox International, Inc.

iHarmony works in conjunction with your iComfort thermostat. Whenever you make a settings change to one of the iHarmony thermostats, zone dampers (which are basically flaps or valves) in your HVAC system's ductwork open or close as needed to direct airflow to precisely the room that needs it. It's a nice feature that certainly ups the Awesome Factor for the iComfort system.

Lennox has offered a great home automation product in the iComfort system. Check out www.lennox.com/icomfortwifi/ to read about all the specs.

Trane

Trane is another hardware manufacturer that is offering its own version of a smart thermostat, the ComfortLink II XL950 (see Figure 4-14).

Figure 4-14:
Nothing
can stop a
Trane! The
ComfortLink
II XL950
smart
thermostat
controls
your HVAC
system.

Image courtesy of Trane.

Trane's ComfortLink (that's what I call it from now on to keep from getting too tongue-tied) system touts itself as not just a thermostat, but an "energy command center."

This is not a slam of the ComfortLink system when I say that it does pretty much what the Lennox iComfort does — the difference being (of course) that it's built primarily for Trane by Trane. If you already have Trane equipment and are pleased with it, it makes sense to stay with a brand you're familiar with. Having said that, the ComfortLink works with any HVAC brand.

Check out www.trane.com/residential/en/products/thermostats-and-controls/connected-controls/comfortlink_ii.html for more information on the base system itself.

Third-party apps and self-installation blues

As with other devices of its kind, there's an app for the ComfortLink. However, this app is developed by Nexia, which is a home automation company that develops apps for several other companies. The Nexia Home Intelligence app, seen in Figure 4-15, can handle all sorts of home automation tasks, and controlling your Trane smart thermostat is one of them.

I have to say, it's a bit off-putting to have one company's app control another company's thermostat, but hey — that's just my opinion. If you're someone who's used to using Nexia's app for controlling home automation devices, then this will probably not be a deal breaker for you, but if you aren't familiar with Nexia, this might be a strong factor when considering the Trane ComfortLink thermostat for your home's heating and cooling needs. Again, that's just my two pence.

One more thing that kind of gets my goat is that Trane also wants installation of your ComfortLink system to be performed by a dealer only. Again, I understand the company wants this work for its dealers, but it seems there should be a user-installable option to go along with the dealer-installable one.

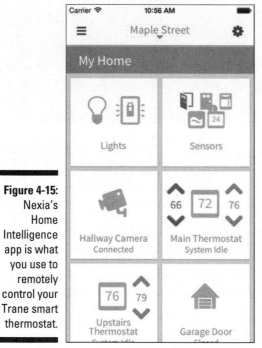

Figure 4-15: Nexia's Home Intelligence app is what you use to remotely control your Trane smart thermostat.

Image courtesy of Nexia Home Intelligence.

ComfortLink zoning

One big plus for the ComfortLink system is the inclusion of zoning. Like Lennox, Trane provides all the hardware for a system, ensuring that everything works together seamlessly.

Zoning allows your Trane HVAC system to direct heating and cooling to specific rooms in specific amounts, effectively reducing your energy costs over the long haul. Like the Lennox zoning features, dampers inside your air ducts open and close as much or little as needed, depending on what temps are set for individual zones.

Go to www.trane.com/residential/en/products/add-on-components/zoning.html to see what all the ComfortLink II Zoning System has to offer. There's a good brochure that you can open on the site.

Click or tap the Find A Dealer button on the Trane URLs I mention earlier and you'll be able to get hold of a "Traned" professional (get it?) who can help answer your questions and solve your problems.

Venstar

Last, but by no means least, are our friends at Venstar. Venstar offers the ColorTouch thermostat (see Figure 4-16) to round out this list of smart thermostats.

Figure 4-16: The ColorTouch smart thermostat is compatible with most HVAC systems.

Image courtesy of Venstar Incorporated.

The ColorTouch is loaded with features:

- ✔ A nice touchscreen interface makes it simple to use and to find what you're looking for in the menus.

- ✔ You can upload items such as personal pictures to use as wallpaper on your ColorTouch touchscreen. Holiday and nature themes are already loaded into the ColorTouch, but you can customize if you like. Who doesn't want to put a picture of her granddaughter on the front of her thermostat?

- ✔ ColorTouch is compatible with the vast majority of systems and wiring conditions, but you need to contact a local Venstar distributor to find out whether ColorTouch will work for yours.

- ✔ ColorTouch can speak your language, assuming it's English, Spanish, or French.

- ✔ You can prevent anyone from "accidentally" changing your thermostat's settings by using a super-secret passcode that Bond himself couldn't break.

- ✔ ColorTouch uses SkyPort technology to allow it to communicate with your Wi-Fi and therefore your smart devices. You can control your ColorTouch on the road as well as at home using the Venstar SkyPort app.

Venstar's ColorTouch is a nice addition to the products surveyed in this chapter, but if you want to get your hands on one, you'll have to find a Venstar dealer on its website. Go to www.venstar.com and click or tap the Distributors tab to find one near you.

Chapter 5

Nice and Tidy Does It!

In This Chapter

▶ Cleaning your home while you're away

▶ Automating some household chores

▶ Working with the right manufacturers and tools for the job

Cleaning house is simply the most fun one can have on a daily basis. I don't know anyone who would rather be at the beach or taking a Caribbean cruise when he or she could be cleaning windows or vacuuming the floor. There's simply no comparison: laundry detergent over tanning lotion any day of the week, right?

Oh, who am I kidding? The previous paragraph was aimed more at impressing my mom than expressing the actual disdain of most folks for breaking their backs cleaning the house every evening after a long day at the office. Truth be told, if we could just close our eyes and twitch our noses to make all the trash go away, we'd all be quite pleased.

Let's step out of fantasyland for a moment. There's always washing of some kind to be done, trash of some kind to be tossed out, items of some kind to be put away, flooring surfaces of some kind to be cleaned, and glass of every kind that needs wiping. And if you have children, multiply those tasks exponentially!

Let's step back into fantasyland again. Wouldn't it be awesome if some (or even better, all) of your everyday cleaning needs could be taken care of automatically? Instead of pushing a vacuum all over your apartment, why not catch up on your reading or do some Netflix binge watching while the carpet is cleaned without your having to lift a finger? What if your aquarium could be cleaned by a robot and you didn't even have to hand it the Windex? Did I say, "Let's step back into fantasyland?" This is no fantasy, folks — indeed, it's a reality!

Cleaning Up While You're Away

We are truly stepping into the future that we, and even our parents, all dreamed about as kids when we begin automating typical household chores. George Jetson and family can't be more than a couple of generations away, I'm thinking. Let's talk about the benefits of automating your daily chores and which ones can be automated today.

Keeping clean while on the go

Some of you may be thinking that this is the biggest no-brainer chapter heading in *Home Automation For Dummies,* but I might have come up with a benefit or two you haven't considered. Please bear with the more obvious points in this list:

- The job gets done, even if you don't feel like it because of illness, your crazy-busy schedule, or what-have-you.
- Saving time is certainly a huge benefit, and may be the top "duh" comment in this short list. There are simply too many ways in which these devices can save you time to mention here, but I bet you can think of a million of them on your own.
- People who suffer from a disability can use automated cleaning devices to clean their homes with little effort on their part. They'll also save money by not having to employ other folks to do the jobs for them.

Automating cleaning chores

Myriad cleaning chores can be automated these days. The following list is a good one, but by no means do I claim it to be an exhaustive one:

- Dust mopping
- Damp mopping
- Vacuuming
- Floor scrubbing
- Cleaning your grill
- Removing muck from your aquarium

Many more cleaning chores can be automated, but we would be here all day listing and reading them. In Chapter 17, I discuss ten others that are done less frequently than on a daily basis.

Understanding how it all works

Unfortunately, most of the automated home cleaning products don't allow for control via smartphones, tablets, or computers. The majority of them are devices that you set into motion and they complete tasks for you. While this isn't the ultimate ideal, it's certainly better in many respects than doing it all yourself. The technology behind each device basically includes some sort of wheels or treads for locomotion, sensors to prevent bumping into things, and some form of cleaning apparatus (sucking, scrubbing, wiping, and so forth).

 While the upcoming product recommendations are extremely helpful and time-saving, keep in mind that nothing replaces good old-fashioned elbow grease. Still, you may find that you tackle cleaning chores more often if all you have to do is push a button!

Introducing a Who's Who of the Remote Cleaning World

Computers and smartphones have Apple, automobiles have General Motors, kitchens have Betty Crocker, dolls have Barbie, and home-automated cleaning has the following list of companies and their products that are fast becoming its icons.

iRobot

iRobot has been in the automated home cleaning business for more than a decade, and it is the creator of the famous Roomba, the world's first automated vacuum.

The Roomba (shown in Figure 5-1) was, and still is, a runaway success, and as a result, iRobot (www.irobot.com) has blossomed into much more than just a vacuum company. Boasting of several products for home use, iRobot also develops products for the defense and security sectors (they're pretty cool devices; check them out on iRobot's website if you're interested).

Figure 5-1:
iRobot's
Roomba is
the grand-
daddy of
automatic
vacuums.

Image courtesy of iRobot Corporation.

From this point forward I mention different flooring types that can be cleaned by the devices in this chapter. But before making any purchase — and certainly before turning any of these devices loose in your home — check with the manufacturer to make absolutely certain that your flooring is supported for use with its device. This is in no way meant to deter you from using these devices; I just want you to be certain that the flooring in your home is protected from possible damage.

Roomba

More than 10 million units have sold since its introduction to the market; that's a bunch of robotic vacuums!

The basic idea behind the Roomba is to let it do the vacuuming while you do something else: That's it. The neater features of a Roomba include:

- Press the Clean button on the top of the Roomba unit and it begins cleaning, not stopping until either the job is complete or it needs a battery charge.

- Roomba automatically returns to the charging station once a job is finished or its battery is too low.

- The unit is smart and knows where to go. Roomba won't fall down stairs and can detect walls, furniture, and other items that it should go around.

✔ An indicator light on the top of the unit alerts you when the dust bin is near full.

✔ You can program a daily schedule for Roomba so that you're not having to push the Clean button every time you want Roomba to get on the job.

✔ Roomba doesn't just have to do an entire room or area; it's also great for spot cleaning.

Roomba is currently offered in one of three series (600, 700, and 800), and its features grow as the series number grows. The 600 series includes the most basic models, the 700 models are a step above, and the 800 series are the crème de la crème of robotic vacuuming. You can learn more about Roomba, its features, and the models offered by visiting www.irobot.com/us/learn/home/roomba.aspx.

iRobot offers a product it calls the Virtual Wall that prevents your Roomba from venturing where you don't want it to. The Virtual Wall emits an infrared beam that the Roomba detects; when it sees the beam, Roomba will turn around, as if it has run into a real wall or obstacle. iRobot offers a "smart" version of the Virtual Wall called the Virtual Wall Lighthouse. The Lighthouse will keep Roomba in one room until the job is finished, and then allow it to move on to other rooms. Check with iRobot to see which versions of the Roomba will work with the Virtual Wall Lighthouse.

Scooba

Scooba is much like its cousin, Roomba, in that it cleans your floors automatically. These two cousins can even use the same charging stations and accessories, such as a Virtual Wall (discussed in the preceding section). The difference is that Roomba is meant for vacuuming dust and debris, while Scooba (shown in Figure 5-2) is meant to scrub the muck and grime from your hard floors. (See the following list of the kinds of floors that Scooba works on.)

Scooba does use water (or iRobot's special cleaning solution for hard floors) to scrub your floors automatically. That said, be careful when walking on slick, wet floors while the Scooba is cleaning.

Scooba's fluid tank is super-easy to fill with either water or a cleaning solution formulated for hard floor surfaces. Here's how Scooba gets the job done:

✔ First, Scooba gives your floor a quick sweep to remove any loose debris, and then gives the floor a presoak to help loosen any stuck-on gunk. (I hope I'm not getting too technical.)

✔ Second, the unit scrubs (and I mean *scrubs*) your floor with a brush that spins at over 600 RPM! After the scrubbing, Scooba's squeegee vacuum sucks up any dirt, debris, and leftover water.

✔ Finally, Scooba gives your floor another once-over with the squeegee to be sure that everything possible has been cleaned from the floor.

According to iRobot, this process helps Scooba to remove up to 99.3 percent of household bacteria — and it can run either a 40-minute or a 20-minute cycle. Your Scooba will also be able to clean most hard floor surfaces, including:

✔ Linoleum

✔ Tile

✔ Slate

✔ Sealed hardwoods

✔ Stone

✔ Marble

Piqued your interest? Find out more about Scooba at `www.irobot.com/us/learn/home/scooba.aspx`.

iRobot sells the DryDock Charging and Drying Stand as an accessory for your Scooba. The advantages to this stand over the basic power adapter/charger is that it will dry your Scooba, preventing bacteria buildup, and it also provides a compact storage area.

Figure 5-2:
Scooba scrubs your hard floors at more than 600 RPMs until all the hard, stuck-on grime is gone.

Image courtesy of iRobot Corporation.

Braava

Have you gotten the impression that the folks at iRobot like clean floors? So far, you have the Roomba for vacuuming, and the Scooba for removing stuck-on gunk you often find on hard floors. Next up: Braava.

Braava, shown in Figure 5-3, is your hard floor's mopping buddy, and it does the everyday mopping chores that tend to break your back. The Braava won't even break a sweat. Bravo for Braava!

Braava can mop your floors using either a dry or damp cloth:

 ✔ When using a dry cloth, Braava moves around the room in a straight path to simply sweep up dust and debris.

 ✔ When in damp-cloth mode, Braava moves in small back-and-forth motions, which helps it to better clean the surface of the floor.

Braava uses what amounts to a customized GPS system to navigate your rooms. iRobot developed the NorthStar Navigation System (housed in their NorthStar Navigation Cubes, one of which comes with your Braava), which bounces a signal off your ceiling, and the signal is then received by the Braava. This helps the Braava to map the room, and even know and remember its location within it. If you have to stop your Braava to change cleaning pads, you can just set Braava back down on the floor and it will remember where it left off in the room. That is both cool and a little scary that a mop is so doggone smart.

You can purchase multiple NorthStar Navigation Cubes, which will extend the cleaning range of your Braava.

Figure 5-3:
Braava is
iRobot's
way of
telling your
dust mop to
take a hike.

Image courtesy of iRobot Corporation.

Check out `www.irobot.com/us/learn/home/Braava.aspx` to see more information about Braava, as well as watch a great video that shows the NorthStar Navigation System in action.

Stay tuned for more great iRobot products in upcoming chapters.

LG

Most everyone recognizes LG, a company that has its proverbial fingers in all the technology pots, from cellphones to refrigerators. For the topic of this book, however, take a quick look at how LG can help you do your laundry.

LG's line of Smart ThinQ appliances brings the Internet into devices that at one time had no interaction with anything or anyone unless he was standing directly in front of the unit. However, Smart ThinQ appliances, which run the gamut from refrigerators to ranges to laundry devices, can use the Internet to update their software and to allow communication with their owners. Smart ThinQ technology allows the following interactions:

- Your washer and dryer can download new and improved wash and dry cycles from LG, as well as any other software updates, through your home's Wi-Fi. And did I mention for free?
- The washer and dryer can notify you when cycles begin, finish, or are interrupted.
- The LG Smart Laundry app, shown in Figure 5-4, allows you to monitor and control washer and dryer cycles no matter where you are. You can also use it to download the aforementioned wash and dry cycles and software updates.

For more information on LG's line of Smart ThinQ washers and dryers, visit `www.lg.com/us/discover/smartthinq/laundry.jsp`. And if cooking is (or is not) your thing, check out Chapter 8, where I discuss LG Smart ThinQ kitchen appliances.

RoboMop

You've seen some pretty high-tech devices up to this point in the chapter, and there are more to come. However, I thought I'd change the pace just a tad and move to a decidedly low-tech automated home cleaning solution: the RoboMop.

Figure 5-4:
LG's Smart
Laundry
app allows
remote
access to
and control
of your
Smart ThinQ
washer and
dryer.

Image courtesy of LG Electronics.

RoboMop has one function in life: to keep your hard floor surfaces clean from dust and small debris. But that's not the low-tech part I'm speaking of. You'll have to get a load of RoboMop's ultra-simplistic design, on display in Figure 5-5, to appreciate just how low-tech I'm going.

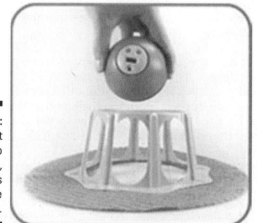

Figure 5-5:
There's not
much to
RoboMop,
but it gets
its simple
job done.

RoboMop isn't designed to look cool or feel like it will last for decades. It's made for chasing those rabid dust bunnies while remaining extremely afford-able. RoboMop uses a robotic (I use the term loosely) ball placed inside a plastic frame that holds a cleaning pad. Here are the steps to follow to get RoboMop embarking on its dust-bunny sentry duty:

1. **Charge the ball for three hours.**

2. **Secure the cleaning pad to the bottom of the plastic frame and place it on the floor.**

3. **Use the ball's built-in timer to select how long you want RoboMop to clean.**

4. **Place the ball in the top opening of the frame, and away it goes.**

   RoboMop will run for the selected amount of time, hopefully having completely eradicated your dust bunny problem.

In spite of how neat an idea and inexpensive RoboMop is, it isn't just some-thing for which you can run down to the local store and grab off the shelf. However, you can order RoboMop through several online retailers, including Amazon. You can also view a short video about how to use RoboMop at the company's website, `www.robomop.com`.

And just in case you're wondering, no, the RoboMop is not accompanied by an iOS or Android app.

Neato Robotics

Before you even know about its products, you've gotta love its name: Neato Robotics. Any kid growing up in the 1970s and 1980s who was a sci-fi aficio-nado or computer geek has used the word "neato" to describe cool technol-ogy at one point or another. The fact that someone incorporated it into a company name just makes sense.

Neato Robotics does what its name implies: It makes neato robots. However, its robots have simple missions in life: to keep your hard floors and carpets clean, clean, clean. Neato Robotics is also not an iRobot clone; while the robotic vacuums may resemble those of iRobot in the fact that they're small and can automatically go back to their charging stations when they need more juice in the batteries, they do have significant differences:

- Neato Robotics' vacuums use a flat edge on the front of their robots, making for a wider brush. That, of course, means it covers more ground.

- Neato uses lasers to scan and map the room it's cleaning (the technology is called BotVision), and develops a plan to tackle the job. As the com-pany points out on its website, its robots aren't "just bumping around."

✔ Neato supplies you with Boundary Markers — magnetic strips that you can place on your floor to make a boundary that the Neato 'bots won't cross over. You can cut the Boundary Markers to fit your doorways and other areas that may need a custom fit.

✔ Neato believes in the "bigger is better" approach to some things. The large dirt bin, extra-large filters, and wider brushes attest to that philosophy.

Neato has two lines of vacuuming robots: the BotVac series and the XV series. The BotVac series (one of which is shown in Figure 5-6) includes higher-end machines with wider brushes, and are therefore more expensive than their XV brothers. But honestly, you really can't go wrong with either model type. These devices have all been praised by the likes of CNET, and you can read a slew of reviews in the News section of the Neato website: www.neatorobotics.com.

Figure 5-6: The BotVac 70e is just one of the great BotVac and XV series of robotic vacuums from Neato Robotics.

Image courtesy of Neato Robotics Incorporated.

Grillbot

Listen up, all you Masters of the Grill: Cleaning everyone's favorite cooking device just got awesome-easy. I'm talking ROBOTIC-easy. That's right: No more stabbing yourself with a thousand tiny metal bristles or scrubbing your knuckles off; we have a robot that can clean the grill for you!

The Grillbot is the dream gizmo of everyone who loves to grill but hates to clean up the darned things. Grillbot comes standard with three brass bristle brushes, which it uses to blast the grate of your grill for up to 30 minutes. The brushes are dishwasher safe and easy to remove and reinstall.

Grillbot offers stainless steel brushes that are a bit more durable than the brass brushes. (Stainless steel brushes can handle the tougher jobs without wearing out as quickly.) You can purchase them from the Grillbot website, www.grillbots.com.

Here's how the whole thing goes down:

1. **Grill your favorite meat and veggies and enjoy!**

2. **Allow your grill to cool down to at least 250 degrees Fahrenheit (cooler is better).**

   NEVER use the Grillbot over an open flame!

3. **Place the Grillbot on the grill's grate, as shown in Figure 5-7.**

4. **Press the button on the Grillbot once for a 10-minute cycle, twice for a 20-minute cycle, and three times for 30 minutes of grate-grinding fun.**

5. **Grillbot will begin cleaning after a 5-second delay, to give you time to close the grill's lid before it gets started.**

6. **Grillbot will stop when the cycle is complete and will emit an alert to inform you it's done its job.**

Figure 5-7:
Grillbot is destined to become the avid griller's best friend.

Image courtesy of Grillbots.

Be sure to close the top of the grill! Grillbot will start churning away on your grate five seconds after you set the timer. When it starts to work, there's very little shielding to keep the bits and pieces of grill-gunk from flying in your eyes.

Hopefully, someday the people at Grillbots will come up with a device that cleans the ashes for charcoal grills. Until then, you'd be hard-pressed to find a better Father's Day gift than this puppy. Hint, hint, wink, wink to my family.

RoboSnail

I can imagine that there's some segment of my readers who saw the title of this section and simply put the book down or skipped ahead a few pages. If you're one of those who stuck around, I'd like you to know that I won't be talking about slimy critters in this section — just slime. Aquarium slime, to be more precise. RoboSnail is not an ill-conceived sequel to the *Robocop* movies, in which a fatally wounded snail is paired with robotic technology that renews its life and turns it into a super-snail that cleans up crime-ridden gardens. As cool as that sounds, the real RoboSnail will sound just as awesome to aquarium owners.

RoboSnail cleans not your floors or even your grill, but your aquarium. The device (see Figure 5-8) is the world's first automatic cleaning tool for aquariums, taking on the daily mission of scouring the glass in your aquarium to keep it free from algae buildup.

Figure 5-8: RoboSnail keeps algae from taking over your aquarium's glass, making it easier for your fish to spy on you.

Image courtesy of AquaGenesis International, Inc.

RoboSnail consists of two moving parts that work in tandem to keep algae from overtaking the denizens of your aquarium. The first is the RoboSnail apparatus itself, which attaches to the outside (dry side) of your aquarium. This apparatus is what actually drives the whole show. The second part of the RoboSnail partnership is the Sweeper unit, which attaches to the inside (wet side) of the aquarium's glass. The two units are held together through the glass by a very strong magnet. No worries about the magnet affecting your fish, though, unless they happen to be alien robots that are using your aquarium as a launching pad for their invasion of Earth, in which case it's a bonus for us.

RoboSnail (`www.robosnail.com`) cleans your glass on a daily schedule, so it will need periodic maintenance to keep up the pace. However, the maintenance is a small price to pay when compared to the time and expense of cleaning the algae out of your aquarium once it's built up on the glass. That's a nasty job that all aquarium hobbyists loathe. Rejoice, people: RoboSnail is here to save the day!

Chapter 6

I'm in the Mood for . . . Anything: Automated Lighting

In This Chapter

▶ Automating your home's lighting

▶ Understanding the technology behind automated lighting

▶ Seeing the best automated lighting products from the best manufacturers

*I*t was a dark and stormy night . . .

And there you were, hiding under the covers.

Whether you consider the "dark and stormy night" line to be one of the best or worst in the history of novels, dark and stormy nights are no laughing matter to some folks.

Especially if, amid the clatter of the storm raging outside, you hear another clatter. Only this time, it's coming from the general direction of the kitchen. Chances of you getting up to see what's going on? Zero. Zilch. Nada.

Wouldn't it be great if you could turn on the lights without even having to get out of bed? How cool would it be to flip on the lights in the kitchen to see if someone lets out a "yelp" and takes off? It sure beats going in there, you know, where it's *dark*.

Suddenly you remember that you have newly installed automated lighting, and you can simply grab your smartphone off the nightstand and turn on the kitchen lights using your trusty app, coupled with a few swipes and taps of your finger!

Click! The lights come on and you hear a scramble! Just then you see your husband running from the kitchen, freshly made turkey sandwich in hand, bolting for the garage to hide the fact that he's been cheating on his diet again. That scoundrel would've gotten away with it, too, if it weren't for your automated lighting. Technology to the rescue!

Lighting Your Life Automatically

From the first sparks of fire in a cave who-knows-how-many years ago right up until the late 1870s, fire has always been how we lit up the darkness in our lives. From campfires to wooden torches to candles to oil-filled lamps, the flame was how we made cave paintings, read parchments, and conducted outdoor events in the dark of night.

That changed forever, though, in 1879, when Thomas Edison finally struck a notion to use carbonized bamboo as the material for the filament in his new-fangled electric light bulbs. From that moment on, we've taken great strides in lighting our way in dark places. I love to look at photos taken from space of the dark side of our planet and see all the lights dotting the earth. As you can see in Figure 6-1, most of us owe Thomas Edison an incredible amount of gratitude. Like most conveniences, we rarely give lighting much thought until we have a problem with it or don't have access to it. Then all heck breaks loose.

Now that we have electric lighting, we must learn how to maximize its potential while minimizing its impact on the environment and our wallets. Automated lighting is a great step in the right direction.

Reasons for automatic lighting

As technology gets better and people's knowledge grows, so does the need to be more responsible with the world's resources. Since the bulk of energy use is tied to lighting people's homes and the places we frequent, it only makes sense to move to automatic lighting.

Figure 6-1:
This NASA photo shows how much of our world is lit at night. Stunning!

Image courtesy of NASA.

The benefits of automatic lighting are obvious — and not so obvious. Consider:

✔ Automated lighting helps keep lights on when they need to be and off when they should be. Although it sounds elementary, simply turning lights on when entering a room and off when leaving it saves a ton of money and energy.

✔ Lighting often deters folks from doing things they ought not be doing. Lighted houses are much less likely to be broken into than those that aren't. Automated lighting helps you keep a light on when you may not be home.

✔ Lights that automatically dim based on other lighting conditions (sunlight, for example) save you big time on your energy bill.

✔ Being able to remotely control your lights is nothing short of awesome. If you accidentally leave the lights on all over the house when you dash out the door for work, just pull out your trusty smartphone and turn the lights off when you get a moment. Why fill the energy company's coffers any more than necessary?

✔ Automated lighting ups the safety value of your home. For example, when your little ones get out of bed at night, motion sensors can trigger lights to come on and go off through the house, following your child to and from her night-time destinations.

Auto-lighting technology

Automated lighting is one of the "it" factors when it comes to home automation. Everyone automatically thinks of turning the lights on and off when the subject of home automation is broached, and for good reason: It's really, really awesome to remotely and/or automatically control anything, especially something so prevalent in our lives as lighting. Now is a good place to start exploring what you can do with today's automated lighting technologies.

Some of the lighting technologies I'm about to discuss employ specific types of bulbs, and others do not. To max out your power savings and achieve a superior experience with your automatic lighting solution, it's always best to use energy-saving light bulbs. It saves you money in both the power they consume and the infrequency with which they need to be replaced.

Here are just a few of the things that you can do today in your home once you implement an automated lighting solution:

✔ Set schedules for your home's lights to turn on or off when you want them to.

✔ Dim lights automatically, saving you on your power bills and also dramatically extending the life of your bulbs.

✔ Use a series of preset conditions that adjust your home's lighting to fit certain conditions. For example, if you are planning to have a romantic evening with that special someone, you can use your Date Night setting to immediately set the lights in certain rooms to low, turn other lights off completely, and otherwise turn your pad into the most romantic getaway in town. Other settings ideas include:

  • *Sleep:* These settings turn off most of the lights in the home, leaving just a few on in strategic places like the bathroom and front porch.

  • *Party:* This combination of settings turns most of the lights in the house on, setting a few to dim and creating specific moods. You can even use this setting to control your lava lamps and disco ball.

  • *Morning:* This setting turns on the bathroom and kitchen lights, as well as those in the garage, so you can make your way safely to the car in those wee early hours.

✔ Motion sensors can be employed in your home auto-lighting solution. As you enter one room, the lights come on for you, and after you leave the previous room, its lights go off. The lights appear to follow you throughout your home as you move from room to room, and the energy company begins to wonder how you're getting away with using so much less electricity lately. Motion sensors also detect when the residence is occupied, adding even more control to your lighting solution.

These are but a few of the things that automated lighting can do to make your life better. Check out the following section of who's who in the field of automated lighting, and begin improving the quality of your life and the sum in your bank account today. Something tells me that your power company won't go belly up any time soon, so you can switch to automated lighting with a clear conscience.

Illuminating the Kings of Automatic Lighting

Automated lighting has some heavyweight contenders who want you to light up your life with their products. You've probably heard of some of these folks before, but others might be new to you. Rest assured, though, that when it comes to smart home lighting, these folks know their stuff.

Philips

Philips has long been a giant in the lighting world, and it's taken quite a large step into the world of automated lighting. Philips has developed a system of automated lighting that changes the way you see your world. That sounds like one big overblown statement to make, but once you see what the company is up to, I suspect you'll be inclined to agree.

hue

The fine folks at Philips have conjured up a little thing they call hue. The hue isn't a single device, but rather a line of devices that redefines how you light the spaces around you. "Redefines" seems like an awfully bold word to toss around when it comes to something like lighting, but I can't gush enough about Philips's hue products and how they work to affect your daily life.

Next, I explain what hue products do.

The hue range of products uses LED lighting, so they aren't conventional bulbs, but they will fit into your current light sockets because they are the same size as standard A19 (the same size as most incandescent bulbs we're all used to) bulbs. But that's not all.

The hue bulbs connect wirelessly (using ZigBee, which you can find more about in Chapter 1) to the hue bridge (all of which can be seen in Figure 6-2), which connects to your Wi-Fi, allowing you to control your hue system via your smartphone or tablet with the hue app.

Figure 6-2:
The hue
A19 starter
pack
includes
three bulbs
and a
bridge.

Image courtesy of Koninklijke Philips N.V.

A hue bulb is able to light your home with brilliant white light. But that's not all. It also can light your home with every shade of color in the spectrum. That's right, I said it: every shade, from one bulb.

Here are a few other tidbits about hue:

- ✔ You can control 50 hue bulbs from one bridge.

- ✔ Mix and match colors throughout your home to make incredible combinations of colors.

- ✔ Use the hue app to create Lighting Recipes. These recipes are groups of settings that you can combine to make a recipe, which the app can easily recall and implement. Here are some recipe ideas that are already built into the app:

  - • *Reading:* Your hue lights will automatically give you the perfect light for reading conditions.

  - • *Concentrate:* This combination of lighting helps you maintain your focus.

  - • *Energize:* This is perfectly suited to giving you that extra pep when you need it.

- ✔ The hue app enables you to easily customize colors by increasing or decreasing combinations of color within the app.

- ✔ You can set your hue bulbs to pulsate, or flicker, or any combination of flashes to help remind you of events or alert you about activities. For example, you could set your hue bulbs to flash three times when you receive an important email.

- ✔ Set up schedules to automatically turn your hue bulbs on or off at preset times.

- ✔ Geofencing capabilities let hue know when you're close to home so that when you are within a preset distance to the house, the lights will be on and waiting to welcome you.

- ✔ The app enables you to create custom colors that match those in pictures that reside on your smartphone or tablet, as shown in Figure 6-3. For example, if the sky is so perfectly blue that you just have to take a picture of it so that you don't forget it, you can use the hue app to "see" that particular shade of blue and it will create that same color in your bulb(s).

The hue's recipes are based on sound science. Color really can impact you and your moods in ways most of us have never thought of, or at least don't spend much time dwelling on. Philips has put together a great site aimed at teaching you all about lighting and how it can help you (as well as hurt you). That site is the Lighting University, and you can access it by going to www. lighting.philips.com/main/connect/lighting_university/.

Figure 6-3:
The hue app can customize your bulbs' colors using pictures stored on your smartphone or tablet. Just pick a color and your room will be bathed in it.

Image courtesy of Koninklijke Philips N.V.

Setting up hue

Setting up a hue system is ridiculously simple:

1. **Replace your old standard bulbs with hue bulbs and turn on the light switch.**

2. **Connect the hue bridge to your Wi-Fi hub using the Ethernet cable provided by Philips.**

3. **Download the hue app to your iOS or Android device.**

4. **Fire up the hue app and find your bridge on it.**

5. **Once you've selected your bridge, you can discover the bulbs you installed in Step 1.**

Now you have complete control over your hue system. It's simple to add more bulbs to the mix as you see fit, too. You can even add other hue products to your system; you don't have to be stuck with standard A19 bulbs, or other styles, if you started your hue system with one of the starter packs.

hue tap

If there could be a con to owning the hue lighting system, it would have to be this: The only way to control your lights is via the app on your iOS or Android device. You can no longer turn your light switches on and off like you've done from the time Mom and Dad first started pestering you about it way back when. You can imagine what a hassle this could potentially turn into, especially if you aren't the only person occupying your home. Your kids will dutifully turn lights on and off at the switch as you taught them to, your spouse will have his own lighting ideas and recipes, and all other manner of higgledy-piggledy will take place. Bank on it.

The folks at Philips heard the complaints and totally understood, so they went to work doing something about it. That something is the hue tap. The tap, seen in Figure 6-4, is a four-button switch that you can take anywhere in the home with you, or you can mount it in a location of your choosing. The tap controls your hue system without the need of your app (once you've set it up, that is). Don't worry, though: Your hue system still works with your app. It's just that with the tap you won't have to constantly be on the lookout for your smartphone or tablet.

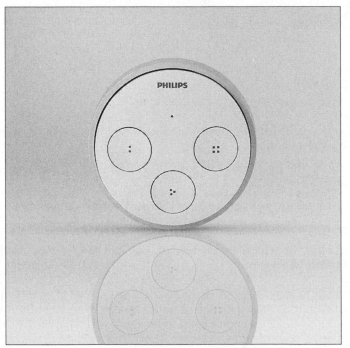

Figure 6-4
The hue tap functions as a standalone light switch for your hue lighting system.

Image courtesy of Koninklijke Philips N.V.

I mention earlier that the tap has four buttons; at first glance, though, it only looks like there are three. The other button is actually the biggest part of the tap; the other three buttons are actually inside of the larger button.

Features of the hue tap include:

✔ Use the hue app to set up your tap. You can assign different functions to its four buttons from here.

✔ Take tap with you anywhere in the house; it's completely portable.

✔ The tap never needs batteries! It actually uses kinetic energy as its power source, meaning that it's powered by your touch. That, my friends, is worth the price of admission.

You can find the entire line of hue products, including where to buy them, at www2.meethue.com/. It has great videos and support materials, too.

INSTEON

INSTEON has been doing the home automation thing for more than 20 years, and that experience shows in its polished and expansive line of home automation products. If it's home automation, INSTEON dabbles in it. Here are several examples of the company's offerings:

✔ Security

✔ Motion sensors

✔ Sprinkler controls

✔ Energy monitoring

✔ Wi-Fi cameras

✔ Smoke detection

✔ Thermostats

✔ Remote controls

In my opinion, INSTEON shines with its work in home lighting. From bulbs to dimmers to switches, INSTEON has this automated lighting stuff down cold. The LED bulbs save tons of money and energy. INSTEON excels at dimmers and switches, which also save you money and energy by using less of the latter — even in lighting devices that don't support dimming themselves. The company also has developed a smart hub that enables you, dear reader, to control all the lighting devices remotely. You're about to dive head first into INSTEON's home automated lighting and see for yourself what I'm raving about.

As you begin to investigate INSTEON you'll most likely run into the term dual-band. *Dual-band* refers to how INSTEON manages communications among its devices in your home. INSTEON uses a dual approach, utilizing your home's built-in wiring as well as RF (radio frequency) to converse among devices. This ensures that no matter how far an INSTEON device may be from other INSTEON devices or hubs, they'll still stay in contact. Thumbs up, INSTEON!

LED bulbs

Since this chapter concentrates on lighting, I start the INSTEON section with a look at its LED light bulbs, one of which you can see in Figure 6-5. INSTEON LED bulbs are much more energy efficient than standard light bulbs, using anywhere from 9 watts to 12 watts (depending on the bulb) and providing light that's equivalent to a 60-watt standard bulb.

Figure 6-5: INSTEON LED bulbs, like the A19 shown here, can save you a great deal of money in energy costs and bulb purchases.

Image courtesy of INSTEON.

INSTEON's LED bulbs are the world's first networked dimmable bulb, and there's more to them than meets the eye:

- LED bulbs fit right into your standard bulb sockets (A19 for typical bulbs and PAR38 for recessed lights), so there's no need to buy new lighting sockets.

- Create custom lighting scenes using different levels (preset brightness) and ramp rates (how long it takes your bulb to turn on or off).

- Color temperature for INSTEON bulbs are set to 2,700k, which gives you a rich, warm light (the same as the incandescent bulbs that we're all used to).

- INSTEON LED bulbs are built to last for 52,000 hours, compared to only 1,000 hours for typical bulbs. "Cha-ching," says the wallet.

- According to INSTEON, its bulbs will cost an average of 96 cents a year to operate, compared to more than $7 a year for standard bulbs.

- INSTEON bulbs are built to dim, which is not something that all LED bulbs can boast.

INSTEON bulbs do indeed dim, but you need INSTEON dimmers, or the INSTEON hub paired with the INSTEON app, to perform this action. And no, you cannot use INSTEON bulbs with your standard dimming switches; they simply won't work.

Find out more about INSTEON bulbs here: www.INSTEON.com/267x-led-bulbs.html.

Couple your INSTEON light bulbs with INSTEON motion sensors. With this kind of setup, you can have your lights come on when motion is detected in the room you're entering, or to go off once you leave the room.

INSTEON dimmers and switches

INSTEON LED bulbs are great, but to maximize their usefulness you need to get your hands on INSTEON dimmers and switches, too. These little fellows are built to work with INSTEON products, so they fit seamlessly into your INSTEON environment.

INSTEON's SwitchLinc dimmers and switches are award-winning devices. Four models are available, each with a slightly different purpose in mind:

- **2474DWH:** This puppy is designed for junction boxes that have no neutral wire. The first caveat is that it will only communicate in RF, not dually through RF and your home's wiring. The second is that it will only work with dimmable incandescent lights, not LEDs.

- **2477DH:** This bad boy is the dimmer switch for high wattage needs. It can dim and switch up to 1,000 watts. It does require the presence of a neutral wire in the junction box.

- **2477S:** This on/off switch does only two things: turns them on or off, no dimming available. However, it does still connect to your INSTEON network, and it does enable you to remotely control more than just lights, including items such as ceiling fans.

✔ **2477D:** This dimmer, shown in Figure 6-6, is the most popular of the four. It is used to dim and switch on or off most of the lighting in your home. If your lights are dimmable and you have a neutral wire in the junction box you want to install it in, this model is for you.

Figure 6-6:
INSTEON's 2477D dimmer can handle most dimming and switching needs, and it also enables remote control of said functions.

Image courtesy of INSTEON.

Those of you who like a bit of style to go along with your tech, have no fear: INSTEON dimmers and switches don't just come in white. They come in a variety of designer colors to suit almost any decor need.

See more of these really innovative dimmers and switches by visiting www.INSTEON.com/2477-wall-switches.html.

INSTEON app and hub

INSTEON is rocking with the lights, dimmers, and switches, but this is the age of the smartphone, where people demand that everything from controlling their lights to making a pot of coffee can be done with a tap or swipe of the screen. This isn't lost on the good people at INSTEON, as evidenced by their attention to detail in their smart hub and apps for iOS and Android devices.

The INSTEON hub, shown in Figure 6-7, is the center of your INSTEON-enabled home. It not only connects all your INSTEON devices in one location, but also provides access to your devices via the previously mentioned app.

Figure 6-7:
The
INSTEON
hub enables
you to
remotely
control your
lighting
(among
other home
automation
activities).

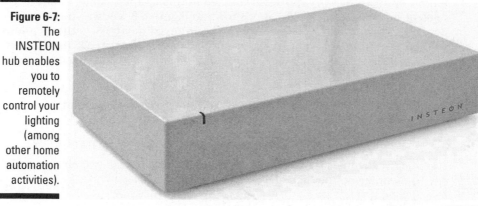

Image courtesy of INSTEON.

While INSTEON's hub does handle a slew (yes, that's a numeric term, where I come from) of functions, this chapter is mainly concerned with lighting, of course. The hub can help you with lighting control in several ways:

- You are always connected to your home's lighting, whether you're there or halfway around the world (as long as you have Internet access, of course).

- All your settings are stored in the cloud, so no matter how many smartphones or tablets you have, you can use and access the same settings from all of them.

- Receive email or instant message alerts whenever a problem or other incident arises.

- Your purchase of the hub is a one-time expense; no monthly fees with INSTEON! (That's a huge advantage of INSTEON, in my opinion.)

- The hub also utilizes the dual-band technology I discuss earlier. Dual-band allows INSTEON to use both the power lines in your home and RF to communicate among INSTEON devices.

- Access your hub and interact with your INSTEON devices via the iOS or Android app on your smart devices, or via a web browser on your computer.

I mention the INSTEON app several times in this chapter, so let's take a peek at it now. The INSTEON app, shown in Figure 6-8, allows you to control all your INSTEON devices from your smart device, whether a phone or tablet, as long as it runs a relatively recent version of an iOS or Android operating system. In terms of controlling your INSTEON lighting, though, here's what you can do:

- ✔ Control individual lighting devices within your home, including bulbs and/or dimmers and switches.
- ✔ Set up lighting scenes, and implement them whether home or away.
- ✔ Make schedules for your lights to come on or go off as you please, depending on the time of day or night.
- ✔ Adjust levels and ramp rates on the fly.

To see the myriad ways the INSTEON hub can help you control your lighting and most other home automation needs, go to www.INSTEON.com/hub. Tell 'em Dwight sent you.

TCP

TCP has been a player in the energy-efficient lighting market for more than 20 years, and it's put its hat in the smart home ring with its line of Connected light bulbs.

Figure 6-8: INSTEON's app allows you to control your lighting from any Internet-connected iOS or Android smartphone or tablet from anywhere.

Image courtesy of INSTEON.

The Connected system uses LED bulbs (see Figure 6-9) to brighten your day (and night), and those bulbs are quite nice. Here are some of their features:

- ✔ The brightness of the bulbs is 800 lumens, which is about as bright as a standard 60-watt bulb. The Connected bulbs are among the brightest of those discussed so far in this chapter.

- ✔ These bulbs are also smart, communicating with the Connect Lighting Gateway so that you can control them from anywhere in your home (or out of it, as you see in a bit).

- ✔ The bulbs come in two sizes: A19 to fit standard bulb sockets, and BR30 for recessed lighting.

- ✔ Both sizes come in either soft white or daylight, and you can mix the two if you like.

The best way to get going with a TCP Connected system is by getting a starter kit, which consists of:

- ✔ Three bulbs (two starter kits are available, one for each bulb size)
- ✔ One Lighting Gateway
- ✔ One remote control

Figure 6-9:
TCP's LED bulbs come very close to equaling the light given off by standard 60-watt bulbs.

CONNECTED
automated home lighting system

60
WATT EQUIVALENT
SOFT WHITE

Brightness
800 lumens

Estimated Energy Cost
$1.32 per year

LED A19

Image courtesy of TCP International Holdings, Ltd.

Setting up your Connected system is simple:

1. **Turn off power to the light sockets at the wall switch.**

2. **Replace your existing bulbs with new Connected bulbs.**

3. **Turn the wall light switches back on.**

4. **Hook the Lighting Gateway to your Wi-Fi router using the supplied Ethernet cable and the power cable.**

5. **Download the TCP Lighting app from the iOS or Android App Store.**

6. **Walk through the on-screen instructions for setting up your Connected bulbs.**

   The app will automatically discover the bulbs once you open it on your smart device.

I implore you to run, not walk, to the nearest computer and use your favorite browser to check out the home automation goodies on TCP's site at `http://go.tcpi.com/GetConnected`.

 The TCP Connected bulbs are compatible with the Wink system (see Chapter 14 for more information about Wink). This means that if you already have the Wink hub, all you now need to purchase are individual TCP bulbs, as opposed to needing a starter kit. The Wink hub takes the place of TCP's Lighting Gateway, and the Wink app can handle the remote control of your lights on both iOS and Android devices.

SmartThings

SmartThings is another company with an eye on home automation. Not to say that others aren't on top of the home automation game, too, but SmartThings has been a company on the move for a few years now, and it continues to grow in popularity.

Its home automation philosophy revolves around the SmartThings Hub, which is the control center for devices that are compatible with the SmartThings universe. The Hub, shown in Figure 6-10, is, of course, interacted with by use of a really great app.

"Okay, so it has a hub and an app, but so do other companies."

I knew you were going to say that!

Figure 6-10:
The SmartThings Hub keeps your SmartThings-compatible devices in constant communication with you.

Image courtesy of SmartThings, Inc.

The SmartThings app may be one of the best home automation apps out there, in my humble opinion. The interface alone is just beautiful to look at, but its functionality is also second to none. However, it isn't just the hub and the app that make SmartThings, well, smart; it's the number of vendors who work with them to supply cutting-edge home automation products for you. Since this chapter focuses on lighting, I stick to that topic here. Some of the companies that have teamed up with SmartThings include:

- GE
- Aeon Labs
- Jasco
- SmartPower

SmartThings offers stand-alone products and offers starter kits that cater to how you might want to kick-start your home automation habit. There are kits for water leak detection, security, and energy saving. For the purposes in this chapter, though, I talk only about the lighting automation kit, which you can see in Figure 6-11. This kit contains one of each of the following items:

- **SmartThings Hub:** Control all the SmartThings-compatible devices you're sure to invest in once you get your feet wet (not literally, of course — water and electricity don't mix!).

✔ **SmartPower Outlet:** You can plug your lights (or any other electrical device, for that matter) into it. You can then control the outlet itself, turning your lights on and off with it, and even get alerts if you've left the lights on. And of course you can use the SmartThings app to turn them off.

✔ **Jasco Pluggable Light Dimmer Outlet:** This outlet plugs into a standard wall outlet, giving you one additional outlet along with a Z-Wave AC outlet that you can control through your SmartThings hub and app. This baby works as advertised, allowing you to control and even dim your connected lights.

✔ **Aeon Labs Minimote:** This is essentially a remote control for your SmartThings-compatible devices. You can control lighting with this remote instead of having to use your smartphone or tablet, which is convenient if you're charging your device or just don't want to have to go through a myriad of swipes and taps to turn your lights on or off.

You can download and take the SmartThings Mobile app for a trial spin if you want to just see how it works. I stand by the facts that it's both functional and beautiful, and giving it a test run is free, so why not?

Go to www.smartthings.com, friend. Just go.

Figure 6-11:
The SmartThings lighting automation kit contains everything you need to get started automating your home's existing lighting.

Belkin

Chapter 4 shows you how Belkin's WeMo products can help you control your thermostats, but now you're going to find out how the exact same apps and products can make you master of your home's lighting.

WeMo's LED Lighting Starter Set

WeMo's LED Lighting Starter Set (is there an echo in here?) comes loaded with everything you need to get started in the world of automated lighting — the WeMo way.

The Starter Set, shown in Figure 6-12, comes with the following goodies:

- **Two WeMo Smart LED Bulbs:** The bulbs give off roughly the same amount of light as a typical 60-watt bulb. They can also be dimmed to help set the mood and save your cash.

- **One WeMo Link:** The Link acts as the central control hub for up to 50 WeMo Smart LED Bulbs, so your whole house can get into the act.

Figure 6-12: The WeMo Lighting Starter Set gets you started automating the lighting in your home simply and affordably.

Image courtesy of Belkin.

Your lighting is then controlled via the WeMo app. Simply install your bulbs, connect the Link to your home's Wi-Fi network, and download the app. When you fire it up, it will automatically find your bulbs and get you rolling.

The WeMo Switch

Another option from Belkin is the WeMo Switch, which allows you to control whatever electrical device you see fit to plug into it. The Switch plugs into a standard 120v outlet in your home, at which time you can connect any electrical device to it. You can plug any lamp into the Switch and control it from a million miles away, so long as your Internet connection reaches that far.

The free WeMo app for iOS or Android devices allows you full control over whatever lighting device you plug into your Switch. This is how to do it:

1. **Plug your Switch into the outlet of your choice (or your dreams, if you're really into outlets).**

2. **Download the WeMo app on your iOS or Android smartphone or tablet.**

3. **Your Switch will create a WeMo network; just connect to the WeMo network as you would any other network on your device.**

4. **Open the WeMo app and choose your home's Wi-Fi network to connect your Switch to it.**

5. **Name your Switch with a descriptive name so you can easily tell which lighting device it controls in your home.**

   Choose an icon for the Switch to indicate the type of device it controls (a light, in this case), and then tap Done. The newly configured Switch will appear in your list of controlled devices.

6. **Tap the power switch icon next to your device in the list to turn it on or off.**

   Green shows you the device is on, and gray is off.

While this is probably the simplest lighting automation setup this chapter explores, it is by no means less. The WeMo Switch does what it is intended to do, and does it very well.

Check out www.wemothat.com to see what else the WeMo product line has to offer.

Chapter 7

Safe, Sound, and Hunkered Down

In This Chapter

▶ Keeping an eye on your home while you're away

▶ Things you can do to automate home security

▶ Getting to know smart home security devices and companies

*J*oe the caveman (yes, Joe's been a common name for quite a while, it seems) has it all:

- ✔ Jane, his lovely cavewife

- ✔ Three adorable cavekids

- ✔ This round stone thing that's good for getting around quickly (he's thinking about calling it a wheel or a cog, but he's having a tough time deciding which)

- ✔ A group of other cavemen with whom he likes to go hunting every day

- ✔ A set of clubs that would make Tiger Woods jealous (but used for entirely different purposes, of course)

- ✔ A great job down at the quarry (apologies to the Flintstones)

- ✔ A three-bedroom/two-bath cave on the south side of the mountain where the breeze doesn't blow in

Life is great for Joe, but in an instant his life could change if threatened. That's why Joe is heavy into modern security for his home and loved ones:

- ✔ Brutus, his trusty pet dinosaur, has been trained as an attack dino, but he's also great with the kids.

- ✔ Joe has an awesome fire pit situated right near the cave entrance, so it not only keeps the cave warm, but it also wards off any critters that might be skulking around.

- ✔ His collection of clubs are strategically placed around the cave so he can get to them quickly should the need arise.

As you can see, Joe is all about keeping those he loves, and the possessions he has, safe.

You and I are just as concerned about security for the people and things that matter the most to us, just as Joe was back in the day. But we do things a little differently.

Establishing Security in the Automatic Age

Passwords are everywhere. If passwords were tangible things, our world would be one huge alphanumeric soup, with letters and numbers and symbols lying all about, falling from the sky, dangling from trees, and generally creating all manner of chaos. They proliferate everything in our digital lives. You, I, and everyone else with electronic devices have passwords (and usernames — we mustn't forget those) for accessing the following and more:

- ✔ Computer
- ✔ Smartphone
- ✔ Tablet
- ✔ Email
- ✔ Bank account
- ✔ App store accounts
- ✔ Social media accounts (Facebook, Twitter, Google+, and the list goes on and on)
- ✔ Streaming video subscriptions (Netflix, Hulu, and so forth)
- ✔ Online retail stores (Amazon and the like)
- ✔ Viewing your kids' grades online
- ✔ Internet service provider account
- ✔ Television service provider account
- ✔ Accounts for all the home automation devices you'll purchase after reading this book

There are even software constructs, such as Apple's Keychain in its OS X operating system, which keeps all the passwords you have for all your accounts in one encrypted, safe place. Of course, you have to remember your Keychain password, but remembering one is better than remembering 50.

Keeping electronic things secure has become a way of life for most of us, and keeping our homes secure has been a priority since man moved into his first cave a few millennia ago.

Keeping your eyes homeward

There are any number of scenarios you can dream up for keeping tabs on your home while you aren't there:

- ✔ What happens if your kids are home but don't have their keys? They can call you and you could use the passcode on your iPhone's app to unlock the deadbolt, or they could use their own smartphones to do so.

- ✔ You're on vacation and no one is home, but you get a motion-detection alert on your Android tablet. Time to call the police to check it out.

- ✔ The baby is sleeping but you're afraid to go wash clothes on the other end of the house because you might not hear her if she wakes. No problem: Just use the Wi-Fi camera in her room and its app on your smart device to keep an eye on and an ear out for her.

That barely scratches the surface of what homeowners and parents can imagine when it comes to security needs, but you get the picture.

Locking things down

You have four main ways to making your home more secure, and I quickly explore them all in this section of the chapter.

Alarms

Home alarms have been around for decades, but these days, your alarm won't just make a loud noise to wake the neighbors, or alert only the security company. You can now be advised, via an app on your smart device, when an alarm has been triggered. You can also reset the alarm from afar, without having to get up from your beach chair when on vacation.

Locks

You can lock or unlock smart locks with an app on your smart device. Some of them even allow access to your locks from computers through a web browser. And for those moments when you feel like going old school, you can also still use a key.

Cameras

Web cameras have been around for a while, too, and you've even been able to view their streams from remote computers using web browsers. Now that smartphones and tablets are here, you can view your webcam from just about anywhere, provided you have access to the Internet.

Motion detectors

Again, motion detectors are nothing new for some folks, but the way you can interact with them from your smart devices opens a whole new world of security possibilities.

Staking Out the Wardens of Home Security

As smart home technology takes off, home security is one of the areas that has seen a real proliferation in devices. Security is more important to most folks than, say, vacuuming the floor or cleaning the fish tank, so devices catering to that market tend to spring up faster than some others. In this part of the chapter, you meet a few of the major players in the arena of smart home security.

SmartThings

One of the more popular functions of the SmartThings home automation system is home security. So much so, in fact, that the company has developed a kit that caters specifically to home security. Actually, it has three separate kits for catering to those concerned with home security: Smart Home Security kit, Smarter Home Security kit, and the Smartest Home Security kit (see Figure 7-1). Take a look at what each kit offers.

The Smart Home Security kit contains:

- ✔ **One SmartThings hub:** This is the nerve center of the SmartThings home automation system. You need this so that you and your devices can communicate.

- ✔ **One SmartSense Motion Sensor:** This will detect movement in whatever room you place it in.

- ✔ **One SmartSense Moisture Sensor:** This will help you know when potential leaks are occurring.

- ✔ **One SmartPower Outlet:** You can plug any electrical device into it and control how and when it operates.

- ✔ **One SmartSense Presence Sensor:** This little device is something that people or animals (as shown in Figure 7-2) carry on themselves. When they come within, or go outside of, range of the SmartThings hub or other sensor in your home automation environment, the system will trigger an alert or some other action.

- ✔ **One SmartSense Open/Closed Sensor:** This sensor will alert you when a door or window is opened or closed. You can even configure it to trigger your heating or cooling units if they are attached to a smart thermostat, which you read about in Chapter 4.

Figure 7-1:
The Smartest Home Security kit from SmartThings comes with a veritable cornucopia of security-minded devices.

Image courtesy of SmartThings, Inc.

Figure 7-2:
The SmartSense Presence Sensor alerts your SmartThings system when a person or animal (or car) is in proximity of it.

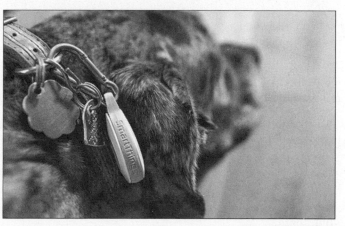

Image courtesy of SmartThings, Inc.

The Smarter Home Security comes with everything the Smart Home Security kit does, plus:

- **One FortrezZ Siren Strobe Alarm,** intended to scare the socks off of anyone who may be entering your home without your permission
- **Three additional SmartSense Open/Closed Sensors** (total of four)
- **One additional SmartSense Motion Sensor** (total of two)
- **One additional SmartPower Outlet** (total of two)

Now it's time to get really smart, with the Smartest Home Security kit, containing the same items as the Smart and Smarter Home Security kits, along with the following:

- **One Jasco Pluggable Light Dimmer Outlet**
- **One additional SmartSense Motion Sensor** (total of three)
- **One additional SmartSense Moisture Sensor** (total of two)
- **One additional SmartSense Presence Sensor** (total of two)

As you can see, SmartThings has you covered in the security department. Controlling your home security devices is a snap using the SmartThings app on your iOS or Android smart device. Visit www.smartthings.com/benefits/home-security/ for more information on getting smart about your home security.

SmartThings offers other home security devices as well, other than those included in the kits, so browse its website for more items that might fit your needs.

Belkin

Belkin's WeMo home automation system is a great one for the budget-conscious. That's not to say the devices are cheap by any means; they are simply more affordable than some others and they get the job done well.

In the home security arena, Belkin has what you need when it comes to the basics:

- Webcams that allow you to see the goings-on inside your home, even when you aren't there
- Motion sensors to alert you when movement is detected in certain areas of your home

I discuss Belkin's NetCam web cameras in detail in Chapter 15, so I urge you to mosey on over there to learn more about them.

The WeMo Motion motion sensor is a great little device that just does what it advertises: It detects motion and reports it to you on your iOS or Android smart device. Unfortunately, you can't buy the Motion sensor by itself; you have to buy it with a WeMo Switch as a bundle (see Figure 7-3).

The Motion can be paired with the Switch to turn lights, fans, or other devices on or off when motion is detected. This is a great way to get started with home automation and enhance your personal level of security, all at the same time. You can also tell the Motion to send you text messages when it detects movement.

Check out the Switch + Motion at `www.belkin.com/us/F5Z0340-Belkin/p/P-F5Z0340` to learn more.

Figure 7-3: The WeMo Switch and Motion work together to turn electrical devices on or off when movement is detected.

Image courtesy of Belkin.

Alarm.com

If you're someone who doesn't want to skimp on accessories, does want 24/7 monitoring by a third-party security company, and the cost of the whole thing is something you aren't overly concerned about, then Alarm.com just may be what you're looking for.

Alarm.com provides every security feature a smart home owner could need or want:

- The Alarm.com system uses wireless cellular technology to communicate your home's status to third-party security teams. This ensures that even if an intruder cuts communication lines going into your home, your system is still up and running wirelessly. This alone is a great feature of Alarm.com.

- The entire system has a battery backup should the power go out. So, for up to 24 hours after a power interruption, your family and home are still safe.

- Alarm.com's Image Sensor not only alerts you when motion is detected in a certain area of the home, but it also takes a high-quality picture and allows you to view it on your smart device or on your personalized Alarm.com website.

- You can tie your home security and home automation together in ways others can't do. One example from Alarm.com's website states that you can configure your system to shut down your HVAC in the event that carbon monoxide or smoke is detected, helping to slow down their spread throughout the home.

- You have full control over your Alarm.com system through the Internet using your smartphone, tablet, or computer, as shown in Figure 7-4.

Figure 7-4: Alarm.com enables you to take command of your entire system through its apps and website.

Image courtesy of Alarm.com.

I could say so much more about Alarm.com, but there's just too much information to give you in this format. Alarm.com is a full-service security and home automation outfit; it can do it all, and it also gives you full control over your security solution through its apps and website. You owe it to yourself to at least give this company and its products a look by visiting www.alarm.com.

Alarm.com does more than home security; it also is quite fluent in the languages of home automation, energy management, personal wellness, and more.

ADT

ADT has been in the security business for more than a century; we've all seen the company's signs in yards of customers who use its systems. You don't stick around that long unless you're good at what you do, and ADT is among the best when it comes to home security. As a forward-thinking company, ADT has made the move into home automation as well, blending the convenience of home automation with top-notch home security.

ADT's Pulse system combines security and automation into one package. ADT provides the following features:

✔ Monitors your Pulse system 24/7.

✔ Sends alerts to your smartphone or tablet.

✔ Enables you to control your home's lights and thermostats.

✔ Allows you to remotely arm and disarm the system.

✔ Uses Z-Wave technology, so it may be compatible with your existing home automation devices.

✔ Utilizes a wall-mounted touchscreen for easy control in your home.

✔ The Pulse web portal allows you to access your system from any web browser on any computer, so long as you have Internet access.

✔ Pulse Voice allows you to speak commands to your security system, such as "Arm the security system" or "Unlock the front door."

✔ View live camera feeds from your computer or smart device (see Figure 7-5).

✔ Use the Pulse app on your iOS or Android smartphone or tablet to remotely control and adjust settings for your system.

Image courtesy of ADT Security Systems.

Figure 7-5:
View live camera feeds using the Pulse app on your smartphone or tablet.

Of course, ADT charges a monthly fee to monitor your home. If that's not something that puts you off, however, then ADT Pulse is well worth looking into. Check out more information, including some very nice video tutorials, at `www.adt.com/pulse`.

Vivint

Once upon a time, there was a company called APX Alarm. APX changed its name to Vivint in 2010, combining the words "vive" and "intelligent," which means "to live intelligently." It was an apt name change, as helping its customers to live intelligently is exactly what Vivint does.

Vivint has become one of the biggest players when it comes to home automation, insofar as a company that does the whole thing for you. Vivint installs the components and quotes you a monthly price for monitoring. This isn't a bad thing, but it's the reason you don't see this company mentioned in other parts of this book: The book focuses mainly on do-it-yourself smart home automation. But since I'm talking about security, and I mention companies like ADT and Alarm.com, which provide 24/7 monitoring for a fee, I would be remiss to leave out a group as good at the craft as Vivint.

Here are some of the best features of Vivint's Smart Home Security package:

- Vivint's team monitors your home 24 hours, 7 days a week, 365¼ days a year (and all day February 29 in leap years when there are 366 days).
- The entire system is wireless, so no need to worry about intruders cutting wires or any such nonsense.

✔ A touchscreen mounted on a wall in your home allows for easy access to your security settings.

✔ Create nonemergency alerts that tell you when an event occurs, such as when a certain door, like the one to your toddler's room, is opened or closed.

✔ Motion detectors let you know when activity is taking place in a part of your home that you want to keep an eye on.

✔ Receive text alerts when potential problems arise, such as a smoke alarm being triggered or the system's alarm going off.

✔ Vivint Sky is Vivint's smart home technology that you can control from your touchscreen (see Figure 7-6), smart device, or computer.

The Vivint Smart Home Security package includes the following equipment:

✔ **1 touchscreen,** which utilizes the Vivint Sky technology for making and changing settings to your system.

✔ **1 motion detector.**

✔ **1 Vivint yard sign** (it's a high-tech one, I'm sure).

✔ **1 key fob,** which allows you to arm or disarm your system, and to even call Vivint, without having to use your smart device or touchscreen. This really comes in handy if you've left your smartphone at the office.

✔ **3 door/window sensors,** which alert you to when doors or windows open or close.

Figure 7-6: Vivint Sky technology helps you control your home security system at home or on the go.

Image courtesy of Vivint, Inc.

I don't know about you, but not including the yard sign would've been a deal breaker for me. While the preceding list doesn't sound like much, you are able to add more devices as you see a need. Some optional devices include:

- ✔ Smoke detectors
- ✔ Carbon monoxide detectors
- ✔ Panic pendants, which you wear on your clothing or carry in your pocket. It can be used in case of an accident to notify Vivint you have an emergency, so long as you're in range of your system.
- ✔ Glass-break detectors, which alert you to broken glass in your home. No, it won't go off if you knock a glass off the kitchen counter, but it will monitor windows for breakage. This is a pretty neat and unique device: two thumbs up.

If the idea of 24/7 monitoring sounds like your idea of home security (and who wouldn't think so?), go to `www.vivint.com/solutions/packages/home-security` to find out more.

As of this writing, you'll find a chart on Vivint's website that compares its offerings to other home security providers, but pay it no mind. Either it's simply outdated and needs revision, or it is comparing apples to oranges. For example, the chart claims that Vivint provides a touchscreen panel and ADT does not, but that is not the case. There are other such discrepancies in the chart, so simply pay it no mind in determining which company you'll want to use for monitored home security options.

Schlage

Walter Schlage began creating door locks way back in 1909, and the company bearing his name remains one of the stalwarts of door locks to this day. His first patent was for a door knob that not only locked but could turn lights on and off — in 1909! This kind of innovation is what has kept Schlage on top of its game over the years, and it continues into the age of the smart home.

Schlage has introduced the Connect and Touch lines of keyless locks, which also offer you connectivity with many of the major home automation companies so that you can control your electronic locks remotely.

The Connect line, one of which can be seen in Figure 7-7, is a bit pricy, but also a bit more top-of-the-line, offering the following features:

- ✔ It has been awarded the highest security grade in the industry, a Grade 1 rating.
- ✔ It features a motorized deadbolt.

✔ You can create and delete up to 30 access codes at a time.

✔ It uses Z-Wave technology to connect with home automation systems from third parties.

✔ You can remotely control your lock using your home automation system's app.

✔ It comes with a built-in alarm that sounds when the lock is tampered with.

✔ Activity Alerts let you know when folks come in or go out.

✔ It can tell when someone is using a lot of force to open the door, and then instantly send you a notification on your smart device.

✔ It enables you to go totally keyless or use a key, whichever you prefer.

Figure 7-7:
The Schlage Connect line of locks can use codes or a third-party home automation system to lock or unlock your door.

Image courtesy of Allegion plc.

The Touch line, shown in Figure 7-8, is also a great line of locks, but there are some key (pun intended) differences in features:

✔ It sports a Grade 2 security rating, which is high — but it ain't a 1.

✔ When Schlage says this lock is keyless, it means it; there is no key with the Touch line of locks. You use the keypad, an app, or you stay locked out.

✔ According to Schlage, this line is 100 percent pick-proof.

✔ It remembers up to 19 codes at a time.

✔ A built-in light helps you see what numbers you're pressing on the keypad.

Image courtesy of Allegion plc.

Figure 7-8:
Touch
electronic
locks
are truly
keyless.

Schlage electronic locks work with quite a few home automation systems that provide apps for controlling smart home devices. Some of those systems that make nice with Schlage include:

- Alarm.com
- Elan
- Honeywell
- Iris (Lowes)
- Leviton
- Nexia
- Revolv
- SmartThings
- Staples Connect
- Vera
- Wink (Home Depot)

If your home automation system provider is not listed, check its website to see if it's compatible with the Schlage line of electronic locks before purchasing a Schlage lock.

Visit `www.schlage.com/en/home/keyless-deadbolt-locks.html` to learn more. But be warned: The website is extremely clunky to navigate. Scrolling is cumbersome and some links tend to overlap. A bit surprising, really, but don't let a website deter you from the product. Schlage is good stuff.

August

While August has been around for only a short time (just a few months at the time of this writing), I have to confess that I'm intrigued by the company and its Smart Lock. This little guy (shown in Figure 7-9) is a nifty piece of engineering, and is a welcome addition to any smart home automation setup.

The August Smart Lock lets you unlock or lock your deadbolt with your iOS or Android smartphone. You can either manually use the August app on your smartphone to control the lock, or you can program it to automatically unlock when you (and your phone) are within a certain range of the deadbolt.

The August app and the August website (www.august.com) allow you to change codes for your lock, and to also invite others to use your lock by sending them their own codes. You can use this feature in a variety of ways:

- Give your housekeeper a key that only works during certain hours of the day, and adjust the hours if you need to.
- Create individual keys for each family member so that you know who's coming and going.
- Allow your trusted neighbors to have a temporary key while you're away, say, on vacation or a business trip. Don't worry; you'll be notified the moment anyone enters the house using the key, so you can keep tabs on who's in the house and when.

Those are just a few examples, but you get the idea.

Figure 7-9:
August's Smart Lock allows you to lock or unlock it with your smartphone.

Image courtesy of August.

The August Smart Lock works with Bluetooth, so you won't have to worry about wiring the new lock or whether electrical outages will be a problem. The only downside to that is you have to leave Bluetooth running on your smartphone, which could diminish its battery life. It's fairly simple to turn Bluetooth on and off on most smart devices, but who wants the hassle? Just leave it on and deal with having to recharge more often.

The encryption August uses in its locks and key codes is the same stuff used by banks to secure online banking transactions. I'd say that's pretty safe, wouldn't you? Nothing's foolproof, of course, but neither is your current deadbolt.

Here's the genius of the August Smart Lock, though: It replaces the interior portion of your currently installed deadbolt, as shown in Figure 7-10. Nothing changes on the outside of your door, and you can still manually open the door from the inside by simply turning the outer rim of the Smart Lock, just like you would a door knob.

Installation is simple and only takes about 15 minutes per lock. The Smart Lock even comes with three different adapters and three different mounting plates to ensure a proper fit to your current hardware. The folks at August have really thought this thing through.

The process of setting up an account involves several steps, which include verifying your identity through both text message and email, but as August explains on its support site, the goal is to make sure you are safe and secure with your purchase. A few extra steps to ensure my family's safety? Sounds good to me.

If you want to take a look at the lock in a retail setting, cruise on over to your local Apple Store, where you'll find an August Smart Lock sitting on a shelf.

Figure 7-10:
The August Smart Lock replaces the interior portion of the deadbolt you already have installed.

Image courtesy of August.

At the time of this writing, August isn't able to function remotely using third-party home automation systems, but the company is planning to unveil that feature in the future. For now, all updates to the lock's software must be done through the app with the phone in close proximity. That really is my only beef with the August Smart Lock, and it won't be a problem for long, it seems.

Curious about whether your iOS or Android device (yes, iPads are supported after initial setup, but no Android tablets are listed) will work with your new August lock? Visit www.august.com/phones to see if your device makes the grade.

I implore you to go to www.august.com to see more information on August, as well as viewing the four different styles offered to suit any decor.

Use your smartphone's security features, such as a passcode or fingerprint recognition, to protect your phone and your home in case your smartphone is lost or stolen. In the event that this does happen, you can also log in to your account at www.august.com and change the codes to your lock.

Yale

Yale claims to be the "world's favorite lock," and it's hard to argue that claim since the company's products are available in more than 125 countries. As one of the oldest and most trusted brands of locks in the world, it's only natural that Yale would join the fray with its own line of smart locks.

The Yale Real Living line of products is designed to work with your current home automation setup. Yale offers touchscreen and push-button varieties of deadbolt locks, including both keyed and keyless types, that work with your existing (or soon-to-be-installed) Z-Wave- or ZigBee-compatible home automation system. Offering both Z-Wave and ZigBee options is a good move by Yale.

The Touchscreen Lever Lock, seen in Figure 7-11, offers the convenience of keyless entry, the functionality of a lever lock, and remote control through your home automation system.

Yale partners with several of the most popular home automation companies. If you have a system from one of these companies, chances are your Yale smart lock will work with it:

- Alarm.com
- Control4
- ELK Products

✔ HomeSeer

✔ Honeywell

✔ Vera

Figure 7-11:
Yale's Real Living line of smart locks, like the Touchscreen Lever Lock seen here, allows you to remotely control access to your home.

Image courtesy of Yale Security, Inc.

Although they aren't listed on Yale's website, I'm confident that other Z-Wave- and ZigBee-compatible home automation systems will work with the Yale Real Living locks. Still, I urge you to speak to someone at Yale or the manufacturer of your system to find out more before you invest in a Yale product.

Check out the Yale Real Living lineup of locks (there are several models, each with various styles to suit your home's needs) by going to `www.yaleresidential.com/en/yale/yaleresidential-com/Residential/` and clicking the Yale Real Living link on the left side of the browser window. While Yale's site isn't as fancy-shmancy as some of the others in this chapter, it does what it should: give you the facts about each product in the Yale Real Living lineup.

Lockitron

The folks at Lockitron have something really cool going on. They have only been at the smart lock game for a while, but they are already creating a splash when it comes to remotely controlling your deadbolts.

Like the August Smart Lock I mention earlier, Lockitron works with your currently installed deadbolt. However, unlike the August Lock, Lockitron doesn't replace the interior hardware: It fits over it. That's right; I said "fits over it." The Lockitron people have put tons of research and Q&A into the product, and it shows.

Lockitron, shown in Figure 7-12, will fit over most locks, which is good. But unlike August, Lockitron does communicate via Wi-Fi right out of the box. (Again, as of this writing, August promises this for the future.) This means that you can control your Lockitron from anywhere you have a smart device or a computer, which is huge.

Figure 7-12:
Lockitron
fits over
your current
deadbolt,
making
installation
and removal
a snap.

Image courtesy of Lockitron.com.

Installing your Lockitron is fairly straightforward:

1. **Download the Lockitron app for your iOS or Android smart device, create an account, and register your Lockitron.**

2. **Insert the included batteries into the Lockitron.**

    It will power on automatically.

3. **Follow the instructions in the Lockitron app to set up your Lockitron with your Wi-Fi.**

4. **Loosen, don't remove, the two screws on your deadbolt's inner plate.**

5. **Slide Lockitron's C-plate behind the deadbolt's plate.**

6. **Tighten the two screws on your deadbolt's plate to hold it and the C-plate in place.**

7. **Place the main body of your Lockitron over the C-plate and line the notches up. Turn the main body clockwise until they lock, but be careful not to force it.**

8. **Unlock your deadbolt and tell the Lockitron app on your smart device that it is unlocked.**

9. **Slide the Lockitron rubber insert over the deadbolt's knob and line it up with the inner notches of Lockitron's main body.**

10. **Line the knob on the Lockitron faceplate with the deadbolt's knob and snap it into place.**

   Done! All that's left to do is give the whole thing a try using the Lockitron app, as shown in Figure 7-13.

Now that your Lockitron is in place, there are a few things you should know that it can do:

   ✔ Share access to your home by having others download the Lockitron app and use the codes you give them.

   ✔ Lockitron can automatically lock and unlock doors, depending on your phone's proximity to it.

   ✔ Lockitron will tell you when someone is knocking on your door.

   ✔ Receive notifications whenever anyone enters or leaves your home.

   ✔ For $5 a month, you can set up Lockitron to use SMS text messages to lock and unlock. This is for those in your circle of trusted individuals who don't have a smart device on which to download the Lockitron app.

   ✔ Batteries can last up to six months before needing replacement. If they give up the ghost before you can replace them, don't sweat it: Just use the knob on the inside of your home and use the key on the outside (don't worry, it's only temporary).

Figure 7-13: Lockitron's app is ready to roll once you install the Lockitron on your deadbolt.

Image courtesy of Lockitron.com.

August Smart Lock versus Lockitron

First, believe me when I say that I have no dog in this fight. I think both products are very good at what they do. However, they are both similar in their approach to automating locks, in that they work with your currently installed deadbolt. On the plus side for August, its Smart Lock seems to be a much cleaner approach and is much more visually appealing. On the minus side for August, coming to market without Wi-Fi access is not the best idea in my humble opinion. Positives for Lockitron are that Wi-Fi is included out of the box and this solution seems to make more sense for those who travel a lot and want to take their locks with them, or for those who are renting. (The Lockitron won't damage the current deadbolt hardwire.) A negative for Lockitron has to be its outward appearance. While not just straight-up ugly, it doesn't seem to fit the standard design for door hardware; to be honest, it sticks out like a sore thumb, but I still like the device. This one basically comes down to what features you deem the most important to you at decision time.

Lockitron is a great home automation gadget that I highly suggest you take a peek at by checking out `www.lockitron.com`.

Kwikset

If you've ever gone shopping for locks in a hardware store, you've run into the good products at Kwikset. Kwikset has been doing locks for a long time, and it's got a new one that has folks talking: the Kevo.

Kevo is a deadbolt that is smart enough to work with your smart devices to secure your home. It has lots in common with other locks that I discuss throughout this chapter:

- ✔ Share ekeys (electronic keys) with other folks in your life so they can gain access to your home.
- ✔ Use your smartphone or tablet to gain access to your lock: no key required.
- ✔ Key fobs can be used to gain access if you or someone you want to have access doesn't have a supported smartphone.
- ✔ You can use a real honest-to-goodness physical key if you like.
- ✔ The Kevo app, shown in Figure 7-14, allows you to control your home's access, view a history of folks who have come and gone, change ekeys, send ekeys, and more.

Figure 7-14:
The Kevo
app is your
phone's
gateway
into your
Kevo lock.

Image courtesy of Spectrum Brands, Inc.

Kevo does have some features that set it apart from the other locks in this chapter, though:

- ✔ A colored light ring around the keyhole of the Kevo indicates when actions are taking place or when the system needs to alert you to something, such as low battery life. The Kevo support site includes a video, along with written details that explain the functionality of the lights and what the different colors mean. You can access that information by going here: `www.kwikset.com/kevo/support/articles/200732416-What-do-the-colors-on-the-light-ring-mean-`.

- ✔ Kevo is pick-resistant and bump-proof.

- ✔ Kwikset's SmartKey technology makes it easy for owners to rekey their own locks.

- ✔ Grant access to as many users as you can come up with, and grant different levels of access to them all on a case-by-case basis.

- ✔ Kevo's Inside-Outside technology is a real boon, preventing anyone who is unauthorized to unlock the door when authorized users, with their phone or key fob on them, come into range on the inside of the door.

In other words, if someone knocks on your door and you walk up to it while inside your home, your Kevo won't automatically unlock for the person on the outside. You must calibrate your fobs and phones in order for this functionality to enable, but a little extra time when installing and setting up your Kevo is well worth it these days.

One thing I haven't told you is how Kevo unlocks your door. Yes, you can use a key, but what about when you have a fob or an authorized phone? Simply walking within range of the Kevo, which you see along with a fob in Figure 7-15, won't lock or unlock the deadbolt. A user must first touch the lock with his or her finger, prompting the Kevo to look for authorized devices in the vicinity. Once Kevo recognizes an authorized user, the door unlocks or locks, as the case may be.

Figure 7-15:
The Kevo
lock with
a key fob,
showing off
its light ring,
which helps
you know
what mode
the Kevo is
in or what
task it is
performing.

Image courtesy of Spectrum Brands, Inc.

The Kevo smart lock is a great device, and has won numerous awards because of Kwikset's level of attention to detail and functionality. It comes in three finishes, so it's sure to match your home's decor, too. You can get your hands on a Kevo by ordering one from several online stores (or by visiting the brick-and-mortar stores):

✔ Amazon

✔ Apple

✔ Best Buy

✔ Build.com

✔ GoKeyless

✔ Home Depot

 ✔ Lowes

 ✔ Menards

 ✔ New Egg

 ✔ Verizon

Just search for Kevo on each website, or go to www.kwikset.com/kevo/order and click on the link for the stores you'd like to do business with.

For more information on the Kevo, and to view lots of great videos describing everything from how it works to how to set it up, go to www.kwikset.com/kevo/.

Kevo is currently only supported through iOS devices, so if you have an Android device you will probably want to wait until Android devices support the Kwikset app. An Android beta program is currently going on, so if you're interested in participating in that, visit https://mykevo.com/beta/android for more information.

Piper

Piper might be last in this chapter, but I would certainly not say it's the least. Piper is an elegant home security solution for today's smart home. It's loaded to the gills with home security features that you'll be surprised to find in one small device, which is shown hanging out on a shelf in Figure 7-16.

Figure 7-16: Piper is standing guard over your home and family.

Image courtesy of Icontrol Networks.

Piper is a stand-alone unit that works with your Wi-Fi network and your smartphone or tablet to keep things under control at home. Some of the built-in features include:

✔ Receive notifications in one of four ways (or any combination of them):

  • Email

  • Push notifications to your smartphone or tablet

  • Phone call

  • Text message

✔ Use the built-in camera to keep watch over an entire room (depending on placement), with a 180-degree field of view.

✔ See HD-quality video, live or recorded.

✔ Use the built-in speaker and microphone for two-way communication.

✔ Scare the proverbial pants off any intruders (or your teenager sneaking in after curfew) with the built-in siren that goes off upon motion being detected.

✔ A multicolored LED lets you get a quick glance at Piper's status.

✔ Piper's functionality can be easily upgraded by adding new Z-Wave devices to your network. Piper supports a number of different device types:

  • Smart switches

  • Door and window sensors

  • Smart dimmers

✔ Keep track of what's going on in your home with the Piper app, seen in Figure 7-17. Piper works with both iOS and Android smart devices, so you won't need to worry about compatibility.

Figure 7-17:
Piper's app opens up your home to you no matter where you go, so long as you have a way to connect to the Internet.

Image courtesy of Icontrol Networks.

One of the best features about Piper in my book: no monthly fees. Ever. Gotta love that!

Piper is affordable, too (at least in comparison to some of the devices I discuss so far), so you may want multiple Pipers for your home. I highly suggest making `https://getpiper.com/` a stop on your list of home security websites to explore.

Chapter 8

Home, Home on the Automatic Range: The Automated Kitchen

In This Chapter

▶ Cooking when you're not even home

▶ Deciding to automate some of your kitchen tasks

▶ Keeping up with who's who in automated kitchens

*T*rekkie (or is it Trekker?) or not, you've most likely seen how the folks on board the U.S.S. *Enterprise* get their nachos and cheese: just push a button and — voila! — a steaming pile of crunchy nachos smothered in melted cheese.

Okay, I honestly can't recall ever seeing a character on any of the *Star Trek* episodes or movies eating nachos, but I can't claim to have watched them all, either. Plus, I understand that nachos and cheese is considered an underground delicacy on Vulcan, but those who indulge in the yummy crunchies won't admit to it.

The idea of a food replicator has both intrigued and terrified food lovers for decades. Popular shows like *Star Trek* and *The Jetsons* made it look to be truly the simplest of tasks, and the characters at least acted as though they enjoyed the "food stuff" it produced for them, so why not? Cooking would just be one less thing to bother with, right? Well, actually some folks would say no to such tech, because cooking is a pure joy, and even therapeutic in some cases, for many people.

But let's be honest: Although the replicator may not be ideal for many of us, we do love it when gadgets come along that help the cooking process to go a bit smoother. This is especially true when one is working late or has a family to prepare a meal for.

How about automating some of your cooking? Well, that's the subject I tackle in this chapter, but have no fear, dear reader. None of the devices I discuss produce some kind of foodlike substance, unless, of course, that's what you put into them.

Cooking Without Being in the Kitchen, and Other Kitchen Awesomeness

I need to go ahead and burst the bubble on this idea: No, remotely and automatically performing some cooking tasks doesn't mean that you'll be able to outfit your kitchen with robotic arms that will whir about your kitchen, grabbing ingredients from here and there, throwing them all together and then placing the whole thing in the oven. I'm not sure you would want such a contraption anyway, especially if you have pets or small children; things could get a bit dicey.

However, home automation and smartphones and tablets are making the kitchen a place where things can get done faster and simpler than ever, as you're about to find out.

If you're already saying, "What good is any of this if it can't do it all for me, without requiring me to step into the kitchen, much less even lift a finger?" then this chapter might not be for you. But if you are truly intrigued by how today's kitchen technology can help better your life, here are a few good reasons to proceed:

- You're running behind because of heavy traffic, and the kids are texting and calling, barely able to speak because they are so weak from waiting for you to cook something (never mind they just ate a snack two hours ago). When you get home, you'll just toss a pizza in the oven, but it takes longer for your oven to preheat than it does to cook the pizza. Hang up on the kids, open up your oven's app, and begin preheating the oven while you're sitting in traffic. Hopefully, none of the kids will pass out before the pizza's ready, but at least you'll lower the chances with this little trick.

- You've set your oven to begin cooking at a certain time, but your flight is running late (as usual). The answer to this problem is to open an app on your iOS or Android tablet and change the schedule. Done.

- You want to preheat your oven remotely, but you can't remember the correct temperature. No worries; your oven can recall the recipe that you uploaded to it and set the correct temp by itself.

- ✔ Be alerted via a text message when your food reaches the proper temperature.

- ✔ The kids call and tell you the milk has ice floating in it. Adjust your refrigerator and freezer temperatures from work without getting up.

- ✔ How neat would it be to have your refrigerator keep up with the items inside of it? And even neater, what if it would alert you on your smartphone or tablet when it was time to buy more butter?

These are but a few of the benefits of automating the most important room in your home, the kitchen. Another benefit of the automated kitchen comes from the tried and true adage, "nobody's happy unless momma's happy." If momma knows how to use a smart device, rest assured she'll be happy with outfitting her kitchen with devices that can communicate with it.

Checking Out the Top Home Automation Chefs

With home automation on the rise around the world, the best-known appliance makers are already on the ball developing products that are not only practical for the kitchen but also tie into today's Wi-Fi and Internet lifestyle. The wave of smart devices has also given rise to new companies that have innovative ideas on transforming old technology into things useful to those of us who are beginning to get used to the mobile way of doing stuff. Time to meet a few of the companies, both old and new, vying to better your lives through bettering your kitchen.

Crock-Pot with WeMo

Before you know it, Belkin's WeMo will have its hands into just about every kind of device you can think of. It's already working with light bulbs and humidifiers, and now it's in the kitchen with its partnership with one of your mother's and *her* mother's favorite cooking appliances: the Crock-Pot. Crock-Pot slow cookers have been around for more than 40 years, and with the inclusion of WeMo, they've stepped into the connected world and appear to be headed for another 40-plus years (at least) in the world's kitchens.

The Crock-Pot Smart Slow Cooker, shown in Figure 8-1, is enabled with WeMo technology, which means you can control it from your smartphone or tablet using the WeMo app.

Figure 8-1:
The WeMo-
enabled
Crock-Pot
lets you do
your cook-
ing slow and
easy — and
remotely.

Image courtesy of Belkin.

As you already know, convenience is the key to a good home automation device, and this one certainly fits the bill. Sure, you have to put the ingredients into the cooker, but that's a given until the day comes when kitchen robots can do that part of the job.

Crock-Pot's WeMo-enabled slow cooker sports the following features:

- 6-quart capacity, which is plenteous, to say the least.

- Enables you to adjust cooking time and temperature, set your food to warm only, or simply turn the cooker off. You can do this from the cooker itself or via the WeMo app.

- And more typical Crock-Pot goodness:

  - Cool-to-the-touch handles.

  - Cord storage on the side of the cooker.

  - Dishwasher-safe lid and stoneware.

If you've ever tasted the goodness that comes from a slow cooker, you don't need me to talk you into this one. If you've never eaten a roast, chicken, or anything else from a slow cooker, I implore you — nay, I beseech thee — please do so now. Do not go through life depriving yourself of one of the modern kitchen's true joys.

If you find yourself in the market for a slow cooker, check out `www.crock-pot.com/wemo-landing-page.html` and give the Crock-Pot Smart Slow Cooker some serious thought.

I think I know what's for dinner in the Spivey home tonight. I just typed myself into some slow-cooked "deliciosity."

LG

Chapter 5 explains how LG's Smart ThinQ washer and dryer can fit right into the automated home, but LG wants to occupy your kitchen, too. The company applied Smart ThinQ technology to a refrigerator and an oven, bringing those appliances to life for you and your family, too.

Smart ThinQ helps you connect with your refrigerator and oven via your Wi-Fi network and the Internet. No matter where you are, as long as you have an Internet connection you can control your appliance from your smartphone or tablet, and you will receive alerts about those smart devices, too.

Smart ThinQ Refrigerator

The Smart ThinQ Refrigerator connects to your home's Wi-Fi so that it can communicate with you wherever inside or outside the home you may be. There are several reasons to call this refrigerator "smart":

- ✔ Keep track of what food is in your refrigerator, using the built-in touchscreen display (see Figure 8-2) or the Smart Access app on your smart device.

- ✔ Be alerted to food expiration dates on your smart device or from the touchscreen.

- ✔ Use the touchscreen to create a shopping list, which is sent to your smartphone or tablet for convenience.

- ✔ Discover new Food Channel recipes based on what ingredients your refrigerator knows it already contains.

- ✔ Send your chosen recipe to your Smart ThinQ Range so that it can begin heating up for action.

- ✔ Customize the touchscreen by uploading favorite pictures to it.

- ✔ Check the weather using the weather app on the touchscreen, or check your schedule using the calendar feature. I have to say, though, that neither of these features sells the refrigerator. You can already do this with your smart device or computer anyway. I don't know many folks who will hang out to read the fridge's weather report, but I could certainly be wrong. Believe me, if these two items are what tilts you in favor of the Smart ThinQ, there are other technology issues we need to resolve for you before you start thinking about a smart refrigerator.

Figure 8-2:
The built-in
touchscreen
works with
you to make
sure you
know what's
in your
fridge and
what you
need to get
more of.

Image courtesy of LG Electronics.

I would advise heading on over to www.lg.com/us/discover/smart-thinq/refrigerator.jsp to learn more, or head out to your nearest LG appliance dealer to see one in action firsthand.

Oh, and yes, it does keep your food cold, too.

Smart ThinQ Range

You've got that shiny new Smart ThinQ Refrigerator sitting over there full of food; now you need something equally as smart to cook that food, right?

LG's Smart ThinQ Range, which you can see in Figure 8-3, makes the perfect companion to the refrigerator, and I don't mean just because they come from the same company and have stainless steel looks. The Smart ThinQ devices really do work with one another, making things that much more convenient.

LG has packed this range with the great cooking technology you would expect from a high-end device:

- Faster cooking times
- A huge 6.3 cubic feet capacity
- Convection heating
- Infrared grilling
- An element dedicated to fast boiling times

Figure 8-3:
The Smart
ThinQ
Range can
be con-
trolled from
your iOS
or Android
smart
device, and
is loaded
with the
latest and
greatest
cooking
technology.

Image courtesy of LG Electronics.

What really makes this a smart range, though, is its capability to connect to you, and you to it, through your home's Wi-Fi and the Internet. You can use the Smart Access Range app to:

✔ Set cooking times and temps.

✔ Check on your food as it cooks.

✔ See when the oven is in use.

✔ Make sure everything is off.

✔ Receive recipes from the Smart ThinQ Refrigerator or from the Smart Access app on your iOS or Android smart device so that it can heat the oven and set cooking time automatically.

Read more about it at www.lg.com/us/discover/smartthinq/range.jsp.

Whirlpool

Whirlpool is one of the tried and true brands that we all are familiar with. It's been around as long as it has for a good reason: It's one of the best at what it does, and that's making appliances. Whirlpool also is obviously very forward-thinking, as it's moving ahead with connecting its appliances to your Wi-Fi and smart devices.

Whirlpool's foray into smart appliances starts with a refrigerator and a dishwasher. Each appliance uses Whirlpool's 6th Sense Live Technology to communicate with your home's Wi-Fi network, and you can monitor and control it from your iOS or Android smart device. You can also view the appliance from a web browser on your favorite computer.

Whirlpool Smart Side-by-Side Refrigerator with 6th Sense Live Technology

Whirlpool incorporates its 6th Sense Live Technology into its Smart refrigerator (see Figure 8-4) so that you can know, via the My Smart Appliances app, what's going on with your fridge at all times.

The 6th Sense Live tech notifies you of the goings-on of your fridge through what Whirlpool dubs Smart Nudges and Smart Alerts. Smart Nudges are friendly reminders that something minor is going on, such as someone leaving the fridge door open. Smart Alerts, though, barge in and tell you when something is really wrong with your fridge, such as the power being out.

What's better, the smart fridge helps you monitor the energy you're using to keep things cool, and will even tell you an estimate of how much your energy costs will be for the device. This feature will at least give you more "real-time" information than the little tag that's on the refrigerator when you see it in a store.

Whirlpool Smart Dishwasher with 6th Sense Live Technology

How would you like your dishwasher to tell you when the washing cycle is over? Or when someone opens the door on it? Whirlpool's Smart Dishwasher will tell you that whether you're close by or far away, using the My Smart Appliances app, shown in Figure 8-5.

Figure 8-4: Whirlpool has jumped into the smart appliance market with the Smart Side-by-Side Refrigerator with 6th Sense Live Technology.

Image courtesy of Whirlpool.

Figure 8-5:
Whirlpool
uses the
My Smart
Appliances
app to allow
you remote
control
and moni-
toring of
your smart
Whirlpool
appliances.

Image courtesy of Whirlpool.

This isn't just a regular old dishwasher with Wi-Fi built-in, though. The Smart Dishwasher employs a wide array of great washing technology to make washing your dishes more energy- and water-efficient, too.

See the entire range of Whirlpool smart appliances at `www.whirlpool.com/smart-appliances/`, or contact a local Whirlpool distributor to see about getting a live demo.

GE

General Electric has been in the appliance ball game for quite the while, and that's probably a huge understatement. Everyone is familiar with the GE logo; it's a cultural icon, instantly recognizable for most folks who weren't raised on the moon.

GE is known for quality products, and the company's braving the waters of the connected smart home with its Brillion technology. As of this writing, GE has only three types of appliances on the Brillion team: single-wall ovens, like the GE Profile Series 30-inch built-in single convection wall oven shown in Figure 8-6, double-wall ovens, and free-standing ranges. The company claims it's busy adding more products to the Brillion line, so stay tuned.

Figure 8-6: GE's line of Brillion-enabled devices are limited to ovens and ranges for the time being.

Image courtesy of General Electric Company.

The Brillion app is available for iOS and Android smart devices. As GE releases more Brillion-enabled devices, I'm certain the app will be updated with the capability to control their features. For now, though, the Brillion app, shown in Figure 8-7, is very good at what it does: controlling your single- or double-wall oven. You can

- Be alerted when food is finished cooking.
- Start cooking remotely.
- Adjust temperatures and cooking times on the fly.
- Control top and bottom sections of a double-wall oven.

GE takes the security of your networked appliances seriously. It has built security functions into its Brillion-enabled appliances, and is working hard to maintain a secured environment between your appliances and the Brillion app. Check out www.geappliances.com/connected-home-smart-appliances/data-security.htm for a breakdown of the measures GE is taking to make your home more secure.

To find out more about GE's Brillion initiative, visit www.geappliances.com/connected-home-smart-appliances/.

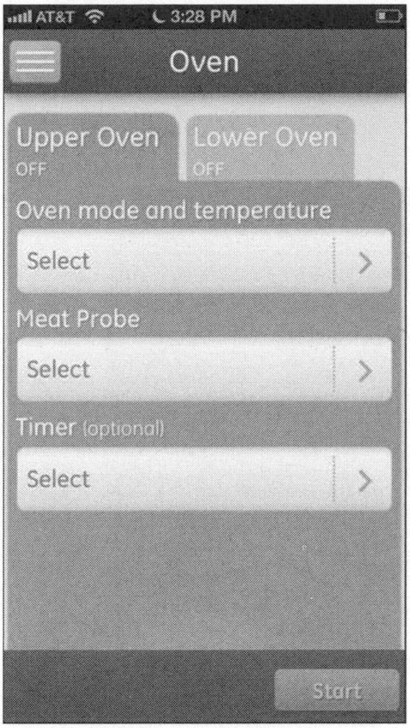

Figure 8-7:
GE's Brillion
app is a wiz
at control-
ling your
Brillion-
enabled
oven's func-
tions and
features.

Image courtesy of General Electric Company.

iDevices

iDevices is one of those companies that sprang up with the advent of the smartphone. Since the company's introduction of the iGrill in 2009, iDevices has taken off, introducing a series of smart cooking devices that are catching on at an amazing rate. And with Apple's announcement of HomeKit (see Chapter 14 for more on that), iDevices is ramping up for even more home automation goodness.

iGrill

The iGrill was the brainchild of iDevices founder Christopher Allen way back in the dinosaur days of 2009. iGrill has since garnered the praises and attention of folks ranging from professional grilling teams, such as the Smokin' Hoggz BBQ Competition team, to the weekday morning stages of NBC's *Today* show.

iGrill 2

"So, what the heck is iGrill, already?"

I'm glad you asked! iGrill is the dream of every person who's ever grilled meat or vegetables on a grill of any kind. iGrill (shown in one of its latest incarnations as the iGrill 2 in Figure 8-8) is a thermometer for your grill, and there isn't another like it anywhere.

Figure 8-8:
iGrill 2 will keep an eye on the grill for you, freeing you up to work on other food you might be preparing.

Image courtesy of iDevices, LLC.

iGrill 2 communicates with your smartphone via Bluetooth, which is a communication protocol that creates local wireless networks between two devices running it — in this case, your iOS or Android Bluetooth-enabled smartphone or tablet and the iGrill 2.

Here's how iGrill makes your grilling life even sweeter than it already is:

1. Fire up your grill and get it good and hot!

2. Prepare your meat for cooking.

3. Insert the iGrill temperature probes into the thickest part of the food you're cooking.

4. Connect the temp probes to the iGrill 2.

5. Make sure that Bluetooth is turned on for your smart device.

6. Power on your iGrill 2.

7. Open the iDevices Connected App on your smart device and select iGrill 2 from the Devices Manager. The iGrill 2 automatically pairs up with your smart device.

8. In the iDevices Connected App, select the type of meat you're cooking and the desired temperature.

Do not place your iGrill 2 on the surface of the grill or on any surface that is too hot for you to touch. While the probes are meant to withstand the heat, the iGrill 2 itself can take only so much before going belly up.

"I've already got a food thermometer, so why in the world do I need this little guy?"

I'm glad you asked that, too, dear reader!

It's at this point that iGrill 2 shows its quality. Snap up your smart device and walk away. That's right, I said walk away. There's no need to hover over your grill with a food thermometer in hand, poking holes in the meat every couple of minutes to see what the temperature is (although you might need to flip it occasionally). iGrill 2 monitors the internal temperature of the meat for you, and you can keep track of it from the iDevices Connected APP (see Figure 8-9). What's more, when the meat reaches the temperature you set back in Step 8, the app will notify you that it's time to snatch the perfectly cooked meat off the grill and dig in (it might not put it in those terms, but you get my drift).

The iGrill 2 comes with two temperature probes, but if you're a pro or have a large number of folks to feed, you can add up to two more probes. Of course, if you need more, you can always get another iGrill 2 . . .

iGrill mini

iDevices has another iGrill that will meet the needs of people who live alone or those who don't grill more than a few pieces of meat at a time: the iGrill mini. The iGrill mini uses the iDevices Connected App to report temps to your smart device, just like the iGrill 2. But unlike the iGrill 2, iGrill mini only supports one temp probe.

iGrill mini has a really cool feature to help you keep tabs on how soon your meat will be done. The LED light on top of the iGrill mini changes colors based on the meat's temp:

- ✔ Green means you're just getting started.
- ✔ Yellow lets you know you're about 15 degrees away.
- ✔ Orange tells you when you're 5 degrees from the temperature you need.
- ✔ Red means it's time to eat!

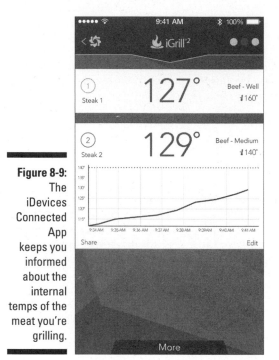

Image courtesy of iDevices, LLC.

Figure 8-9:
The iDevices Connected App keeps you informed about the internal temps of the meat you're grilling.

The iGrill mini, shown in Figure 8-10, is able to detect when you're too far away to see its LED light (based on the proximity of your smart device), at which time it will go into a low power mode and won't display the colors. Saving battery power is saving wallet power, and that's always good.

See all there is to know about the iGrill line of devices by visiting http:// idevicesinc.com/igrill/.

iGrill is good for smoking, too

iGrill is not only for grillers, but also for folks who prefer to smoke their meats. iDevices sells an ambient temperature probe that sits in your smoker or your grill to detect the temperature within it. Using the iDevices Connected App, you set the minimum and maximum temperatures for your smoking session, and iGrill will notify you if temperatures drop below it or get too high. The ambient temperature probe works with both the iGrill 2 and iGrill mini.

Image courtesy of iDevices, LLC.

Figure 8-10:
While only able to use one temp probe at a time, the iGrill mini is still a great and afford-able tool for the master griller in all of us.

Kitchen Thermometer

While iDevices do great on the grill, they are equally as great in the kitchen. iGrill is the choice when grilling or even smoking your favorite meats, but when it comes to working in the kitchen, the iDevices Kitchen Thermometer, shown in Figure 8-11, is where it's at.

The Kitchen Thermometer (the name says it all, doesn't it?) works like the iGrill, in that it uses temperature probes inserted into the meat you're cooking to keep up with internal temps. The difference: It is designed for cooking in the home, not outside in the elements (you do grill in the snow and rain, right?).

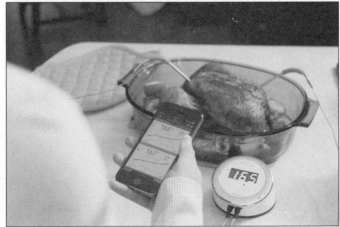

Figure 8-11:
The iDevices Kitchen Thermom-eter on the job, making sure this chicken cooks to perfection.

Image courtesy of iDevices, LLC.

The Kitchen Thermometer supports up to two temperature probes, so you can either use it to monitor two different meats at the same time, or to make sure that something large, like a good-sized turkey, cooks evenly.

Again, the iDevices Connected App is how you stay in touch with your meat's temps if you're away from the Kitchen Thermometer, which also uses Bluetooth to communicate with your iOS or Android smart device. If you're near the Kitchen Thermometer, though, you can just use its touch interface to see the temperatures being reported by one or both probes.

When cooking, a real foodie might want to share the dish he's been working over for the last hour or more. Well, the iDevices Connected App allows you to do that with ease. You can share your culinary creations with other iDevices users via the iDevices community, or you could use your social media accounts to do your braggin', as shown in Figure 8-12.

The iDevices Connected App also lets you see what others in the iDevices community are cooking up, and helps find great new recipes for you to try. And you get all this for free with the app. Can't beat that!

Figure 8-12:
Share your dishes with the iDevices community or on social media with the iDevices Connected App.

Image courtesy of iDevices, LLC.

The Kitchen Thermometer mini

The Kitchen Thermometer mini is to the Kitchen Thermometer what the iGrill mini is to the iGrill 2: a smaller, but still very powerful and fun-to-use version of its big brother.

The Kitchen Thermometer mini supports only one temperature probe, and it also uses the same LED lighting method as the iGrill mini when you are near it: green telling you it's just getting going and red letting you know it's done, while yellow and orange fit in the middle, letting you know when cooking is nearing completion.

The Kitchen Thermometer mini, shown hard at work in Figure 8-13, also uses the iDevices Connected app to communicate with you from a distance. You also use the app to select a target temperature for the KT mini.

A great feature of all the iDevices thermometers, iGrill's included, is that they can mount on metal surfaces with a built-in magnet. I know it sounds like no big deal at first, but when your countertops and your stovetop are covered with cooking utensils, dishes, and other assorted cooking "stuffs," being able to mount the thermometer to the side of the oven or some other surface is a bonus. The probes are stored in wraps, which are also magnetized, so when you go to store your iDevices thermometer you can just stack the probe wraps onto it and keep everything organized and in one spot. The iDevices folks are thinking this stuff through, people. Great job!

Figure 8-13: Attractive, small, and quite able to get the job done; that's the KT mini to a tee.

Image courtesy of iDevices, LLC.

One more thing

My Mamaw can make fudge and other candy like nobody's business, and my mom learned how to do it just as well from cooking with her. While they both are still flawless with their confections, I'll bet they both would love to get their hands on another little doodad from the folks at iDevices: its Pro Candy Probe.

The Pro Candy Probe (see Figure 8-14) is a probe designed specifically for gauging the temperature in candies as they're cooking. This little wonder takes the guesswork out of the temps needed to make perfect candies. Pro Candy Probe works with the iGrill and Kitchen Thermometer line of devices, including the mini versions of both.

This probe isn't just for candy making, though: It can also be used to monitor the temperatures in frying oils! Grandmama Spivey would have loved this thing, too! I think the designers and engineers at iDevices must have had their mothers and grandmothers in mind when they created this probe.

Pro Candy Probe can be found on the iDevices store, along with a lot of other accessories, including additional temperature probes: `http://store.idevicesinc.com/`.

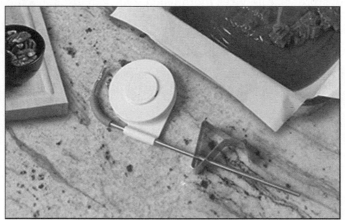

Figure 8-14:
Pro Candy
Probe from
iDevices
helps keep
the candy
makers in
the fam-
ily happy,
along with
the grill
masters.

Image courtesy of iDevices, LLC.

Quirky

Your spouse is getting ready to bake up something great, as always, when she opens up the fridge only to find that there are no eggs. That's when she gives you "that look" and you realize that she asked you last night to get more eggs. You give her your puppy dog eyes, hoping to score a point or two, but she only points to the door. The game will have to wait, bud; you're off to the store.

This unfortunate scenario could have been avoided entirely had you, one, remembered what she said about the eggs the night before, and two, invested in the Quirky Egg Minder, like your best friend told you to do over a month ago. You see, the Egg Minder would have reminded you, via your iOS or Android smartphone, that the eggs were near or entirely empty, and you would have at the same time remembered your wife's words, saving you another trip and from missing the entire first quarter of the game.

The Quirky Egg Minder, shown in Figure 8-15, is the brainchild of one Rafael Hwang, and it is saving folks from similar scenarios the world over. Here's how:

1. Purchase your Egg Minder.

2. Turn on the Egg Minder once you get it (there's a switch on the bottom).

3. Download the Wink app on your iOS or Android device (if you don't already have it) and open it.

4. Click Add a New Device in the Wink app.

5. Find the house icon on the top of the Egg Minder; it should be blinking orange.

6. Start the countdown when prompted in the Wink app and hold your smartphone right over the blinking orange house icon on the Egg Minder.

7. Once the Egg Minder has been registered with your Wink app, you'll hear a chime and will be greeted by "Success!" on the smartphone.

8. Place your eggs into the Egg Minder and place the lid on top.

9. When you're ready to use some eggs, take the lid off the Egg Minder and a light near the oldest egg will blink. That's the egg you should start with so that you're using the oldest eggs first. Whenever you remove the oldest egg, the light near the next oldest egg will blink, and so on it goes.

Figure 8-15:
The Quirky Egg Minder keeps you on top of when eggs are running low and which you should use first.

Image courtesy of Quirky Incorporated.

That's it! Egg Minder is always available to view in the Wink app so that you can know exactly how many eggs you have left. You can even set reminders in the Wink app so that you're notified when your egg supply is running low.

Take a gander at the Egg Minder here: www.quirky.com/shop/619.

Chapter 9

Monitoring Water Use and Detecting Leaks

In This Chapter

▶ Keeping an eye on the amount of water you're using

▶ Detecting leaks before they get out of hand

▶ Wading through automated water-monitoring products

*I*n my experience, there aren't many monthly bills that elicit as much of a jolt response as that of an unexpectedly high water bill. When other bills, such as electric or natural gas, are high, the reason is almost always that you simply consumed more than usual of the resource. But when it comes to water, the mind immediately starts racing:

✔ Is there a leak somewhere?

✔ Are the kids taking hour-long showers?

✔ Is the neighbor using our water hose to fill his pool again?

While each of those is troublesome, water leaks tend to strike the most terror into the heart of a homeowner. You scramble around the house, checking every pipe, fixture, commode, and spigot for that steady "drip . . . drip . . . drip . . ." that causes you to grip your wallet ever so tightly.

This chapter discusses water usage and how you can use today's technology to not only keep an eye out for leaks (and therefore prevent the subsequent damage), but also how to keep tabs on your daily use of one of the most precious resources.

Watching Your Water Usage

Few things are as important to people on a daily basis as water, and that is no stretch of the truth. Water is so much a part of daily life that humans simply don't think about it much until it's time to pay for it or they are without it. This section examines the need for monitoring your usage of water, as well as how you can go about it.

The why's of monitoring water

Take a moment to think seriously about the role that water plays in your life and how much you actually use it. Some of your most basic daily activities involve water:

- You drink water every day, in some form or another. Even if you don't pour yourself a glass of cold water, it's near a guarantee that if you drink a liquid it will include some level of water. Iced tea, coffee, soft drinks, and even adult beverages all contain some measure of water in them.

- You wash your dishes, clothes, cars, and your body with water.

- Water keeps crops from drying up, thereby keeping you not only hydrated, but also fed.

- You use water when you go to the restroom, both in the toilet and when you (hopefully) wash your hands.

- You brush your teeth and rinse with water.

- You incorporate water into your leisure activities, whether at the beach or simply in the backyard with a water hose.

Water enriches people's lives in countless other ways every day. Suffice to say, it's probably a good idea to keep an eye on how much of this incredible resource you use. Not only do you want to maintain this resource, but you also want to maintain your monthly budgets (water's not expensive, but it isn't free either).

Coming at this from another viewpoint, for as much as people benefit from water, it can also be very damaging if not kept in check. Water damage in a home can be catastrophic, leading to expensive fixes, the loss of a home, or even personal injury. Finding a water leak too late can be devastating to a homeowner's pocketbook and even lead to health issues caused by mold and mildew. Knowing when a leak first occurs can prevent a world of problems.

So, water should be monitored for two main reasons:

✔ Discover inordinate amounts of water usage to prevent waste and unexpectedly high monthly bills.

✔ Make yourself aware of leaks before serious damage can be inflicted on your property.

The how's of monitoring water

The best way for you to monitor water usage (call it Plan A) is to station one member of your household, armed with a walkie-talkie, at every major water outlet. Place your spouse in the master bath, your oldest daughter at the spigot in the backyard, your son next to the kitchen sink, your youngest daughter should spy the washing machine hoses, and grandma can man the bathroom in the front of the house.

Okay, I sense that some of you might be objecting to that plan for one reason or another, so let's move on to Plans B and C.

Plan B consists of detection devices that discover leaks and report them to you instantly via text, email, or some other notification on your smartphone, tablet, or computer. These devices are simple sensors that detect the presence of water where it shouldn't be, and they report the moisture to a smart hub or similar device, which then relays the problem to you.

Plan C employs the help of a "smart" water meter that tracks real-time water usage and reports it to your smartphone, tablet, or computer. Through the use of an app, you can see the amount of water that you're using on a daily basis, and review various statistics, such as an estimate of your monthly bill or comparisons of monthly water usage.

The upcoming section details companies that excel in monitoring water in such ways, and will free your family members from their duties outlined in Plan A earlier in this chapter.

Assessing the Water Monitoring Mavens

Several companies monitor water usage and detect leaks, but many of them are either not the most user friendly or are geared more toward industrial uses for their technologies. Those that I discuss in this section are aiming to benefit homeowners with brilliant new technologies that make the chore of water monitoring almost entertaining, for lack of a better description.

Wally

The name "Wally" may bring your thoughts to the gentle robotic fellow of Pixar fame, but the two don't bare any resemblance. No, the Wally I'm discussing with you, shown in Figure 9-1, will spare you from many a water-leakage headache, not entertain you in the movie theater.

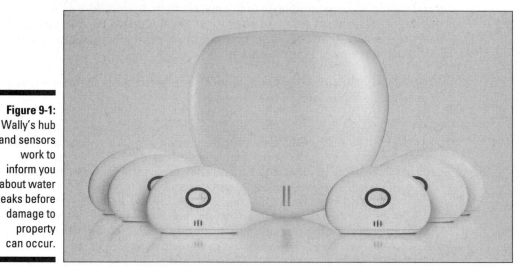

Figure 9-1: Wally's hub and sensors work to inform you about water leaks before damage to property can occur.

Wally, a product by the good people at SNUPI Technologies, serves one purpose in life: to warn you about any water leaks in your home. Wally performs its only job quite well, and feels right at home within your home automation environment.

Wally does its job through the assistance of its own smart hub and sensors that you place in areas of your home most likely to experience a water leak. The sensors report detected water to the hub, and the hub notifies you with a text or an email. The sensors communicate with the hub through the copper electrical wiring that already exists in your home, and their batteries can last for up to ten years. Wally's sensors report on the temperature, humidity, and moisture of the area in which they're placed.

I implore you to visit www.wallyhome.com to learn about Wally and how it works. Click the Buy Now link in the upper-right area of the page to go to the Wally Store. Once there, you can purchase WallyHome, which is the basic Wally starter kit. WallyHome includes everything you need to get started:

- ✔ One hub
- ✔ Six sensors
- ✔ One power cord
- ✔ One Ethernet cable

You can also purchase individual sensors or multipacks of sensors after, or in addition to, your initial WallyHome purchase. The hub can communicate with up to 1,024 sensors (wow!), so you most likely won't have to worry about needing too many sensors.

SNUPI Technologies is the company behind Wally, and it's the SNUPI tech that makes the whole thing click. SNUPI stands for Sensor Nodes Utilizing Powerline Infrastructure. For those of you who really want to know the inner-workings of the tech in your WallyHome units, go to www.wallyhome.com, click the How It Works link near the upper-right area of the page, scroll all the way down the next page, and click the Download Whitepapers button to get a PDF detailing the technology.

I would be remiss if I didn't mention the main way that you actually interact with Wally: through the Wally app. The Wally app, shown in Figure 9-2, not only alerts you (in detail, I might add) to water leaks, but also:

- ✔ Instructs you on the best areas of your home to place your Wally sensors.
- ✔ Allows you to make sensitivity adjustments to the sensors.
- ✔ Enables you to activate and deactivate sensors.
- ✔ Helps you keep track of multiple Wally hubs and sensors in more than one location (such as a vacation home or your office).

You can also administer your My Wally account(s) from the Wally app, along with several other tasks.

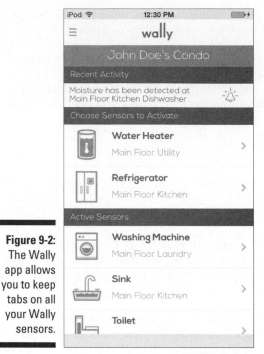

Figure 9-2:
The Wally app allows you to keep tabs on all your Wally sensors.

Driblet

The folks at Driblet have two lofty goals: They want to help you and the world save money and water. For some, the idea of saving money may trump that of conserving water, and for others, the main concern is the conservation of nature's most precious resource. I think most people's preferences fit somewhere in the middle: They recognize the immense importance of water to daily life, but the need to keep money in the bank ranks pretty high, too. Regardless of your personal motivations, Driblet is a combination hardware/software product that will help you achieve both. Mind you, Driblet will not control the amount of water you use; Driblet alerts you to how much water you are using, helping you to create better water habits in your daily routines.

The hardware part of Driblet is a smart meter that connects to water pipes in your home, such as a showerhead (see Figure 9-3) or a sink. Driblet keeps track of how much water is passing through the meter and sends this information to cloud-based servers.

Figure 9-3:
The Driblet smart water meter collects information about the amount of water used at various locations in your home.

Image courtesy of Driblet Labs, Inc.

A few things to note regarding the Driblet meter:

- ✔ The meter is self-powering, using the water that passes through it to generate power. There's never a need for batteries or to charge the meter. How cool is that?

- ✔ You can connect the meter to any half-inch pipe.

- ✔ The meter measures not only the amount of water passing through, but also its temperature.

- ✔ The meter communicates with Driblet's cloud-based servers through your Wi-Fi connection.

This is where the software part of Driblet kicks in: The information collected by the meter can be accessed through your favorite web browser on a computer or by using the Driblet app on your smartphone or tablet. At this point, you can monitor your water consumption from each Driblet meter in your home. The information is transmitted in real-time to your smartphone or tablet, or you can view it on your computer's web browser.

Using the software in the app (see Figure 9-4) or on the browser, you can create alerts for each Driblet meter so that you will be notified when certain user-defined thresholds are met. For example, you can set the Driblet in your shower to notify you once a certain amount of water has been used. Once the alert has been given, you can then alert your teenager that he won't be able to drain Lake Erie with the shower this time because you're keeping an eye on how much water he's using.

Image courtesy of Driblet Labs, Inc.

Figure 9-4:
The Driblet app is your water-conservation friend, alerting you when you've used a custom-set amount of water.

Find much more information on Driblet at `www.driblet.io`. As of this writing, Driblet is available for pre-order. The product itself is already garnering the well-deserved attention of governments, corporations, and individual homeowners around the world.

INSTEON

INSTEON fans, rejoice! There's a water leak sensor tailor-made for your home and the INSTEON hub you're already using.

The INSTEON Leak Sensor, which can be found at `www.insteon.com/2852-222-leak-sensor.html`, is a sturdy device that does one thing and does it well: It detects water leaks (the name speaks for itself, no?). While it may seem similar in function (identical, really) to you if you already read the earlier Wally section of this chapter, the INSTEON Leak Sensor does have one very obvious advantage over similar devices: If you've already incorporated INSTEON hubs and devices into your home, then you won't need to purchase a hub to begin monitoring for water leaks.

To get started with the INSTEON Leak Sensor, follow these steps:

1. **Purchase one or more sensors at `www.insteon.com`, or from another reputable INSTEON dealer.**

2. **Place the sensor in a location where it might discover a water leak. INSTEON recommends the following locations as potential leak hazards:**
   - Basements
   - Dishwashers
   - Refrigerators
   - Sinks
   - Toilets
   - Washing machines
   - Water heaters
   - Water softeners

3. **Open the INSTEON app on your smartphone or tablet, and follow the on-screen instructions for adding the sensor to your INSTEON hub.**

4. **Configure the app to alert you when the sensor detects a water leak.**

Your INSTEON Leak Sensor, shown in Figure 9-5, will make it easy for you to own it. The only time you need to check it is if it does indeed alert you to a leak, or ten years from now when it needs a new battery. Yes, you read it correctly: The INSTEON Leak Sensor only needs one AA lithium battery every ten years.

Figure 9-5:
The INSTEON Leak Sensor is on duty 24/7, and a single battery will last for ten years!

The Creek Watch app helps track water conditions

IBM has developed a great app that helps local and national watershed groups, scientists, and other concerned agencies keep track of water conditions. The app is called Creek Watch, and is available for download on the Apple App Store.

If you're concerned about helping keep track of water conditions in your area, you can help by downloading the Creek Watch app to your iPhone or iPad and collecting four conditions of your water: a picture of the water body, the amount of trash it contains, how fast the water is flowing, and how much water is contained in the body.

Doing something so simple can go a long way toward keeping the earth's water clean and usable for generations to come.

Chapter 10

Smart Home Entertainment

. . . .

In This Chapter

▶ Getting rid of remote control clutter

▶ Using your smartphone or tablet to control your home entertainment

▶ Discovering who can help you do what with home entertainment

. . . .

M ost of us recall at some point being told by our parents, and especially our grandparents, how things have changed in the world and just how easy we have it in this day and age.

The "We Used to Walk Barefooted 10 Miles in the Snow, Uphill, Both Ways to Get to School" story has been passed down from generation to generation, ad nauseam. And sadly, I find myself repeating it to this day, faithfully passing the "oh, woe is my generation" torch to my kids, and most assuredly to their kids. Gotta keep the flame going, you know!

Although I can't tell my kids I had to trek through the snow barefooted for miles, I can give them my own sordid tale of woe. You see, I can still remember the days when we had to get off the couch or chair we were sitting in to change the television channel (all three or four . . .). To make matters worse, there were these knobs labeled VHF and UHF: Turn the wrong one and — KABLOOEY! — you'd have to call one of the adults to come change the channel back from something that vaguely resembled a digital snow storm. Imagine the horror! I remember how my eyes welled up with tears the first time I saw a TV remote control in our local Montgomery Ward store. And I can't begin to adequately explain the euphoria that swept through our home the first time we brought a remote control into our own abode. Pure. Sheer. Ecstasy. Period.

These days, my kids fight over whether to watch streaming video from Netflix or Amazon Prime, and should they watch it on the iPad or cast it to our Internet-enabled television using our Google Chromecast.

The times they are a-changin'.

Modernizing Home Entertainment

Most of you probably have at least vague memories of the televisions I describe in the introduction to this chapter, but other than having to turn knobs on TVs, how else has technology changed in regards to entertainment? I can think of a few areas:

- Remember CDs? These shiny little discs seemed like something straight out of *Star Trek* when we first saw them.

- How about cassette tapes? Or, dare I ask, 8-tracks?

- Vinyl records were the best way to listen to music for decades. (There was a time where you just couldn't find vinyl anywhere, but as fate would have it, vinyl is making a comeback.)

- My children's first introduction to the Sony Walkman occurred in summer 2014, while watching Marvel's *Guardians of the Galaxy* in our local cinema. The film's main character frequently listened to his Walkman so as to remind him of good things in his past.

- My grandparents had one of those ornate wooden entertainment consoles that included a turntable for vinyl records, an 8-track player, an AM/FM radio, and internal storage of records and 8-tracks, all book-ended by a pair of really good speakers (for the time). The thing took up as much space as their couch. (It was probably just as heavy to move, too!)

Needless to say, that's not how we roll these days.

Home entertainment today

Apple single-handedly changed entertainment forever with the advent of the iPod and iTunes. Ever since then, Apple and its competitors have transformed how you get and consume your music, books, movies, and even television.

You get your entertainment digitally, and in several different ways:

- Purchasing media through an online store like iTunes or Google Play

- Streaming media via Internet-connected players (or "set top boxes," as some may refer to them) like Roku or Apple TV

- Subscribing to media services like Netflix and Hulu

- Buying electronic books on a Kindle or similar device

After you acquire your entertainment of choice, you can enjoy it in several new ways:

- ✔ On your computer through web browsers and dedicated apps
- ✔ Using apps from various providers (such as Netflix, Amazon, or even television service providers, like DirecTV) on your smartphone and tablet, like those in Figure 10-1
- ✔ On your television using media players like Roku, Apple TV, or even a gaming console
- ✔ Through dedicated apps from Hulu and the like, if you have a "smart" Internet-enabled television

Figure 10-1: Apps like the one from Netflix allow you to watch your subscription content on multiple devices.

Image courtesy of Netflix, Inc.

Smart home entertainment technology

Wi-Fi and the Internet are the way many folks are choosing to view or listen to their entertainment options these days, and this is only going to be a growing market. Many people (myself included), and more every single day, are saying goodbye to the old way of doing things (cable and satellite providers) and are relying on the newest technologies:

- ✔ Wi-Fi networks and Wi-Fi–enabled televisions, stereos, and speakers are making it easier to stream Internet content to your entertainment appliances.

- ✔ Subscription services, like those offered by Amazon (Amazon Prime) and Netflix, allow you to pay a low monthly or annual fee to enjoy unlimited streaming of their video content. Others, such as Pandora, offer free alternatives for listening to music.

- ✔ Online social media sites like YouTube (one of the three most popular in the world, behind only Google and Facebook) have changed the way people get their video fix.

- ✔ Devices, such as Google's Chromecast, allow you to open a video or website on a device such as your computer or tablet and play it through a Wi-Fi network on your televisions.

- ✔ Many sound system manufacturers, such as Bose and Pioneer, have developed Wi-Fi–enabled systems that you can control with an app on your smartphone or tablet.

And this is how we're doing things at the beginning of this home entertainment revolution. As the tech gets smarter, so do our homes and the way we bring entertainment into them.

Introducing the Smart Home Entertainment Gurus

Some of the companies you read about in this chapter are those that have been in the tech game a long time and are just expanding their brand into today's new frontiers. However, some of these are companies are relatively, and in some cases, totally new to your entertainment lexicon. Regardless, they all have something rather interesting to add to your home's smart entertainment options.

Roomie

So you have a television, huh? And I'll bet you probably have a cable or satellite television provider, too. A top-of-the-line sound system probably hangs out with the television. You might even have a streaming media player so you can watch Internet-based video on your TV. There's a game console of some sort, as well. Don't forget about all the other televisions and other entertainment equipment scattered throughout your home.

So there you are with all your entertainment options before you. Too bad you can't see or otherwise use them because of the mountain of remote controls that sits between you and them.

"I know how to solve this dilemma," you confidently say, with a nod and a sly wink to boot: "I'll get one of those universal remotes!"

To which I respond, "Ah, my friend, that would have been a great idea — ten years ago. You see, these days one universal remote won't do the job for all the different devices you have. Not to mention, those remotes only work with infrared devices, not those that use Wi-Fi to communicate." That's the real killer: the capability to control devices that are Wi-Fi connected.

What would you say if I told you there is a remote control that could control all your devices, even those using Wi-Fi? That's right, even your infrared ones. Well, there is: the Roomie. Roomie (see Figure 10-2) is a virtual remote. More accurately, Roomie is an app that you install on your iOS smartphone or tablet (or both), giving you access to virtual remote controls for just about any device you own.

No, I'm not kidding. This is for real, I promise.

Roomie even has a list of compatible devices so that you can take a gander to see if your home entertainment devices are supported. The list is divided into three sections:

- ✔ **IP Compatibility** lists devices that connect to your Wi-Fi network natively

- ✔ **Infrared (IR) Compatibility** lists infrared devices that you can control using Roomie. Infrared devices require a Roomie Blaster adapter to work.

- ✔ **Serial Compatibility** lists devices that connect using the RS-232 serial connector, which is the connector older computer monitors use to connect to your computer. These devices require both a Roomie Blaster adapter and a Roomie Serial Cable to work with the Roomie remote.

Table 10-1 lists a small portion of device manufacturers supported by the Roomie remote and the types of devices they manufacture (IP, IR, or serial).

Table 10-1 is not an exhaustive list — not even close. Literally thousands of devices can be controlled by Roomie. Suffice it to say, no matter whether your home automation device is remotely modern, a little worn, or nearly

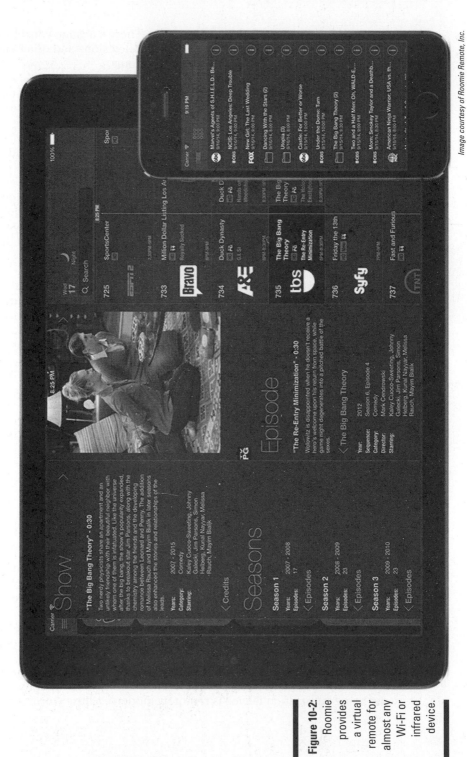

Figure 10-2:
Roomie
provides
a virtual
remote for
almost any
Wi-Fi or
infrared
device.

Table 10-1	Some Manufacturers Supported by Roomie
Manufacturer	*Compatibility Type(s)*
Acer	IR
Apple	IP, IR
Denon	IP, IR, serial
Google	IP, IR
INSTEON	IP, IR
JVC	IP, IR
LG	IP, IR, serial
Lutron	IP, IR
Nest	IP
Onkyo	IP, IR, serial
Panasonic	IP, IR
Philips	IP, IR
Pioneer	IP, IR, serial
Roku	IP, IR
Samsung	IP, IR, serial
Sharp	IP, IR
Sonos	IP, IR
Sony	IP, IR, serial
Tivo	IP, IR
Yamaha	IP, IR, serial

worn out, the odds are pretty good that it will work with Roomie. Not many products can purport that level of compatibility.

And Roomie can even control other home automation devices, such as your window shades and lighting. Told you it was good.

It's not all wine and roses, though. The one beef I have with Roomie is that you can only contact its support team via email. No phone number. No human voice. If you need help right now, well . . . you'll just have to wait, unfortunately.

Go to `www.roomieremote.com` to get the skinny on this great remote control alternative. Remember, click or tap on the Compatibility tab to make sure that your home entertainment components are supported.

Currently, Roomie is an iOS-only device (at the time of this writing). However, Roomie does state on its site that Android compatibility is something it hopes to incorporate in 2015. The company claims this has allowed the development process to proceed much faster than it would have had Roomie supported Android from the outset, and I can't fault that argument.

Blumoo

Blumoo is another company that is providing an escape from the remote control blues by offering its own version of the universal remote. And this time, Android users aren't excluded: Blumoo supports Android and iOS right out of the box.

Blumoo also goes about its business in a slightly different manner than Roomie. Blumoo uses Bluetooth to manage communications between your iOS or Android smartphone or tablet and the Blumoo base station (see Figure 10-3).

Figure 10-3:
Blumoo's base station sends signals to your home automation devices when you issue commands from your smart device.

Image courtesy of Blumoo.

Since Blumoo doesn't use Wi-Fi to communicate, that's one less drain on your network's bandwidth. Another plus is that the Blumoo won't stop communicating with your devices if your Wi-Fi isn't working.

The Blumoo base station contains an IR (infrared) blaster that awesomely bounces IR commands off your walls, cabinets, and just about anything else it needs to in order to make your home entertainment devices jump at every command.

Another cool feature about Blumoo is that you can connect a speaker directly to the base station so you can stream music from your smart device. Connect the Blumoo to your home sound system and you can stream throughout the joint. Sweet.

The Blumoo app allows you the freedom to take control of your home theater:

- ✔ Download preconfigured virtual remotes for all your entertainment devices. More than 225,000 devices are supported!
- ✔ Customize the virtual remotes by moving, deleting, or adding buttons.
- ✔ Create macros that enable you to perform multiple actions with the touch of just one button. For example, create a macro that will power all your entertainment devices on or off at once.

However, the same complaint I have regarding Roomie applies here: The only way to get support for your Blumoo is through email. The actual quote I heard on one of the support videos was that you could send an email if you ran into problems or had questions during setup and someone "will get back to you shortly." Shortly? What does that mean, exactly? A few minutes after you send the email? As soon as possible on the next business day if you happen to be setting up your Blumoo after the company's support team has gone home for the evening? Believe me, I understand that Blumoo isn't a company that staffs its support center 24/7. No problem. But the customer should at least be given a better response time than "shortly."

Do not let my support rant deter you from checking out the Blumoo site at www.blumoo.com. The site actually makes for fun reading.

Logitech

"You know, Dwight," I can hear some of you saying, "I kind of like having a remote control in hand. I have to deal with my smart device all day long, and I like feeling the heft of a remote control chock-full of actual physical buttons."

I hear you, friend, and so does Logitech.

Logitech is the creator of the Harmony line of universal remote controls, and they can scratch right where you itch when it comes to your actual (as opposed to virtual) remote control obsession.

Harmony universal remote controls are IR only, so you won't be able to control any Wi-Fi devices with them. For example, the Google Chromecast is a Wi-Fi–only device, so your Harmony remote won't work with it.

Logitech's Harmony devices vary in their capabilities, and therefore in price, but they all perform quite well in their intended roles.

The Harmony Ultimate One, seen in Figure 10-4, is the sole control you need to command your entertainment system.

Ultimate One features include:

- You can control up to 15 entertainment devices from just one remote.

- Button functions can be customized.

- The built-in touchscreen allows you to swipe through the menu, similar to your smartphone or tablet.

- It's compatible with more than 270,000 home entertainment devices!

- It uses a charging station to recharge its batteries, so you will rarely ever change a battery for this remote, which is certainly a welcome change.

- You can add up to 50 favorite channels so all you need to do to change the channel is touch the icon for the channel you want to view.

Figure 10-4:
Harmony
Ultimate
One is the
remote
you need
if you want
to use one
device to
control your
home enter-
tainment
system.

Image courtesy of Logitech.

The Ultimate One is a great device for handling your home entertainment system, and it's also easy to set up using your Mac or Windows-based PC. Follow these steps:

1. **Open your favorite web browser and go to** www.myharmony.com.

2. **Click on the Sign In/Set Up link near the top of the page.**

3. **Click the Download Now link on the preceding page to download the MyHarmony software necessary for your computer.**

   The site will automatically detect your computer's operating system and download the appropriate version for it.

4. **Install the MyHarmony software and launch it.**

5. **Create an account if you don't already have one, or sign in with your current account.**

6. **Follow the on-screen instructions, as I'm doing in Figure 10-5, to connect your Harmony remote to your computer and begin setting it up for use.**

Once you've gone through the setup process, you can begin controlling your entertainment with an honest-to-goodness in-your-hand remote control, with real buttons and everything.

Go to www.myharmony.com to see a list of Harmony remotes and other accessories, such as a keyboard, to make using your home entertainment devices that much easier.

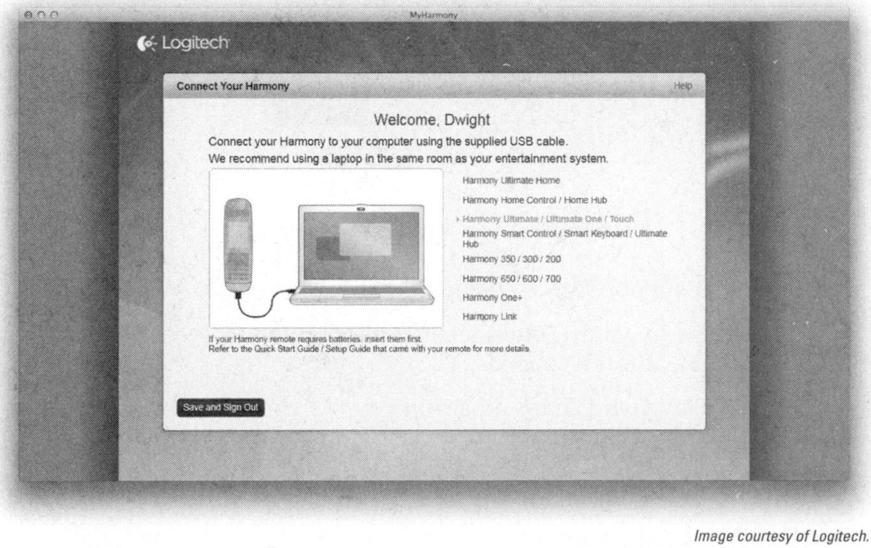

Figure 10-5: Set up your Harmony Ultimate One with software using your Mac or PC.

Image courtesy of Logitech.

Apple

Streaming video has been around on the Internet for quite the while, but only recently has it begun to be viewed on televisions and smart devices by a significant amount of folks. This is due to the advent of streaming media devices that make it simple to put streaming content onto your TV.

One such device, and one of the most popular in its category, is the Apple TV (see Figure 10-6).

Figure 10-6:
Stream video from the Internet, and even from your computer or iOS smart device, with the help of Apple TV.

Image courtesy of Apple, Inc.

Apple TV's features are as long as my arm:

- It supports up to 1080p HD video.
- Set up your iTunes account information to access your iTunes content on your television.
- Play your iTunes music on your TV or speakers.
- Access content through the apps of your favorite providers, such as:
  - Crackle
  - Disney

- ESPN

- Fox

- HBO

- History

- Hulu Plus

- MLB

- NBA

- Netflix

- NFL

- Showtime

- YouTube

✔ Stream content from your Mac or iOS devices using AirPlay.

✔ View content you have stored in iCloud, such as your photos or personal videos.

✔ Watch movies you've created with your Mac with iMovie Theater.

✔ Share content that other family members have purchased using Apple's Family Sharing.

✔ Mirror content from your other devices so that others can watch the action on your TV, as shown in Figure 10-7.

There's even more to Apple TV than I have space to discuss, but you get the picture by now.

Apple TV simply connects to your television with an HDMI cable. Once they're connected, enable Bluetooth on your iPhone or iPad and hold it close to the Apple TV; the Apple TV uses this momentary connection to glean your Wi-Fi network's settings from the iPhone or iPad. Everything will be up and running in no time.

Once you have it working, you can control Apple TV using its remote control, which is included, or you can download and use the Remote app on your iOS smart device. Whether you're an Apple fan or not, whether you have a Mac or Windows PC, you should give the Apple TV a look. Check it out at `www.apple.com/appletv`, or you can see it at your local Apple Store. (Other stores, such as Best Buy, also may have demos of Apple TV for you to see.)

Figure 10-7:
Mirroring
allows you
to show the
exact
content
that's on
your iOS
smart
device or
Mac on your
television.

Image courtesy of Apple, Inc.

The Apple Remote app does much more than just control your Apple TV. You can stream music directly to speakers that are attached to an Airport Express (a wireless network device that plugs into any outlet), synchronize content across devices, queue music or other videos from anywhere in the house, and much more. Go to www.apple.com/apps/remote to see all that can be done with this free app.

Roku

Founded in 2002, Roku is one of the first companies to put forth a streaming media player. As such, it is also one of the most popular, having sold literally millions of its Roku players, like the Roku 3 in Figure 10-8, over the years.

The idea is simple: Build a little box, fill it with streaming media apps from various outlets, connect it to the Internet and your television, and open a world of streaming media that is hard to beat. You'll have thousands of television shows and movies right at your fingertips, and you can watch them all whenever you feel like it.

Roku's been at this a while, and it also doesn't have ties to any other internal interests. For example, Apple wants you to use iTunes, and as such, you can only use Apple TV with it. There are other examples of this practice, as well, but Roku doesn't have any other interests than selling you a streaming media player. Roku doesn't care what TV you use to play the video or listen to the music on (it also supplies music channels, not just video). More than 1,800 channels are available for your perusal on Roku. I know that sounds like an amazing array of TV nirvana, and in some ways, it is (Roku gives you most of the main streaming channels you could hope for, with the notable exception of iTunes), but please understand this: The vast majority of the channels are jokes. Not the funny kind either, but the roll-your-eyes-and-pass-on-by-with-a-disgusted-look kind. But that shouldn't detract from Roku's other shining features. Just don't expect that you'll find something for you and your family on every channel. Ain't gonna happen.

Figure 10-8:
Roku's latest and greatest streaming media player: the Roku 3 (with its accompanying remote control and headphones).

Image courtesy of Roku, Inc.

TIP

You can take your Roku with you when you travel! Your Roku box remembers your credentials, so whenever you go somewhere that has Internet access, you can also hook up your Roku to a television and watch your favorites.

Roku currently offers four versions of its player:

- ✔ Roku 1
- ✔ Roku 2
- ✔ Roku 3
- ✔ Roku Streaming Stick, shown in Figure 10-9

Image courtesy of Roku, Inc.

Figure 10-9:
The Streaming Stick is easy to hide behind your TV.

Every Roku player comes with the following:

- ✔ 1,800+ channels of streaming multimedia
- ✔ Up to 1080p HD
- ✔ Built-in Wi-Fi to stream content from your network
- ✔ Access to the Roku app for your smartphone or tablet
- ✔ A Roku remote, some with built-in headphones (depending on the model)

You can view a head-to-head comparison of all the Roku models so you can determine which best suits your needs: Just visit www.roku.com/products/ compare.

The Roku app affords you another way of controlling your Roku device. You can search for content and instantly send it to your Roku, switch between more than one Roku device, and more. But the best feature to me is that you can use the app as another remote (see Figure 10-10), because in a home with four children you're bound to lose the physical remote at some point. With the Roku app, just fire up your smart device, open the Roku app, and you're back in business.

Roku's website, www.roku.com (fancy that), can answer all your Roku questions, and will also let you see the cornucopia of channels available.

Your smartphone or tablet must be using the same network as your Roku in order for the app to work with it. If you have a problem connecting your smartphone to the Roku, be sure that it's actually on the network and not just using your cellular carrier's signal for its Internet connection.

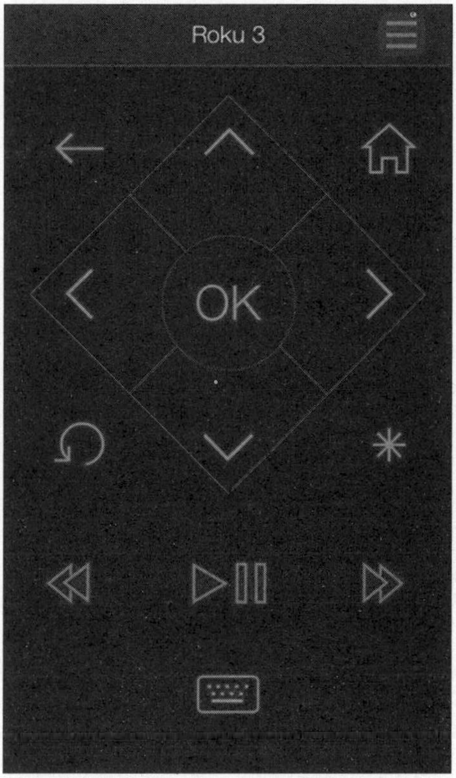

Image courtesy of Roku, Inc.

Figure 10-10: The Roku app can also act as a backup remote, or you can use it as your primary remote if that suits you best: Choice is nice, isn't it?

Google

Google is another of the technology big dogs that started out doing something altogether different (Internet search engine) and has morphed into a company that dabbles in quite a diverse range of ventures. One of those ventures is into television sets.

Google stepped into the television market with the advent of Google TV in 2010, but that might have been better categorized as a slight misstep. Google TV is fading away (as of 2014), and Google has launched the Nexus Player running the Android TV operating system. The Nexus Player, shown in Figure 10-11, has a lot of promise, but since it was just released in November 2014, it has some catching up to do in regards to its competitors. Nexus Player provides the standard apps for watching streaming

Figure 10-11:
Nexus
Player is
Google's
latest
attempt at
giving you
an Android-
based
streaming
media
platform.

Image courtesy of Google.

media, such as Netflix and Hulu, and you can cast shows from your smart devices to it (like Google's own Chromecast, which I discuss next), but more developers need to get on board for the Player to really put a dent in the market.

One big thing about Nexus Player, or more accurately, the Android TV operating system, is that you will be able to use your standard Android apps with it. In other words, apps that you install on your Android smartphone or tablet can also be installed on your Android TV. This will give you tons of flexibility and consistency between your Android devices.

However, Google's main attention-grabber when it comes to getting Internet and computer-based content to your TV is its Chromecast. The Chromecast, shown in Figure 10-12, is a dongle that you plug into the HDMI port on the back of your television.

Chromecast was an instant hit for Google. It has a small footprint and a small price point: $35 is all you need to start casting to your television.

Figure 10-12:
Google's Chromecast allows you to play content from your computer or smart device on your television through your Wi-Fi network.

Image courtesy of Google.

Chromecast is easy to set up. Follow these steps:

1. **Plug your Chromecast into one of the HDMI ports on your television.**

2. **Chromecast uses USB for power, so you can either plug its USB connector into a USB port on your television or connect it to the USB power adapter and plug the adapter into a standard outlet.**

3. **Go to www.google.com/chromecast/setup from any Mac or Windows computer, or from any iOS or Android smart device, and then download the Chromecast app for your device when prompted.**

4. **Open the downloaded Chromecast app and follow the instructions for setting up your Chromecast to work with your network.**

I almost forgot to mention one tiny thing: In order to cast from your Mac or PC, you'll need to download and install Google's Chrome web browser. It's the only browser that can (currently) cast its content to the Chromecast. However, you will need to install the Google Cast extension in order to do so. To get and install the extension, follow these steps:

1. **Open the Chrome browser on your computer.**

   The extension is not supported on mobile web browsers.

2. **Visit www.google.com/chrome/webstore and click the blue Visit Chrome Web Store button.**

3. **Type *Google Cast* into the search field in the upper-left corner of the resulting page and press Enter or Return on your keyboard.**

4. **Find Google Cast under the Extensions heading and click it.**

   You may need to scroll down a bit to find it. A new window opens within the browser window to extol all the features that Google Cast can offer.

5. **Click the blue Free button in the upper-right area of that window to install the extension.**

6. **Restart Google Chrome (completely quit and reopen it) to activate the extension.**

7. **To cast the contents of a page in your Chrome browser, click the Cast button in the upper-right corner of the Chrome window, circled in Figure 10-13.**

The cool part is that anything you view in the Chrome browser can be displayed on your television using the Chromecast.

The Chrome browser, while it is currently my favorite and the favorite of many a web surfer, is known as being a bit of a memory hog. When Chrome was first released, I loved its speed and interface, but eventually had to walk away because it was simply overtaking my computer's memory. (I had this experience on both Macs and Windows machines.) However, I did come back after a few updates had been made to Chrome and have found it more manageable. From time to time, though, I do find myself having to restart the browser to reclaim huge chunks of memory. Chrome is a great browser, but when you first start to notice everything on your computer slowing down, completely quit and restart Chrome to see if that does the trick.

Figure 10-13: Click the Cast button in the Chrome browser to send the contents of the browser window to your TV.

Bose

If you've ever heard Bose speakers, you've never forgotten the great sound they put out. I'm not saying other speaker makers aren't as good as Bose, but I'm not sure that there are many (if any) that surpass it. Bose has been around for 50 years, and it is still a leading innovator in sound technology.

The Bose SoundTouch line of Wi-Fi–enabled speakers, shown in Figure 10-14, are wireless speakers that you can place throughout the house and wirelessly play your tunes on, using your iOS or Android smart device to run the show.

Figure 10-14:
The SoundTouch line of speakers sound great, look great, and are easy to manage from your smartphone or tablet.

Image courtesy of Bose Corporation.

SoundTouch speakers come in three flavors, shown from left to right in Figure 10-14:

- ✔ SoundTouch 30 is made to fill larger spaces with rich Bose sound.
- ✔ SoundTouch 20 is designed for average-sized rooms.
- ✔ SoundTouch Portable is also for average-sized rooms, but is also portable, so you can take it to any room of the house with ease.

All the models share the following features:

- ✔ Connect directly to your favorite streaming music platform (such as Pandora, Spotify, and others) or Internet radio stations.
- ✔ Stream music from your personal music library.

✔ Each model comes with six preset station options. You configure the stations using the SoundTouch app, which comes free with your SoundTouch system, and you can access stations with the press of a single button on the speaker itself.

✔ SoundTouch speakers connect to other SoundTouch speakers, creating their own speaker network throughout your home. You can play the same song throughout your home or play different songs on each speaker.

The SoundTouch app is available for iOS and Android systems. The one feature where iOS users will have an advantage over Android users is that SoundTouch speakers incorporate Apple AirPlay compatibility natively.

Check out the SoundTouch range of speakers, as well as other SoundTouch devices, by going to www.bose.com and clicking on the Wi-Fi Music Systems tab.

Sonos

Since I'm discussing speakers, I would be remiss not to mention the folks who really got the Wi-Fi speaker craze started: Sonos.

Sonos has been on top of its game, and this market segment, since 2002, and it shows no signs of slowing down. While competitors are continually launching products that come close, so far none have surpassed Sonos's line of Wi-Fi–enabled sound systems.

Sonos offers a full range of what it calls HiFi wireless speakers to suit your needs:

✔ **SUB** is a wireless subwoofer that gives you as much bass as you can stand. The SUB, shown in Figure 10-15, pairs with any of the Sonos line of speakers.

✔ **PLAY:1** is a compact speaker that delivers big sound in a small package. This little guy offers what Sonos simply labels as Loud Sound. Get two PLAY:1 speakers to deliver rich stereo sound in small spaces, or to complement a home theater system as great rear speakers.

✔ **PLAY:3** is the Sonos speaker that delivers what the company terms as Really Loud Sound. This speaker is designed for average-sized rooms and provides a deeper level of bass than the PLAY:1, but it can also be used in a home theater system as a great rear speaker.

✔ **PLAY:5** is the big boy of the bunch, providing Crazy Loud Sound (Sonos's description) and Crazy Deep Bass (also from Sonos). The PLAY:5 is meant for larger spaces and is designed to be the main player in your music system.

✔ Already have an existing wired music system, but want to make it wireless? The **CONNECT:AMP** connects to your system and does just that, allowing you to broaden your wired horizons.

✔ **PLAYBAR,** shown in Figure 10-16, is the ultimate offering from Sonos. This bar not only connects to your music system, but also to your television, and the sound that issues forth from it is nearly flawless.

Figure 10-15: Get ready for some seriously d-e-e-p b-a-s-s with Sonos's SUB wireless subwoofer.

Image courtesy of Sonos, Inc.

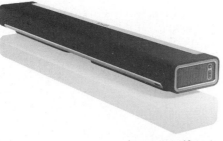

Figure 10-16: Sonos's PLAYBAR is a Wi-Fi music and sound lover's dream, and it looks really cool, too.

Image courtesy of Sonos, Inc.

The entire Sonos system can be controlled from your iOS or Android smart device using the Sonos app. You can control as many Sonos devices as you like using the app, playing different songs on separate speakers, or playing the same tunes throughout your home.

Sonos allows you to connect your speakers directly to your Wi-Fi, but a feature that you'll really love is the capability to create your own separate Sonos Wi-Fi network. This prevents the Sonos devices from using valuable bandwidth that your other wireless devices so desperately crave; it makes your wireless sound more stable (which Sonos devices are already known for being); and it extends your Sonos wireless network with every device you install.

Check out the Sonos website, www.sonos.com, for more information on its wonderful devices than I could ever pack into this chapter.

Happy listening!

Part III
Automating Outside Your Home

Image courtesy of Robert Bosch GmbH.

Find a quick list of links to outdoor home automation devices at www.dummies.com/extras/homeautomation.

In this part . . .

- ✔ Keep track of the weather right in your own backyard.
- ✔ Mow your lawn without getting off the deck chair.
- ✔ Water your lawn automatically.

Chapter 11

Checking the Weather

. . . .

In This Chapter

▶ Staying on top of temperature and humidity levels in your home

▶ Checking the weather with personal weather stations and other products

▶ Keeping tabs on your sun exposure with stylish wearable devices

. . . .

> *Everyone complains about the weather, but nobody ever seems to do anything about it.*
>
> — *Willard Scott*

*E*veryone loves Al Roker, and Willard Scott is simply a legend (the "Walter Cronkite of weather," if you will), but sadly, most of us don't keep tabs on our favorite weather personalities anymore. Mobile devices changed that forever.

The advent of awesome weather apps for smartphones and tablets has made retrieving up-to-the-minute weather information as simple as tapping an app's icon on a screen. In just a few seconds, you can know what's going on right now weather-wise in your hometown or in Rome, Italy (or both simultaneously, if Rome happens to be your hometown, but I digress). But how many times have you checked your favorite weather app, looked at your local weather and was told it was sunny and 0 percent chance of rain, only to be startled by a massive thunderclap and look out your window as drops of rain the size of baseballs hurtled toward you? Once is one time too many, if you ask some folks.

Keeping Tabs on the Weather

Some people collect baseball cards and comic books. Others listen to emergency radio scanners at all hours of the night, keeping up with local law enforcement happenings. Still others steep themselves in sports or hobbies.

We all have our favorite pastimes, and for some of us, keeping up with the weather and understanding every last aspect of it is what floats our boat (pardon the pun).

While it might be neat to know how windy it is in Chile, or how much snow is falling in Siberia, what's it like in your own neighborhood? Or your own backyard, or even inside your home?

"Why in the world would I want to know the weather in my own home? Isn't that what the thermostat is for?"

Great question! And yes, the thermostat can tell you what the temperature is like — in the exact spot it's located. However, it cannot tell you what the temperature is like in your basement, or in the upstairs playroom. Knowing the exact temperature in a given area of your home is just one of many good reasons that you'll want to add personalized weather to your automated home. Here are a few more reasons for your consideration:

- Check carbon monoxide levels in your home or specific areas of it.
- Keep up with humidity levels throughout your home.
- Be informed when your plants need watering.
- Know the exact wind speeds and direction in your own backyard.

All of the preceding readings (and more) can be accomplished with today's home weather stations and technology. There are even wearable items that can make you aware of when you've had enough sun. Read on to find out more about personal weather stations and other ways today's technology can help better your life.

We have personalized music lists and customized cars. You can get a burger made "your way." I think that something as important as weather is to our daily lives is at least as worthy of such close and personal attention and detail as the amount of lettuce, onions, tomatoes, and pickles we imbibe. Don't you agree?

Checking the Weather Automatically

The market for personal weather stations and other personalized weather apparatus (and even apparel) is surprisingly robust. I say "surprisingly," because I'm willing to bet that most of us don't even realize the market exists. It most certainly does exist, and it is full-to-bursting with companies that want to deliver up-close-and-personal weather reporting that is unbeatable in reliability. My aim in this section is not to point you to one solution or another when it comes to personal weather for your automated home, but to simply open your eyes to the many possibilities you have for bringing automated personal weather observation and forecasting to your life.

Netatmo

Netatmo has only been around since 2011, but the company has already earned quite a name for itself. The range of Netatmo products garners great reviews around the globe and the numbers of those great reviews are increasing quite rapidly. For our purposes, we'll stick to just a couple of Netatmo products that will help keep you in the know about local and personal weather conditions.

The Netatmo Weather Station

Netatmo does personal weather, and it does so with style. One peek at the Netatmo Weather Station's indoor and outdoor modules and you'll know what I mean. Their slick silver aluminum cases look really great on the patio and on the sofa table. Blending in with your decor won't be a problem for these devices, as you can tell from Figure 11-1.

You begin building your personalized weather base with Netatmo's Urban Weather Station (that's what Netatmo calls its starter kit). The box ships with one indoor module and one outdoor module, and a USB-adaptable power supply for the indoor module. (The outdoor module operates with two AAA batteries that last up to a year.)

Figure 11-1: The Netatmo Weather Station's indoor (shown here) and outdoor modules look great with any decor.

Image courtesy of Netatmo.

The way it works is really simple, but the amount of information you can gather is anything but. While said info isn't complicated, it is certainly in depth.

The indoor module helps you keep track of:

- ✔ Indoor temperature
- ✔ Indoor relative humidity
- ✔ Indoor air quality
- ✔ Carbon monoxide levels
- ✔ Noise meter

The outdoor module reports the following:

- ✔ Outdoor temperature
- ✔ Outdoor relative humidity
- ✔ Outdoor air quality
- ✔ Barometric pressure
- ✔ Weather

Here's how the whole thing gets done:

1. The outdoor module sends its information to the indoor module.

2. The indoor module uses your Wi-Fi connection to send info from both modules to Netatmo's cloud computing service. You can force an instant information update by pressing the top of the indoor module.

3. You access the information in real time via the Netatmo app on your smartphone or tablet (see Figure 11-2), or in your favorite web browser (see Figure 11-3) by visiting mynetatmo.com, signing in to one or the other (or both, if you please) with your account information.

Windows Phone users, rejoice! Netatmo provides support for you (as well as for iPhone and Android users) — as long as you have Windows Phone 8.0 or newer installed, that is.

The indoor module can also display information on the amount of carbon monoxide in the room directly:

1. Press the top of the unit to begin a manual measurement process.

2. **The long, slender light on the front of the unit will glow with one of the following indicators:**

- *Green means the carbon monoxide levels are perfectly normal in the room.*

- *Yellow lets you know that the carbon monoxide levels are a bit higher than normal.*

- *Red is a warning that carbon monoxide levels are too high and that the room should be ventilated.*

Figure 11-2:
The Netatmo app works great on your favorite smartphone or tablet.

Image courtesy of Netatmo.

Visit www.netatmo.com/en-US/product/weather-station to discover all that you can do with the Weather Station. There's also a nice video on the site that gives an overview of the Weather Station's features and a real-life perspective on how it can be used.

After you kick the tires with the Urban Weather Station starter kit, you may find that one indoor module isn't enough for your needs. Should that be the case, you can order additional modules. For the outdoor monitor, you can even purchase a rain gauge that works seamlessly with your Weather Station, too. Just go to www.netatmo.com and click the Shop button in the upper right to load up your shopping cart.

Figure 11-3:
Your
personal
weather
station
is only a
mouse-click
away on any
computer
(including
those run-
ning Linux)
via a web
browser
and your
Netatmo
account.

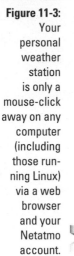

Image courtesy of Netatmo.

The true weather junkie will be thrilled to know about Netatmo's Weather Map website. The site displays weather information from actual Netatmo customer sites all over the globe. You can even customize the way the site displays weather information (such as showing temperatures in Celsius or Fahrenheit) using the buttons in the lower-right corner of the site. The Weather Map site can be accessed at www.netatmo.com/en-US/weathermap.

The Netatmo JUNE

The preceding section explains the personal weather experience that the Netatmo Weather Station affords you. But wait! There's more! Netatmo can get even more personal than that. How would you like to wear a beautifully designed device that keeps up with how much sunlight you are being exposed to, warns you when it is too high, and even suggests the level of sunscreen protection you should be wearing to prevent sunburn? Sun worshippers, prepare to beam with excitement: The Netatmo JUNE (shown being worn on the wrist of the person in Figure 11-4) is precisely that device.

The JUNE is a device that you can wear on your wrist much like a watch, using a leather or silicon band, or you can even attach it to your clothing, like a pendant or broach. JUNE was crafted by a professional jewelry designer (so you know it looks mighty nice) and comes in three colors: platinum, gold, and gunmetal.

Image courtesy of Netatmo.

Figure 11-4: The Netatmo JUNE will help prevent sunburn and premature aging of your skin, if you'll heed its advice.

The good news: JUNE keeps up with how much sunlight you're being exposed to throughout the day, and it will communicate that information to you through your iPhone via Bluetooth. The bad news: As of this writing, the app does not work with Android devices. (Perhaps Netatmo will release an Android-friendly version in the future. We can hope for that, at least!)

The JUNE app asks you a few questions about your skin type after you first install it and sign in to your Netatmo account, as illustrated in Figure 11-5. After you've charged your JUNE using the USB charger it comes with, you can sync your JUNE with your iPhone. Once configured, your JUNE will happily keep you informed about your sun exposure — and what you should do to minimize it.

ARCHOS

ARCHOS is a French technology company that dabbles in the tablet, smart-phone, and smartwatch markets. However, the company also has quite a good handle on the personal weather front (another dastardly pun I just ask you to excuse).

The ARCHOS Weather Station utilizes indoor and outdoor modules that sense the weather and other environmental factors wherever you place them, and they report the information back to your smartphone or tablet using the ARCHOS Weather app. The information is uploaded to the ARCHOS Cloud (isn't the name "Cloud" great for information from weather apps?) through your home's Wi-Fi connection, and can be accessed by your devices at any time.

Image courtesy of Netatmo.

Figure 11-5: Configure the JUNE app so that it can better help you protect your skin from the sun's harmful rays.

The indoor module, shown in Figure 11-6, captures a great deal of information within the room or space it occupies, such as:

- ✔ Temperature
- ✔ Relative humidity
- ✔ Atmospheric pressure
- ✔ Noise level
- ✔ Air quality

The outdoor module allows you to know the temperature and relative humidity on the outside of your home.

You can get instant feedback from the indoor module regarding air quality by simply waving your hand in front of it. The dome will light green if your air quality is just fine, yellow if it's getting iffy, and red if you need to fling all the doors and windows in your home wide open.

Figure 11-6:
The ARCHOS indoor module reports environmental information to your smartphone or tablet via the ARCHOS Cloud.

Image courtesy of ARCHOS.

So far, I'm sure you're thinking that the ARCHOS Weather Station sounds quite a bit like the Netatmo Weather Station — and you're right. They function similarly. But if you think about it, most products are created by more than one manufacturer. For example, General Motors and Honda both make cars that perform nearly or the same functionality, and Samsung and Sony both make televisions. So although both companies make similar products, you may prefer how one company goes about it than the other. It comes down to personal preference.

One thing ARCHOS does differently from Netatmo is that ARCHOS includes a soil module. The soil module, shown in Figure 11-7, is placed in the soil around your plants (yes, you can use multiple modules) to detect temperature and humidity/moisture. The module will alert you when it's time to water your plants, taking the guesswork out of the tedious (at least for me) task. ARCHOS just may be your green thumb's best pal.

For more information on the ARCHOS Weather Station and its modules, go to www.archos.com, click the Connected Objects tab, and then click the Weather Station link. There you'll find a video, a photo gallery, and technical specifications for the modules.

AcuRite

AcuRite, owned by Chaney Instrument Company (which has been around since 1943), has been a purveyor of weather stations for a long time — long before Apple and others even knew what a smartphone or tablet was.

AcuRite offers a multitude of weather devices for both the professional and the wannabe meteorologist, but this section focuses on a specific offering: the AcuRite Weather Environment System.

Image courtesy of ARCHOS.

Figure 11-7:
Add the ARCHOS soil module to your Weather Station. Your plants will love you!

The AcuRite Weather Environment System consists of the following set of devices:

- ✔ A weather station display
- ✔ An AcuLink Internet Bridge
- ✔ The AcuLink app and website
- ✔ A 5-in-1 weather sensor

The AcuLink Internet Bridge, shown in Figure 11-8, gathers the data reported to it by the 5-in-1 sensor and makes it available via the Internet. You can access the data through the AcuLink website, or you can use the AcuLink app, which you can download to your iPhone, iPad, or Android device.

The weather station display is a tabletop device that detects and reports indoor temperature and humidity on its own (unfortunately, it does not detect air quality), and it also displays information sent to it by the 5-in-1 sensor. You can quickly determine the outdoor and indoor weather comings and goings with a quick view of the display. That said, be sure to place it in an easily viewable location in your home.

Figure 11-8: The AcuLink Internet Bridge passes information from your 5-in-1 sensor to the AcuLink website or app.

As you can see in Figure 11-9, the 5-in-1 sensor not only looks like it means business, but it also works as well and professionally as it appears. This bad boy includes five impressively named sensors that work all sorts of weather-gathering wizardry:

- Thermometer (okay, that's not too impressive, but it gets better)
- Hygrometer (that's kind of impressive-sounding)
- Wind speed anemometer (now that's impressive!)
- Wind direction vane (not impressive at all, but certainly useful)
- Rain gauge (ditto)

"Yes, Dwight, it looks cool and the sensors have neat names (some of them, anyway), but what can a hygrometer and anemometer do for me?"

I'm glad you asked, dear reader! The 5-in-1 sensor uses its coolness to report the following for you:

- Your very own personalized weather forecast for morning, noon, and night conditions

✔ Outdoor temperature

✔ Outdoor humidity

✔ Wind speed and direction

✔ Barometric pressure

✔ Wind chill

✔ Rain data

Figure 11-9:
The AcuRite 5-in-1 sensor looks like something Spock would use in *Star Trek*, which is, of course, very cool.

Image courtesy of AcuRite.com.

AcuRite does personal weather really well. It offers a wide variety of sensors and display devices for the home weather fan, and I definitely recommend a visit to the website (www.acurite.com) to see all that the company is up to. To find and view the Weather Environment System discussed here, type **01055A1** in the Search box in the upper-right corner of the AcuRite website and click the resulting link.

Access and share your personal weather with Weather Underground

Weather Underground (`www.wunder-ground.com`) is one of the best weather websites in the world, and you can make it better by linking your AcuRite Weather Station to it. By linking your personal weather station (PWS) with Weather Underground, you'll be providing the site's forecasting model with more accurate and truly local weather data, which it'll use to generate better forecasts for your area. You'll also be able to view your personal weather information on the Weather Underground website. Please go to `www.wunderground.com/weatherstation/about.asp` to find out how to link your PWS to Weather Underground; you'll be joining more than 30,000 (and rapidly growing) other weather enthusiasts who share weather info.

Chapter 12

Your Grandfather's Dream, Your Reality: Automating Lawn Care

In This Chapter

▶ Discovering which lawn care tasks can be automated

▶ Cutting your grass while watching from the kitchen window

▶ Watering the lawn while reading the paper

Some jobs around the house are stereotypically seen as being handled by one of the genders:

- ✔ Mom cooks the meal while dad fixes the sink.
- ✔ Grandfather installs new shelves while grandmother finishes her sewing.
- ✔ Big brother cleans the toilets while little sister watches television.

Just kidding about that last one. It occurs to me that I must have expressed a repressed memory from my childhood — or, to be fair to my parents and sister, at least a repressed perception of a childhood memory.

Males have been firmly affixed as the stereotypical gender that cares for the lawn, hence the title of this chapter. However, I can recall more than a time or two when I've seen my grandmothers, my mom, and my wife handle many a lawn care task. So this chapter's for you, too, ladies.

Many folks love to work on their lawns, but if push came to shove, most of us would prefer to put a couple of cows in the yard and let them take care of it. But since most folks these days don't live in an area that's cow-friendly, we'd love the next best thing: for the tasks to be automatically done using today's tech.

Caring for Your Lawn Doesn't Have to Break Your Back

We like to think that the more our technology advances, the more time we have for the things we love and the less work we have to put into the tasks that drive us crazy. So far, you have seen how home automation can help with the cooking, cleaning, and other chores inside the home. Now it's time to discover what home automation can do for you when it comes to jobs that are outside the confines of your abode's walls, be they humble or otherwise.

Reasons for automating lawn care

You awaken to the sounds of birds chirping on a beautiful Saturday morning and relish the idea of whipping that lawn of yours into shape. You are a lawn connoisseur, having acquired the taste for an immaculately shaped, perfectly cut, and gorgeously green yard from several generations stretching all the way back to your kin in the old country. You grab a cup of coffee, open the garage door, and step into the dew-covered grass to survey the task at hand between sips of java. The coolness of the breeze complements the warmth of the spring sun as you pull the crank cord on your mower. As the mower starts up, you push it to where you'll begin the first row of what will soon be the most manicured yard in the neighborhood.

It's now late afternoon. Your hands are aching from pushing and pulling your mower all over God's creation. Gallons of water have been consumed in the name of keeping you hydrated. Hours have been flushed away trying to fix the mower's blade after you ran over a petrified stump from the stone ages, only to end up having to buy a new blade at the hardware store. Your knuckles are battered and bloody from banging them against your mower's engine in an attempt to remove the gas tank so you could clean the gunk out of it, which you discovered is what's causing the sorry thing to quit on you every couple of laps around the lawn. You're also sporting a nice new bandage on your left ankle after stepping into that hole your 5-year-old dug in the yard last winter, which you didn't see because the grass had grown over it. The sun's beginning to go down, and you now realize you'll have to get back out here again tomorrow to finish the job.

Weekend. Shot.

If you've had much experience with cutting your own grass, the scenario I've just described is an all-too-familiar one. That in itself should explain the basic reasons for automating your lawn care, but here are a few more reasons should you need further convincing:

- ✔ Automation will save you money!
- ✔ Robotic mowers are very low maintenance.
- ✔ Work can be performed at any time, day or night.
- ✔ Robotic mowers are electric, eliminating the need for gasoline.
- ✔ Automation frees up your time.
- ✔ And finally, the most obvious reason: Why break a sweat if you don't have to? (I hope the fitness buffs in the audience will forgive me for that one.)

Now, I know what many of you are thinking, primarily because I had this thought myself: "Don't these kinds of devices just contribute to a lazier society and eliminate what was once a good excuse to go outside and get some exercise?" Let me answer your question with another: "Would you like to give up your clothes washer and dryer, or perhaps your dishwasher?"

I thought not.

Lawn care tasks that you can automate

Well, when it comes to the list of lawn care tasks that you can automate, it won't take very long to read:

- ✔ Mow
- ✔ Water

That's right: There are only two tasks as of this writing, but they're the two biggies. I've researched and researched, but try as I might, I've been unable to discover a robotic lawn edger or a robotic hedge trimmer. I'm sure someone's trying to build them, but as of now they're only a dream for consumers. Believe me, I can feel your disappointment as I type this.

Getting to Know the Top Companies in Lawn Automation

When I was a kid, I had a weird thought (that kind of goes without saying): I envisioned C3PO pushing our lawn mower around the yard while R2D2 weeded the flower bed and trimmed the hedges. R2D2 even wore a big straw hat — no kidding.

I gave you that semi-disturbing look into my psyche to illustrate the point that people have been hoping and dreaming of ways to more easily get the yard work done for quite the while. While the famous robot duo from the *Star Wars* universe aren't about to cut your grass, their distant cousins, today's robotic lawn mowers, will be more than happy to do the job. Robotic mowers are a reality, and many can even be controlled via your smartphone or tablet. The next few sections look into some of the most popular robotic mower companies and explain how each can help you automate that oh-so-burdensome task, keeping the grass nice and trim.

Robomow

Robomow started in 1995 as a company called Friendly Machines, which developed the first robotic lawn mower. Since then, Robomow has become one of the top brands in the robotic mowing world. These mowers can handle the cutting of most lawns that can be cut with a standard push mower. One of Robomow's former taglines reads: "It mows, you don't." In my opinion, the company should have stuck with that one. It says all there is to say about Robomow's products.

Speaking of products, Robomow offers robotic mowers for small yards (one model), medium yards (two models), and large yards (two models). Each model is designed to tackle yards of certain sizes:

- ✔ **RM510:** yards up to 5,500 square feet

- ✔ **RC306:** yards up to 6,500 square feet

- ✔ **RS612:** yards up to 12,900 square feet

- ✔ **RS622:** yards up to 23,700 square feet

- ✔ **RS630** (shown in Figure 12-1): cuts every yard in your neighborhood. Okay, not really, but it does handle yards up to 32,300 square feet.

For yards larger than 32,300 square feet, you will need more than one Robomow. Dual robotic mowers are able to work together in the same yard, but their setup procedures are a bit different than if setting up a single mower. You can contact Robomow for more information on dual mower setups by visiting `www.robomowusa.com/contact.html`.

Figure 12-1:
Robomow's
RS630 is a
grass-eating
machine!

Image courtesy of Robomow.

Determine which mower you need

Just how do the good folks at Robomow expect you to go about measuring your yard's dimensions to find out which mower is best for your needs? Well, I'm surprised at you, gentle reader! You should have known that Robomow has made it super simple for you to get a good idea of how large your yard is by using Google Maps. This is the 21st century we're living in, after all, where knowledge is often a click or a tap away!

Using your favorite web browser, hop on over to `http://robomap.robomow.com/?site=en-US` to begin measuring your yard using the Robomap. Here's how to easily measure your yard:

1. **Once on the site, enter your address information so Robomap can pull up a satellite image of your property. Click Next.**

2. **Center the image of your property in the window by clicking-and-dragging the map image. Click Next.**

   You can also use the zoom slider on the left of the window to help center the image.

3. **Select a brush size from the options on the left side of the screen.**

4. **Using your mouse pointer or trackpad, click-and-drag over the portions of your yard that you typically mow, as I've done for Elvis Presley's yard in Figure 12-2.**

   The light green highlights are the sections of your yard that you're measuring.

5. **Select the eraser tool to remove any areas you mistakenly highlighted.**

6. **When you're finished highlighting, click Next to see a neat illustration of a Robomow mower at work cutting the area of your lawn you highlighted.**

7. **Click the Skip button when asked if you want to share the animation with your Facebook friends (unless you just have to show your friends which part of your yard you're going to mow . . .).**

   Robomap will show you a picture of the model it recommends for you and your yard.

You've got to admit: The yard measurement tool is a great resource to help you determine which model suits your needs. It's also kind of fun to search for famous lawns (like the White House or London's Wembley Stadium) to see what Robomap recommends. In case you're wondering, Wembley Stadium threw the Robomap tool for a loop: "BAD MODELS DATA!" it screamed.

Keeping your mower in your yard

You might be wondering how the mowers stay in your yard, and don't take off down the street, or worse, run over your neighbor's carefully manicured flower beds. The secret is perimeter wire, which is part of the initial setup of your Robomow mower. You'll need to run the wire around your property, creating a virtual fence with the wire that your mower dare not cross. The wire can either be simply pegged to the ground around your yard, or you can bury it. Whenever your mower runs into this virtual fence, the machine simply turns around and heads in another direction, just as it does when it bumps into obstacles such as trees and bushes.

Figure 12-2:
Use
Robomow's
Robomap
tool to
determine
which
mower
model you
need.

Setting up a perimeter can be a little tricky, especially if your yard is irregularly shaped. If you should need help designing a perimeter, Robomow is happy to assist you by designing a custom perimeter plan for your yard (for a reasonable charge).

Other great Robomow features

The Robomow stable of mowers affords you tons of great features:

- The mowers are so quiet they can even go about their task when the rest of your neighborhood is sleeping. Won't your buddy next door be green with envy when he wakes up on Saturday morning to find your lawn is already in tip-top shape?

- Mowers immediately return to their charging station after the job is completed or if they're running really low on charge.

- You can decide whether to cut your lawn in the rain or not (no umbrella required!)

- Your mower can be programmed to require a PIN before it will operate.

- The Robomow app lets you take control of your mower from your iOS or Android device. Visit www.robomow.com/en-USA/mobile-app-en-us for compatibility information.

- The mowers incorporate safety features to keep your automated mowing a positive experience:

    - If the mower is lifted or turns over, it will automatically shut off.

    - A Child Lock feature keeps the mower from being operated by just anyone (children definitely fit that category).

Head on over to www.robomow.com to find out much more about Robomow and its mower models.

Husqvarna

No self-respecting home gardener or lawn care expert is unfamiliar with the name "Husqvarna." These folks have been in the lawn and garden game since the early part of the 20th century, and have been around as a company for nearly 400 years! And no, I didn't know that either, until I researched the information. Over the years, Husqvarna has become known as a top-of-the-line manufacturer of lawn and garden tools, and its reputation is intact when it comes to automatically mowing your lawn, too.

Husqvarna has been robotically cutting lawns for 20 years, and suffice it to say that it has become quite skilled at the task. An interesting tidbit is that Husqvarna's first robotic mower, introduced in 1995, ran on solar power: hence its Solar Mower moniker.

These days, Husqvarna's robotic mowers are called Automowers, and they're excellent tools to have in your home automation arsenal. Backed by Husqvarna's outstanding reputation and quality, these little puppies (the Automower 220 AC shown in Figure 12-3) can take care of your lawn's trimming without you having to lift a finger.

Figure 12-3:
Husqvarna's
Automowers
have 20
years of
research
and develop-
ment behind
them.

Image courtesy of Husqvarna AB.

The Automower line of mowers can cut your grass on a continual basis. You set up your mower, start it on its merry way, and it will cut your lawn, stopping only to recharge when needed. Once recharged, the Automower will continue to cut your lawn. Automower cuts in a random pattern — which eliminates track marks in your lawn and helps your grass to grow stronger since it's being cut from different directions. The Automower also uses razorlike blades that slice through your grass with ease, utilizing a mulching process to feed your lawn its own clippings (no bag!). Over a period of a few weeks, this random pattern and mulching cutting method will return a beautiful lawn that has been strengthened and fertilized by your Automower.

Here are some other features that will cause you to consider Husqvarna's Automower closely before making a decision on which manufacturer will get the honor of keeping your lawn immaculately trimmed:

- ✔ Uses a very low amount of energy, so recharging and mowing don't cost a fortune.
- ✔ Automowers are weatherproof, so you can rest easy during your area's rainy season: The lawn will be kept nice and neat.

- ✔ Husqvarna's engineers have figured out how to equip the Automower to handle steeper inclines than some of its competitors.

- ✔ Like other robotic mowers, Automower uses a boundary wire that you place around your yard to guide it along.

- ✔ If someone tries to swipe your beloved Automower, it uses an alarm and a secured PIN to make sure that the thief doesn't get far.

- ✔ Husqvarna has outfitted Automower with safety features to keep life as simple as possible. Should the mower be tilted up or lifted, the blades will automatically shut off. No missing fingers or toes with the Automower on duty.

- ✔ The built-in settings panel allows you to easily modify Automower's behavior, such as when it cuts and how.

- ✔ A guide wire helps the Automower find its way back to the charging station more quickly, reducing the chances of Automower not making it back to the station before it runs out of power.

- ✔ It's super-simple to adjust the cutting height of your Automower. Turn the knob on top of the mower, shown in Figure 12-4, to the desired cutting height. You no longer have to adjust the height of each individual wheel, as you do on the typical push mower.

Many Automower owners can also use Husqvarna's My Automower app to program and keep track of their Automower. The app can also alert you when there's a problem, such as the mower becoming stuck or having to fend off the neighbor's kid.

Figure 12-4:
The knob on top of your Automower makes it simple to adjust cutting height.

Image courtesy of Husqvarna AB.

I highly recommend you take a trip to the Husqvarna website. Visit www.husqvarna.com, go the Products section, and then select Robotic Mowers to see the selection of Automowers in your part of the world. The site is also chock-full of videos and other tips to help you get your Automower up and running, and to keep it that way.

LawnBott

LawnBott, by Kyodo America, hasn't been around as long as Husqvarna, or even as long as Robomow, but its lineup of robotic mowers is impressive. Not only does LawnBott have the most models to choose from of the three manufacturers discussed up to this point, but its products also can handle a wider range of lawn sizes than the others.

When it comes to style, LawnBott's models leave a little something to be desired (with the exception of the Spyder; it's a pretty neat-looking critter). However, this isn't about style; it's about getting the yard cut without breaking a sweat, and LawnBott does that as well or better than most anyone else.

LawnBott's models include:

- ✔ **LB1200 Spyder:** This little fellow is intended only for small lawns (up to 5,500 square feet); however, it is the only robotic mower on the market to date that doesn't require the use of a perimeter wire. The Spyder (shown in Figure 12-5) uses special sensors to determine when it's no longer over a grassy area.

- ✔ **LB75DX:** This model cuts yards up to 7,000 square feet, and does employ the use of a perimeter wire (as do the rest of the upcoming models).

- ✔ **LB85EL:** The 85EL can take care of yards up to 24,000 square feet.

- ✔ **LB200EL:** The 200EL handles lawns up to 38,000 square feet. To compare, that's nearly 6,000 square feet more than Robomow's best-range mower, the RS630.

- ✔ **LB300EL:** This bad boy of the backyard (and any other yard, for that matter) is unparalleled in the amount of lawn it can cover: 64,000 square feet! This is one mean grass-eating machine.

Figure 12-5:
LawnBott's
Spyder
doesn't
need a
perimeter
wire to stay
on your
lawn.

Image courtesy of LawnBotts.com.

LawnBott's way of getting the job done is similar to the way other robotic mower makers go about it:

✔ Perimeter wire is used to mark the cutting boundaries for your LawnBott (with the exception of the Spyder, as mentioned). Having said that, LawnBott's machines also work within enclosed areas, such as a fenced-in yard, without the need for the perimeter wire, if you wish. Just be careful that you don't have an area within the area (such as a flower bed) that you don't want to be sliced and diced.

✔ LawnBott will follow the perimeter wire back to the recharging station when its batteries are low or when it's completed cutting duty for the day. Again, this isn't applicable to the Spyder.

✔ Based on battery life, cutting time can range from 45 minutes to 10 hours, depending on the model you're using (the 75DX is the shortest time, and the 300EL has the longest).

✔ All models except the Spyder include a rain sensor, which allows the mower to cut or not when it rains, based on your instructions.

✔ LawnBotts can all receive software updates via the Internet using your Wi-Fi connection. That's just awesome.

✔ LawnBotts can be secured with a PIN, without which they will not operate if you choose this security option.

✔ An optional GPS unit can be installed so that you can track down the location of the LawnBott should it be stolen, or shall we say, removed from your property without prior authorization.

✔ LawnBotts can all work on yards with slopes up to 25 degrees, which is to say they can handle a hill pretty well.

✔ Safety is as much a concern to LawnBott as it is to other manufacturers. The device will simply shut off if tilted or picked up.

✔ Each of the EL models also supports SMS as an option, which allows you to receive text notifications from your LawnBott on your cellphone, whether it's "smart" or not.

✔ All models are compatible with the Ambrogio Remote app for iOS and Android, shown in Figure 12-6. Use it to remotely control your LawnBott and to get notifications if things go awry.

It's obvious that LawnBott has covered most, if not all, of the bases when it comes to automatically mowing your lawn. Check out www.lawnbotts.com to find scads more information, including a nifty side-by-side comparison chart of all the LawnBott models.

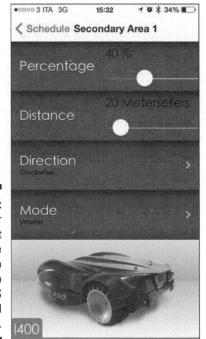

Figure 12-6: Control your LawnBott with the Ambrogio Remote app on your iOS or Android device.

Image courtesy of LawnBotts.com.

Robotic mowers around the world

Those of you living in parts of the world other than North America will be happy to know that your selection of automated mowers is much broader than that for those who do live here. Let's take a look at three of the bigger and better brands.

John Deere

I've lived in the Southeastern part of the United States my entire life, and few companies are more synonymous with these parts than John Deere. Whether it's tractors or riding mowers, John Deere has been right in the thick of things for as long as I can remember. But I have to admit that I was a bit surprised to find out that the company is just as good at robotically mowing a lawn as it is at tilling a field.

John Deere's TANGO E5, seen in Figure 12-7, is the venerable company's foray into the world of automated lawn care and, by most accounts, it's a good one. However, you can't get your hands on one in the Southeastern United States — or any other part of the United States, for that matter.

That you can't buy a particular John Deere product in the United States sounds strange, for sure, but it's not the only company following the practice. The fact is this: Robotic or automatic mowing is super-popular in Europe and in other countries around the world, but it's yet to really take off in the U.S. This is reason enough for some manufacturers to make their products available in places around the world, excluding the United States.

For more information on the TANGO E5, visit www.deere.com/en_INT/ products/equipment/autonomous_mower/autonomous_mower.page.

Two more examples of big-name manufacturers whose automated lawn mowers can't be purchased in the U.S. are Honda and Bosch.

Figure 12-7: John Deere's TANGO E5, available just about every- where ... except the USA.

Image courtesy of Deere & Company.

Honda

Honda's Miimo is a slick grass-cutting hombre, coupling Honda's reputation for reliability with its experience in the area of robotics. The Miimo is quite a machine in both looks and functionality.

You would think that with the popularity of Honda's other products in the U.S. that the company would offer the Miimo within the country's borders, but that isn't the case as of this writing. But if you're someone living in Europe — congratulations! — you can get your hands on one of these little gems with little to no problem.

The Miimo, shown in Figure 12-8, covers the basics of what the other automated lawn mower manufacturers do:

- ✔ It provides a safe mowing experience, with automated shut-off when the device is lifted or tilted too much.

- ✔ It's quiet, so mowing can be performed any time of the day or night without disturbing the neighbors.

- ✔ The Miimo is self-charging, meaning that once its power is low it will seek out the charging station on its own and recharge.

- ✔ Rain is not a problem; the Miimo is waterproof and the blades will cut wet grass as well as dry.

A couple of other features really stand out on the Miimo:

The blades are made of (in Honda's words) "high quality ductile heat-treated steel." This means that should the blades hit a solid object they won't shatter, but instead will either bend or rotate inward.

Figure 12-8:
Honda's Miimo will be right at home in your garage next to your Honda automobile and motorcycle.

Image courtesy of Honda.

You can choose to have your lawn cut in one of three cutting patterns: random, directional, or a mix of the two.

Check out the Miimo at `www.honda.co.uk/garden/miimo/`.

Bosch

The Bosch Indego is yet another great robotic mower option from yet another great company with a reputation for quality. This little blue-green baby can tackle your (non-U.S.) lawn as autonomously as the next robotic mower, and has all the features you've come to expect from these yard-mongers:

- ✔ The Indego can charge itself, returning to the charging station of its own accord.
- ✔ Cutting slopes is a breeze (slopes up to a 35 percent grade, that is).
- ✔ Perimeter wire is used to make certain the Indego never loses its way.
- ✔ A PIN code and alarm prevent folks from sneaking off with your Indego.
- ✔ A yaw sensor helps the Indego regain its footing should it slip on slopes or wet grass.

The Indego (shown in Figure 12-9) has lots of other features, too, including the standard safety features like automatic shut-off. One of the coolest has to do with the cutting technology employed by Bosch: Logicut. You see, Bosch follows the philosophy that a directional pattern is better than a random one, citing time, energy, and cost savings. The Logicut technology has the Indego first map out the lawn and then create an efficient mowing plan that tells the Indego to cut the lawn using parallel lines where possible.

Figure 12-9: The Bosch Indego prefers to cut your lawn in parallel lines rather than using a random pattern.

Image courtesy of Robert Bosch GmbH.

Take a virtual look at the Indego at www.bosch-indego.com. Bosch has packed a great deal more information into its web pages than I can divulge here.

Don't forget your Indego's PIN! If you forget the PIN and attempt to enter it too many times incorrectly, the Indego will shut down. The only way to recover it is to take it and the charging station to a certified Bosch dealer.

Watering Your Lawn Automatically

It doesn't matter what your preference of robotic mower is if you don't have a lawn for it to mow. Moving from mowing your lawn to watering it, let's take a look at how best to automate your lawn-watering tasks. Sure, there have been automatic sprinkler systems since the Stone Age, but only recently have you been able to control your sprinklers via your smartphone.

Cyber Rain

Cyber Rain is a company that connects your existing sprinkler system to the Internet, and since it can do that it allows you to control your system from anywhere you have an Internet connection. Cyber Rain's software and information is entirely cloud-based (get it, "cloud"-based?), which lets you access your irrigation system from any device with an Internet connection and a web browser. Cyber Rain also saves you money over your existing system because it uses your local weather forecast to adjust its watering schedule automatically. Your existing sprinkler system waters on a set schedule, regardless of whether you've just survived a torrential downpour or not.

Here's how to put Cyber Rain to work:

1. **Replace your existing sprinkler system controller with a Cyber Rain controller.**

2. **After mounting the Cyber Rain controller, connect the wires for your irrigation system's water valves to the controller.**

3. **Connect the Cyber Rain Gateway to your home network.**

    This allows the controller and gateway to communicate with one another and share information about your irrigation system.

    You can use as many Cyber Rain controllers as you like with your Cyber Rain Gateway.

4. **Log in to your Cyber Rain account from any computer or smart device that can run a web browser.**

5. **Monitor your water savings, change your irrigation schedules, initiate a manual watering cycle, and more from Cyber Rain's cloud-based software.**

   Sit back and open your next water bill with confidence that you'll see results of savings both in your water consumption and in your bank account.

The Cyber Rain system will alert you to problems encountered in your irrigation system. For example, should the irrigation pipes spring a leak, Cyber Rain will note that water is being used when it shouldn't be, send you a notification of the problem, and shut down watering functions until the alert is cleared.

That you can access your irrigation system's controls through the Internet is a boon, but one might also consider that using an app to control the whole thing is a pretty awesome deal, too. However, the Cyber Rain app (see Figure 12-10) isn't nearly as functional as the web-based version of the controller software. As a matter of fact, the app itself isn't garnering a lot of love from its users, based on feedback I've found on the iOS and Android

Figure 12-10: Cyber Rain's Cloud app is leaving its users feeling a bit let down, especially considering how good the web-based software is at handling your sprinkler system's needs.

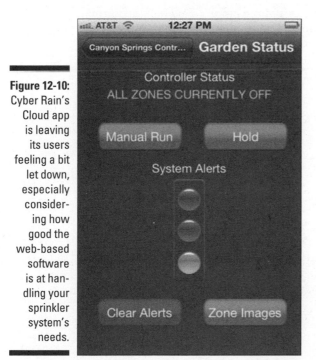

Image courtesy of Cyber Rain.

App stores. The biggest problem with the app is that it is so simplistic, and I've read complaints that some of the features don't work as advertised. The latest version of Cyber Rain's app as of this writing is 1.6; I hope it's been updated since I wrote this book and that the reviews are on the upswing.

I suggest checking the Cyber Rain website (`www.cyber-rain.com`) so you can further investigate its fine irrigation system products. You will find lots of information there, not only about Cyber Rain's residential products, but also about its commercial irrigation systems.

Rachio

Rachio is all about the business of saving you money and conserving water. It goes about these two tasks in much the same way as Cyber Rain:

- ✔ It keeps a real-time look at your area's current weather conditions before scheduling a lawn-watering session, and makes automatic adjustments to said schedule as needed.

- ✔ Rachio uses the Internet and the cloud to exchange information between your irrigation system and your devices (smart devices and computers grant you access to your personalized info).

- ✔ It replaces your current sprinkler system controller with one of its own, called the Iro (see Figure 12-11).

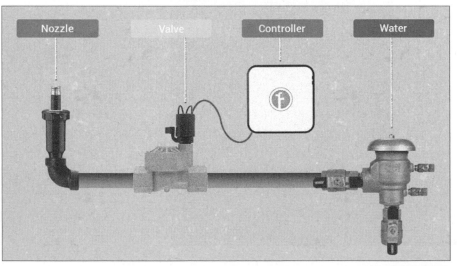

Figure 12-11:
The Iro controller grants you access to your irrigation system from anywhere you can get an Internet connection.

Image courtesy of Rachio.

At first blush, Rachio and Cyber Rain might seem like two companies with the same idea. However, Rachio is aiming to separate its product in a couple of important ways:

✔ Rachio's Iro doesn't require the purchase of a gateway. It simply connects to your Wi-Fi with the help of your smartphone. You use your smartphone to flash the Iro, giving it the same information your smartphone uses to access your home's Wi-Fi network.

✔ While Cyber Rain's smart device app seems to be an afterthought in regards to its functionality, Rachio primarily uses apps on iOS and Android devices to operate the Iro, as illustrated in Figure 12-12. You can access a web-based page dedicated to the Iro on the Rachio website (`https://rach.io`) as well, but anything you need to do with your Iro was designed to be controlled by an app first. Rachio's app is clean, easy to navigate, and packed with features.

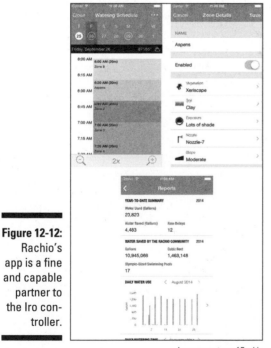

Figure 12-12:
Rachio's app is a fine and capable partner to the Iro controller.

Images courtesy of Rachio.

Part IV

Taking Command of Your Home Automation Systems

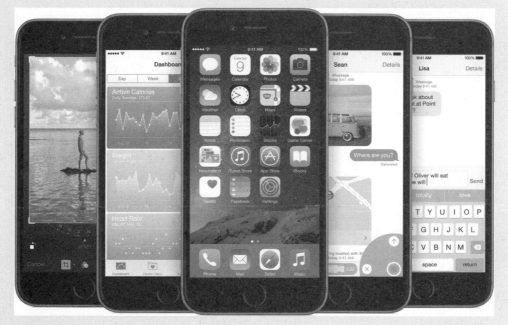

Check out the best smartphones and tablets for your smart home automation system at www.dummies.com/extras/homeautomation.

In this part . . .

- ✔ Discover which devices allow you to remotely control your home automation system.

- ✔ Learn how to keep your home automation apps up-to-date.

- ✔ Find out which companies are striving to bring platform unity to smart home automation.

Chapter 13

Working with Mobile Devices and Computers

In This Chapter

▶ Finding out which smart devices work best with home automation systems

▶ Discovering computers and operating systems that work with home automation tech

▶ Keeping your home automation apps updated

*T*he UPS guy just dropped off enough boxes full of smart home automation devices to keep you busy for the next few weeks, and that's just unboxing everything.

Time zips by and you've got all your home automation gear unboxed and ready to go. You decide to connect your smart hub first so that the other devices can connect to it.

Halfway through the installation process, you get to the part where your iOS or Android smartphone or tablet is required to download an app and create an account.

"Aw, who needs that fancy-shmancy stuff?" you ask, as you whip out your tried-and-true Motorola flip-phone from 2004. You poke around the menu a bit, get frustrated, and even call your cellphone provider for help. Alas, you find no App Store to download your app from. "Bummer," you say, with a tinge of despondency.

And then you notice in the instructions that you can also register your smart hub on the company's website. Eureka! You dash inside, sit down at your desk, pop open a can of your favorite soft drink, and proceed with the five-minute process of booting up your good ol' Commodore 64 computer. After much ballyhoo, the C64 is up and running, but again you're stymied in your attempt to register your smart hub: There's no Internet connection or web browser on your C64! (How'd you ever find this book about smart home automation in the first place? Geez!)

Sorry, Methuselah, but it looks like you might need to upgrade a few electronic thingies around the house: In particular, you'll need a smartphone, a tablet, and/or a contemporary computer to not only register your products, but to even be able to use them.

Discovering Devices Commonly Used for Smart Home Automation

Having the right devices handy will make getting started with and using your smart home automation devices that much easier. In this chapter, I give you an overview of which smart devices and computing platforms are most frequently supported by home automation companies, and also tell you how to get apps and keep them updated.

Smartphones

Most folks using smart home automation tech will find themselves reaching for their smartphones when they need to open a lock or adjust a thermostat remotely. Although most smartphones work quite well with today's home automation tech, some devices might not quite be able to cut it. Take a look at which smartphones and operating systems are most frequently supported and which ones are sketchier in their capability to control your home automation.

iOS

Apple's iOS is the smartphone operating system that started the smartphone craze with the release of the first iPhone in 2007.

There simply can be no denying that iOS changed how many of us live our daily lives. Many of the following tasks we perform with our phones today first became commonplace because of iOS and the first iPhone:

- Surfing the Internet
- Taking and sending pictures and videos
- Sending and receiving email
- Watching Internet-based videos
- Listening to and purchasing music and other multimedia

What is a smartphone?

A smartphone is a cellular phone that is smarter than you and I put together, or at least it seems so sometimes. Actually, they are cellular phones, but they also perform some of the same functions as your computer, use a touchscreen interface, and can connect to the Internet with ease, whether through your cellular provider's network or via your Wi-Fi network.

✔ Connecting to Wi-Fi networks

✔ Creating and sharing events on your calendar

✔ Synchronizing content with your computer

✔ Listening to podcasts

There is so much more, too; I'm only scratching the surface. "You could do some of that before the iPhone!" some of you might retort. You and I both know that you could do some of those things on old-fashioned cellphones (such as taking and sending pictures), but the difference between performing those tasks on the old devices and performing them on the iPhone is as great as that of using pigeons to send messages and using email. Don't get sassy, please.

I spend much time discussing iOS and the iPhone because, frankly, without them, this book might not be written and home automation might still be in the dark ages. That is no exaggeration. Who knows what might have happened if Steve Jobs and company hadn't decided to go forward with the iPhone? Although Android devices are good products these days, who knows where they would be today if not for the push they were given by Apple to up their game?

The iPhone is the only smartphone in the world authorized to use the iOS operating system. While that may turn off some folks, Apple believes its hardware will run its own operating system better than anyone else's hardware will — and you can't argue with results. Most home automation technology companies today support both iOS and Android smart devices, but there are some that still only support iOS. The main reasons for that disparity are:

✔ iOS has been at the game for longer.

✔ iOS is generally more stable than Android.

✔ Hardware and software compatibility issues are kept to a bare minimum since both are from the same manufacturer, Apple.

  ✔ Many home automation developers cut their teeth on iOS and are reluctant (and some downright refusing) to work on the Android platform.

Having said all that, these are the iPhone versions most likely to be supported by the majority of the home automation companies on the market:

  ✔ iPhone 4

  ✔ iPhone 4s

  ✔ iPhone 5

  ✔ iPhone 5c

  ✔ iPhone 5s

  ✔ iPhone 6 (shown in Figure 13-1 on the left)

  ✔ iPhone 6 Plus (shown in Figure 13-1 on the right)

All iPhone versions in the preceding list support at least iOS 7, which is crucial when running most of the home automation apps today. Anything older than iOS 7 just won't do for most of them. Sigh.

Figure 13-1: Apple's latest gems in the iPhone line, iPhone 6 (left) and iPhone 6 Plus (right).

Image courtesy of Apple, Inc.

The current version is iOS 8, so if you're thinking you'll just get an iPhone 4 from your friend, think twice. Sure, the iPhone 4 supports iOS 7, but it doesn't support iOS 8, and in a year or two app versions will only support iOS 8. That trend is just part of the technology game, so be ready for it now and don't force instant obsolescence on yourself by trying to save a few bucks on an old iPhone.

For more on iOS 8 and the iPhone, check out www.apple.com/iphone.

Android

After reading the preceding section on iPhones and iOS, you might think I have a complete aversion to Google's Android operating system, but I assure you that is not the case. Android is a great mobile operating system, particularly the newest versions, and it does everything iOS can do. Granted, Android doesn't enjoy the same stability as iOS, and the fact that multiple hardware vendors use the operating system can play havoc from time to time, but Android as a platform is a good thing.

Android versus iOS reminds me of the battles between Apple's Mac OS and Microsoft's Windows years ago. You don't hear much about that old-time squabble these days, but you do hear and read Android versus iOS comparisons all the time.

Android will do all that you want it to, but the question is, does it do what you want it to in the way that you want it to? That same question can be applied to iOS, as well. It all comes down to your personal preference. I'll leave it at that.

Here's something to be wary of, though: The versions of the Android operating system supported by home automation companies vary wildly. Some companies, like SmartThings, say the versions of their apps you need to install and the version of the Android operating system you need on your smartphone vary by device, as shown in Figure 13-2.

The reason? Smartphone manufacturers that use Android on their phones can tinker with the original Android OS version, and sometimes that tinkering can make things a little less stable than they otherwise would be. In some cases, you may have an app that works great on Phone 1 but has all kinds of issues on Phone 2, even though they are both running the same version of the app and the same core version of Android. Android is open-source software, meaning that anyone can use it and modify it (within reason) to his or her own needs. So companies that use Android can take a core release of the software from Google and pretty much do whatever they want with it. Of course, these manufacturers want more people to buy their smartphones more than their competitors' devices, so they try hard not to break compatibility with other apps — but it's something you need to be aware of. If your home automation app works differently on one Android phone than it does on another, don't automatically assume the app developer is the one that goofed things up.

Figure 13-2:
The version of an Android app you install on your smartphone may vary based on the device's manufacturer.

Apps	Categories ∨ Home Top Charts New Releases			❓ ⚙

My apps
Shop

Games
Editors' Choice

What's New

SmartThings version 1.6.8 includes several bug fixes and overall performance improvements for enhanced stability. Noteworthy changes include the addition of in-app support chat and quick mode switching via the left menu.

Additional information

Updated	Size	Installs	Current Version	Requires Android
November 12, 2014	Varies with device	10,000 - 50,000	Varies with device	Varies with device
Content Rating	Permissions	Report	Offered By	Developer
Low Maturity	View details	Flag as inappropriate	SmartThings	Visit Website
				Email
				support@smartthings.com
				Privacy Policy

Most home automation companies do support Android, so chances are good that if you already have an Android smartphone that you'll be able to use it with the system you're considering purchasing (or have already purchased). If you aren't sure, please find out before plunking down your hard-earned cash on a system you can't use.

Having offered my take on the Android platform, allow me to give you a list of some of the latest smartphones (as of this writing) that run it:

- Samsung Galaxy S5 (shown in Figure 13-3)
- Sony Xperia Z3
- Sony Xperia Z3 Compact
- LG G3
- Samsung Galaxy Note 4
- OnePlus One
- HTC One M8 (shown in Figure 13-4)

For more information about the Android OS, go to www.android.com.

Windows Phone

It seems strange to think that Microsoft is lagging behind rather than being one of the leaders in the field of operating systems, but when it comes to smartphones, the company is trailing Apple and Google by a mile. That isn't to say that the Windows Phone operating system isn't good, but Microsoft got into the game a little late.

Figure 13-3:
Samsung's
Galaxy S5
is a popular
Android-
based
smartphone.

Image courtesy of Samsung.

This being the case, many home automation companies have paid little to no heed to the cries from Windows Phone users for support of their devices. If you are a Windows Phone user, don't be discouraged, though. Some home automation companies, like SmartThings and Alarm.com, are coming around, while others are still holding off, like Belk and Wink. All I can tell you in terms of availability is to contact the companies directly to voice your need for Windows Phone apps. Because availability is a concern, this does limit your choices of home automation systems and devices, I'm afraid.

Another issue you need to be aware of is that those home automation companies that do support Windows Phone tend to favor the latest version, which is 8.1 as of this writing, but there is some support out there for version 8. Good luck finding any support for version 7, though. It's not my intent to bring you down, but I do want you to be informed about the current state of affairs concerning Windows Phones and home automation.

Figure 13-4:
HTC's One M8 is considered by many to be one of the top Android smartphones of 2014.

Image courtesy of HTC Corporation.

If you don't have a Windows Phone app for your home automation system, you may have an alternative. Most home automation systems have dedicated websites you can log into, allowing you to monitor and control everything from there. Your Windows Phone comes with a web browser, right? Well, there you go!

Now, onto the phones! A number of Windows Phones are on the market, but you'll notice after a quick search that the vast majority are by one manufacturer, Nokia. Culling through a list of Windows Phones on Microsoft's website is like taking a tour through Nokia-land (Figure 13-5 sports one of the Nokia models). I kid you not. It's kind of funny when you look for a list of the best Windows Phones and almost all of them are Nokia models (and in one case, one review I found listed nothing but Nokia models).

Fear not, though, if Nokia isn't your thing; other Windows Phone makers includes the likes of HTC and Samsung.

Please do check the world of Windows Phones out for yourself by visiting www.windowsphone.com/.

Image courtesy of Microsoft Mobile.

Figure 13-5: In terms of sheer numbers, Nokia smartphones, like the 635, are dominating the Windows Phone market.

Tablets

As I mention earlier in the chapter, most of you will probably stick to your smartphones when it comes to making adjustments and checking in with your home automation systems, especially when on the go. However, it may be a different story in the home: The tablet may take center stage.

Tablets are essentially overgrown smartphones, without the phone part (at least in most cases). But it is precisely their size that makes them so useful and makes them viable alternatives to full-blown laptop computers. Tablets are lightweight, durable, and have a touchscreen, so getting your work done or catching up on your entertainment is now done in a portable way.

Many of the traditional home automation companies have utilized touch-screens for years with their products, but they were completely customized devices that were specific to the home automation tasks alone: Nothing else could be done with them. Plus, they were often mounted on walls and you were unable to take them around the house with you, much less outside the home.

Today's tablets do offer you the mobility that the old-fashioned kind didn't, plus you can customize them to your heart's content. Check out the following tablet makers that you'll most likely be dealing with in your home automation endeavors for the foreseeable future:

iOS

Hello, Apple! Nice to see you again.

Yep, the Cupertino Fruit Company also has the inside track with tablets in the home automation space, and for the same reasons it holds the slight edge over Android with smartphones.

Apple's tablets run the same operating system that its phones do — iOS. The same version issues apply as well, with version 8 being the most current.

Apple currently offers two models of its popular iPad, the iPad Air (shown in Figure 13-6 on left) and the iPad mini (shown in Figure 13-6 on right).

Figure 13-6:
Apple's iPad Air (left) and iPad mini (right) are among the most popular tablets in the world.

Image courtesy of Apple, Inc.

Both iPad Air and iPad mini come in different configurations, however (Wi-Fi–only and Wi-Fi+Cellular models are available for each configuration, as well):

- ✔ iPad Air 2
  - • Up to 128GB of storage
  - • 9.7-inch display
- ✔ iPad Air
  - • Up to 32GB of storage
  - • 9.7-inch display
- ✔ iPad mini 3
  - • Up to 128GB of storage
  - • 7.9-inch display
- ✔ iPad mini 2
  - • Up to 32GB of storage
  - • 7.9-inch display
- ✔ iPad mini
  - • Up to 16GB of storage
  - • 7.9-inch display

See the range of iPads at www.apple.com/ipad.

Android

Android apps are available for tablets just as they are for smartphones, so don't think you might be missing something when it comes to being able to control your home automation devices.

Apple currently offers a total of five iPads, but if you're in the market for an Android tablet, you are about to hit the mother lode, my friend. There are more Android tablets on the market than there are grains of sand on the beach (at least it seems that way). And this is a good thing, because it means a tablet is available for nearly every budget.

Again, the only issue I would advise you to be wary of is the version of the Android OS your tablet is running. Generally speaking, when it comes to compatibility with the latest home automation devices, newer is better.

Here is a list of some of the best Android tablets on the market:

- **Nvidia Shield Tablet** (`http://shield.nvidia.com/gaming-tablet/`): Don't let the "gaming" tagline fool you; this tablet is just as good for home automation as it is gaming.

- **Samsung Galaxy Tab S** (`www.samsung.com/us/mobile/galaxy-tab`)

- **LG G Pad** (`www.lg.com/us/tablets`)

- **Sony Xperia Z3 Tablet Compact** (`http://sonymobile.com/us/products/tablets/xperia-z3-tablet-compact/`): This puppy's waterproof!

- **Google/HTC Nexus 9** (`www.htc.com/us/tablets/nexus-9/` or `www.google.com/nexus/9/`): This one's shown in Figure 13-7.

Do your homework before buying your Android tablet, though; they are definitely not all created equal. You can pretty much bet on those in the preceding list, but if you'd like to check out offerings from other tablet makers, please do.

When it comes to most things, the adage "you get what you pay for" applies. That is definitely the case when it comes to Android tablets, dear reader.

Figure 13-7:
Google and HTC teamed up to bring you the Nexus 9, which is a sweet Android tablet, to be sure.

Image courtesy of Google.

Computers

Now, this book has focused on remotely controlling your home automation system from smart devices, such as those I just discussed. However, with the Internet and the World Wide Web at your fingertips, computers can be pretty handy, too.

Although most home automation companies don't make native applications for computer-based operating systems (there are some exceptions), they do provide access via a dedicated web page. You can, for example, access your Alarm.com home security system or your Netatmo weather station through a web browser.

Suffice it to say, if you have a relatively modern computer in your home (or office, or wherever else), along with Internet access, you should be able to at least access your home automation system from it, and most likely be allowed to control it, too.

If you have trouble viewing or accessing a site from one web browser, just download and try another.

Macs and OS X

Apple's Mac line of computers running the OS X (that's pronounced OH ESS TEN, for those of you who are new to Apple's parlance) operating system should work with no issues when it comes to accessing and using any home automation company's dedicated website.

OS X comes with the Safari browser, but there are plenty of others to choose from. For example, you can search for any of the following browsers, in OS X's App Store:

- ✔ Google Chrome
- ✔ Mozilla Firefox
- ✔ Opera

If none of those suit your tastes, just keep searching; there are plenty of browsers out there for Mac.

When it comes to native apps that run on your Mac to control your home automation system, there aren't very many. And rightly so for the most part, since you can already do most, if not all, of the tasks I discuss in this book via the Internet (provided the home automation company offers the option, of course).

One exception that comes to mind: Indigo Domotics (`www.indigodomo.com`). These folks are out to help the serious (and advanced) home automation guru get the job done. The company's software is Mac-only, and it is extensive. I definitely advise you to give Indigo Domotics a look if you really want to dig deep into home automation and to run several different home automation protocols from one piece of software.

The next question is, which Mac do you need? Apple offers several models, desktop and laptop alike:

- **MacBook Air** (ultra-slim laptop)

- **MacBook Pro** (full-featured laptop)

- **iMac** (the iconic all-in-one computer)

- **iMac with Retina 5K display** (the iMac, but with a crazy-great display; shown in Figure 13-8)

- **Mac Pro** (loaded to the gills with features for the graphics professional; not necessarily for the average home user)

- **Mac mini** (compact unit that comes with nothing else; you have to supply the keyboard, mouse, and monitor)

Visit your local Apple Store or check it all out at `www.apple.com/mac`.

PCs and Windows

Any PC capable of running Windows 7 or newer should have no problem viewing and using websites by home automation companies that allow you to control your system from the web. Heck, I would even say that if you can run Windows XP, you're pretty safe.

As with OS X, Windows is not in short supply when it comes to compatible web browsers. As you probably know, Internet Explorer is Microsoft's default browser of choice, but you can find others if it doesn't fit the bill, such as:

- Google Chrome

- Mozilla Firefox

- Apple Safari

- Opera

As far as stand-alone home automation software goes, there are a few options for Windows users, but like the Mac, few of them are necessary unless you want to use your computer (as opposed to the cloud) as your primary control hub. If that is what you'd like to do, then you'll want to check out these offerings:

- ✔ Home Control Assistant: `www.hcatech.com`; shown in Figure 13-9
- ✔ HomeSeer: `www.homeseer.com`
- ✔ HouseBot: `www.housebot.com`

Figure 13-8:
The iMac with Retina 5K display just loves your eyes, and they love it right back.

Image courtesy of Apple, Inc.

Windows Tablets

"Why isn't this section on the other pages with iOS and Android tablets?" I can hear my readers and my editors all asking that question right about now.

Well, the reason is simple. Windows tablets are indeed tablets, but you could understandably be misled into thinking they are like iOS or Android tablets. Actually, Windows-based tablets that run Windows 8 are indeed running the full-blown version of Windows 8, not a separate mobile version of the Windows OS. They are completely Windows computers, operating-system-wise, so they belong in the computers discussion.

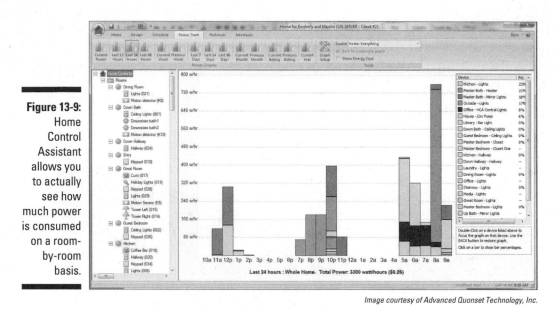

Figure 13-9:
Home
Control
Assistant
allows you
to actually
see how
much power
is consumed
on a room-
by-room
basis.

I won't rehash what I discuss under the previous PCs and Windows section. However, if you want to use a Windows-based portable device that doesn't include a keyboard (or at least has one you can tuck away) to control your home automation system, then a Windows tablet, like the Lenovo ThinkPad 2 shown in Figure 13-10, will be right up your alley. Anything you can do on a Windows PC can be done on the tablets, too.

PCs and Linux

Linux has come a long way in the last few years. The term would generate looks of disgust or apathy among computer users who were used to doing things on Windows or Mac machines. Let's face it: Linux used to be the ugly duckling of the computing world, but much has changed. Linux has become a viable and attractive alternative for folks looking for an inexpensive way to keep their PC up-to-date and for getting things done. Linux itself is free, and it will run on computers using Intel or AMD processors. Today's computer users are able to do what they need to, with tasks such as email, editing pictures, surfing the web, listening to music, watching streaming video, and the like becoming much more user friendly of late. Linux distributions, such as Ubuntu (shown in Figure 13-11), have made installing and using Linux a million times easier than ever before.

When it comes to Linux home automation software, there are several choices out there, but they are not for the faint of heart or the Linux newbie. Choices such as Minerva (www.minervahome.net) and Pytomation (www.pytomation.com) are for the seasoned Linux and home automation veteran.

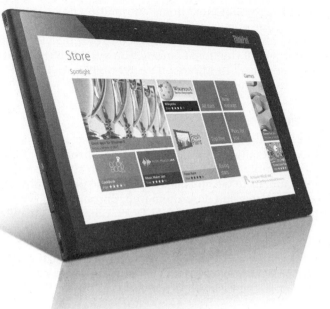

Figure 13-10:
Lenovo's
ThinkPad 2
and other
Windows
tablets
run the full
version of
Windows 8.

Image courtesy of Lenovo.

Figure 13-11:
Ubuntu
is among
the most
popular,
and user-
friendly,
Linux dis-
tributions
available
today.

Image courtesy of Canonical Ltd.

Remember, though, that most home automation companies do offer web logins to your home automation system, so if you're running Linux, there's a good chance you'll be able to control things through your web browser. However, if the home automation system uses technologies such as Adobe's Flash or Microsoft's Silverlight, you'll need to install those software packages.

Chromebooks

The latest PCs to hit the market are Chromebooks, which are slimmed down and inexpensive computers that run Google's Chrome OS. Chrome OS is designed to be super-user-friendly, providing an almost browserlike experience. It's not meant to be a business workhorse or a graphics powerhouse, but it does the basics and does them well. Chrome OS gives you access to all the standard Google apps, such as Docs, Gmail, and Calendar, as well as thousands more via the Chrome Web Store.

Chromebooks, such as Toshiba's Chromebook 2 (shown in Figure 13-12), are great for those who want a laptop, need just the basic computing experience, and aren't tied (for one reason or another) to OS X or Windows.

When it comes to home automation, you're pretty much tied to just accessing your home automation system through the manufacturer's dedicated website. You can't install software on a Chromebook: It is what it is (or maybe I should say it's WYSIWYG, "What you see is what you get").

If the home automation company uses Java or Microsoft's Silverlight to power its website, you're out of luck. Chrome OS doesn't support Java or Silverlight, but Adobe's Flash does come as part of the Chrome browser, so you're in the clear there.

Figure 13-12:
Toshiba's slim Chrome-book 2 is a great option for computer users who just need the basics.

Image courtesy of Toshiba America Information Systems, Inc.

Keeping Apps Up-to-Date

Keeping your apps updated to their latest and greatest versions is a good thing. I know I risk stirring the ire of those who are on the other side of that fence, but I've always believed that updates are good things. Don't get me wrong: I've had my share of some not-so-delightful experiences after performing an update (and sometimes while in the middle of one), but the vast majority of the time it's been a positive thing.

I've found it to be especially true that updating iOS and Android apps is a good idea, because they generally are trying to fix bugs more than they're adding features. You might be more wary of updates that jump from one version to the next (such as from version 2 to version 3), but updates to established versions are almost always a great idea (for example, updating from version 3.1 to version 3.2).

The remainder of this chapter delves into how to update your apps for the devices you'll be using to access your home automation system and devices.

iOS

iOS uses its App Store to keep track of updates to apps you have installed on your iPhone or iPad. The App Store is able to keep track of the apps you've

---

Automatic updates

iOS and Android both allow you to automatically update apps, but I personally don't enable it. Why not? Because I like to have control over the whole process; it's that simple. Go ahead, call me a control freak. It won't bother me ("sticks and stones"). I have a bunch of apps on my phones, but they don't update often enough and in such a quantity that it discourages me from updating manually. However, if you've got a ton of apps and they do update frequently, it will probably save you from headaches if you allow updates to occur automatically. Also, if your smartphone's or tablet's data plan isn't unlimited, it's a good idea to only allow automatic updates when you're connected to Wi-Fi so you don't use up your allotted data. To enable or disable automatic updates on iOS, go to Settings⇨iTunes & App Store and toggle the Updates switch. For Android devices, go to Google Play Store⇨Menu⇨Settings, and under General find and tap Auto-update apps; make a selection. The Menu icon looks like three stacked parallel lines, by the way.

downloaded and of those you currently have installed by using your Apple ID. Whenever a developer updates an app that you have installed, the App Store lets you know in one of two ways:

✔ By displaying a red badge in the upper-right corner of the App Store icon when you're not in the App Store.

✔ By displaying a red badge on the Updates tab when in the App Store; the Updates tab is found at the bottom right of the screen, as shown in Figure 13-13.

You can update your apps in one of two ways:

✔ Update an individual app by tapping the Update button to the right of the app's name in the list.

✔ Update all the available apps at once by tapping the Update All button in the upper right of the screen.

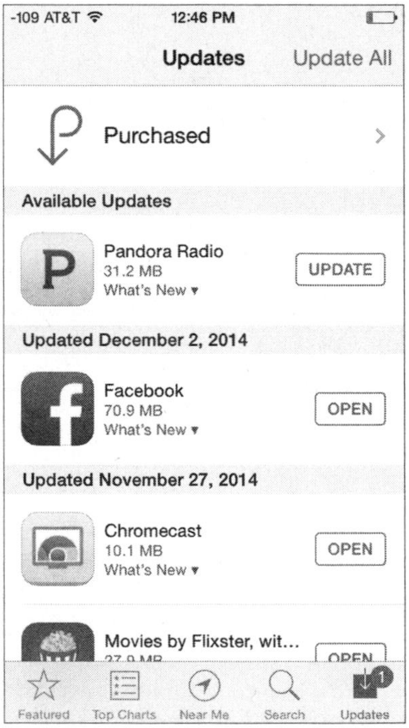

Figure 13-13:
The iOS App Store shows you a list of updates to apps you have installed on your iPhone or iPad.

Android

Updating apps that are installed on your Android device is also a simple process:

1. **Open the Google Play Store app.**
2. **Tap the Menu icon (looks like three stacked parallel lines).**
3. **Tap My Apps.**
4. **Scroll through your list of apps.**

   Apps that have updates available will be labeled as such.

5. **Tap the app you want and then tap Update.**

OS X

If you are running home automation software on your Mac, or if your web browser is getting long in the tooth and things aren't rendering on-screen properly, it's a simple process to update:

1. **Open the App Store (yep, there's one in OS X as well as iOS).**
2. **Click the Updates button at the top right of the window, shown in Figure 13-14.**

   The App Store will check to see if there are updates for any of the apps you have installed. If so, they will appear as a list.

3. **Click the Update All button in the upper-right corner of the list of available updates to do just that, or click the Update button next to each app to update them individually.**

Some software updates require a restart of your computer. If you aren't at a place in your work where you can restart, simply postpone the updates until a better time.

OS X allows you to direct it in how it should install updates to your computer. Go to the Apple menu in the upper left of the screen and select System Preferences, then click App Store. Read through the options and determine those that you prefer to use.

Figure 13-14:
OS X's
App Store
checks for
updates
to your
installed
apps and
lists them
for you.

Windows

Windows 8 has certainly changed how Windows users get around, so updating your software might not be as intuitive if you're new to it. Here's how to check for and install updates in Windows 8:

1. **In the upper-right corner of the screen, you will see Updates; the number of apps you have installed that can be updated appears in parentheses. Click Updates.**

2. **Select the apps you want to update by clicking (or tapping, if you're using a touchscreen) them in the list. You can click or tap Select All in the lower left of the screen to update all the apps at once.**

3. **Click or tap the Install button at the bottom of the screen to install your updates.**

   The Installs screen will show the progress of each individual app as it is updated.

4. **Exit the Store app when finished.**

Done!

Chapter 14

Controlling Your Home from One Platform

In This Chapter

▶ Wading through the muddle of multiple control platforms

▶ Striving for platform unity

▶ Getting to know today's leaders in control unity

All for one and one for all.

— Alexandre Dumas, *The Three Musketeers*

You've done your homework on what systems will make your home automation dreams come true, and you've probably installed some home automation goodies. Life couldn't be sweeter!

Or could it?

Think about it: You've got gadget after gadget, each from a different manufacturer, and each with its own way to control the items inside and outside your home. You have an app that controls your light, another that automates your stove, one that operates the door locks, yet another that coordinates the security system, still another handling the thermostat, and on and on it goes. Where it stops, nobody knows. I think you catch my drift: It's exhausting just thinking about opening an app, closing another one, opening yet another (oh no, the interface is entirely different!) — closing that app, lather, rinse, and repeat.

What to do, my weary home automation friend? What knight in shining armor will save us home automation junkies from the crushing weight of all those apps? It's my aim in this chapter to introduce you to those potential knights who will rescue you from your app distress and make your life much easier.

You discover how several of the top home automation companies are working hard to solve the problem of unity, and how each of the solutions can benefit you now and in the long run.

Examining the Lack of Unity

The word "unity" can be defined in several ways, including:

- ✔ The quality or state of not being multiple
- ✔ A condition of harmony
- ✔ The quality or state of being made one
- ✔ A totality of related parts
- ✔ An entity that is a complex or systematic whole

Why dedicate a chapter of this book to unity? Well, if you're one of the folks I mention in the introduction who have already acquired several home automation products, you will totally understand the reason: Without some kind of cohesion of control over your home automation environment, things can get a little higgledy-piggledy, to use a highly technical term.

Recognizing the "higgledy-piggledy" state of home automation

The focus of *Home Automation For Dummies* is on the burgeoning "smart do-it-yourself" home automation market, where people control their automation products via their smartphones, tablets, or computers. The upscale and customized whole-home type of systems offered by companies like Crestron and Savant provide their own all-in-one control systems that take care of all your automation control needs. The smart do-it-yourself market is a fairly new one, so there hasn't been much push (until very recently) to make everything work together from a central controller. There are myriad reasons for this pickle in which we find ourselves:

- ✔ Individual companies may like you to use only their product offerings.
- ✔ A manufacturer may cater only to specific home automation needs (their apps control your lighting but not your locks, for example).
- ✔ Products may incorporate different communication technologies.

Several home automation communication protocol standards have been around for years, but they don't usually play nice with one another of their own accord. If you buy a device that uses ZigBee, don't expect it to work with other devices in your home that are using Z-Wave, INSTEON, X10, or the like, unless assisted by one of the options mentioned in this chapter.

Seeing ways to achieve platform unity

The obvious need for some sort of unity among the home automation big-wigs won't be accomplished by making everybody sit around a campfire singing "Kumbaya" (although that would be pretty entertaining, I'm sure). Let's be honest: Business is business, even if said business claims to be looking out for you, the consumer. This home automation unity is going to take someone from the outside stepping up, then, before it can be achieved, right? Well, that might be an answer, but that isn't necessarily the only way; established home automation companies are also joining others in the search for unity.

How will this unity be accomplished? There is no one right way, but having many different ways is better than having none at all, I'm sure you'll agree.

Two potential methods for achieving this unity are as follows:

- ✓ **Develop a single platform** that manufacturers incorporate when developing and designing their products. This platform will almost certainly coexist with other competing platforms within a product, but that isn't something that will concern the homeowner so long as the whole thing simply works as it should.

- ✓ **Incorporate most or all of the communication protocol standards** (including necessary software and hardware) into one controller device, or hub. This hub would be able to automatically distinguish which protocols devices in the home are using and control them via specialized "bridge" software. This bridge software acts as a translator between the hub and the devices it is controlling.

Choosing the Single-Platform Path

This unity hiccup in the home automation universe just screams for someone to fix it, and several folks are stepping up to the plate to do just that. I show you a couple of companies that are working to help you in the quest for home automation harmony by providing a single-platform solution.

Peeling Apple's HomeKit

"Did he say 'Apple'?"

Indeed, I did say Apple! And yes, I'm talking about the Mac and iPad maker. I totally understand if you're confused by me leading this part of the chapter off with a company that hasn't been a player in the home automation market on a large scale — at least not when it comes to controlling the devices in your entire home. Sure, Apple has more than dabbled in the home entertainment world (as I describe in Chapter 10), but the late, great Steve Jobs never showed any interest at all in totally running the show in regards to home automation.

Well, the good folks in Cupertino have very recently announced a little thing they call HomeKit, and it will become many a home automation fan's best friend, particularly those using their iPhones or iPads to run their smart home (and let's be honest — that's most of us). With HomeKit, Apple is providing a common communication protocol that home automation device makers can incorporate into their products. When consumers purchase HomeKit-enabled devices, they can use the HomeKit app in iOS 8 to control them all. However, HomeKit does more than just offer simple on and off commands to devices, as you soon discover.

Starting with HomeKit basics

Image courtesy of Apple, Inc.

Before I explain how HomeKit strong-arms your smart home into harmonic submission, take a look at what you need to get started:

- ✔ An iPhone or iPad
- ✔ iOS 8 installed on said iPhone or iPad
- ✔ The HomeKit app
- ✔ A bevy of HomeKit-enabled devices

The first three items on the preceding list are all provided by Apple, but what about the little gems mentioned in that last item? Apple has announced a who's-who list of its initial partners who have all glommed on to the HomeKit initiative, and I'm more than happy to provide that list for you. Table 14-1 gives you the name of Apple's partners and their primary product focus (this does not represent the entirety of some of the company's offerings, mind you) in the home automation market.

Making a scene with HomeKit

Yes, HomeKit can say "light, turn on" and "light, turn off," but it's up to doing more than just those menial chores. HomeKit provides you freedom from ever having to flick or adjust a light switch (and other devices) again by enabling you to program "scenes."

Table 14-1	Apple's HomeKit Partners
Partner	*Product Focus*
August	Locks
Broadcom	Microcontrollers
Chamberlain	Garage door openers
Cree	Lighting
Haier	Appliances, air conditioners
Honeywell	Thermostats
iDevices	Smart Bluetooth-connected devices
iHome	Audio products
Kwikset	Locks
Marvell	Wireless microcontrollers
Netatmo	Weather stations and thermostats
Osram Sylvania	Lighting
Philips	Lighting
Schlage	Locks
Skybell	Smart doorbells
Texas Instruments	Wireless microcontrollers
Withings	Health-focused smart devices

Scenes in HomeKit are sets of commands that you program for single or multiple devices so that they turn on or off or adjust when given a single command. For example, if you're having folks over for a dinner party you could program the following devices to perform the following tasks:

- Front and back porch lights turn on at full strength.

- Hall lights adjust to 75 percent strength.

- The thermostat is set to a comfy 72 degrees.

- The shades are all set to mid-height.

- Music and speakers are turned on and set to a particular station and volume level.

- Lights in the dining room are set to 50 percent.

- Ceiling fans on the back porch are engaged.

Once you've programmed these settings in HomeKit, you give them the title of Dinner Party. When the time comes for guests to begin arriving, you can tell Siri (the name of Apple's voice recognition program used in iOS) to engage the Dinner Party setting. All the commands in the preceding list are enacted instantly, providing your guests with an entertainment atmosphere they'll tell their children's children about. These settings are fixed, changing only when you want them to, so if you frequently host dinner parties you'll be armed and ready the next time you feel like throwing a little soirée.

Of course, you can create all kinds of scenes to set up as you become more familiar with HomeKit, such as:

- **Nighttime:** Lock all the doors, set the alarms, turn out most of the lights, set the bathroom lights to low, turn on the baby monitor, and other sleepy time stuff.

- **Morning:** Get the coffee brewing, set the lights to brighten progressively as the morning marches on, set the kids' alarms to wake them up (so hopefully you don't have to), and so forth.

- **Away from Home:** Set certain lights (perhaps those on the porch, in the kitchen, the garage — you get the drift) to come on at various times of the day or night, set the alarms and locks, enable motion detectors, charge up the electric fence (hey, you never know what some folks will use to secure their homes), and the like.

- **Date Night:** Oh, yeah . . . pipe in the Barry White tunes (yes, he's still the smoothest and the coolest), dim all the right lights, get the fireplace going, and whatever else you can dream up to make the night right.

✔ **Annoying Company:** Make your lights flick on and off like your home is infested with a poltergeist, crank up the stereo with the most annoying sounds known to man (or create a track of your kids at the peak of a Halloween-candy-induced sugar craze), lower the thermostat to 40 degrees, and set your smoke alarms to test. This combination is sure to make even the most ardent of annoying houseguests uncomfortable enough that they'll be seeking asylum elsewhere in mere moments.

The number of scenes you can set up are limited only by your imagination and by the number of home automation devices that occupy your residence.

Much more will be forthcoming from Apple regarding HomeKit. Check their website at `www.apple.com` for updates. However, if you'd like to know more now, especially if you're a techie, visit the HomeKit developer's site at `https://developer.apple.com/homekit/`.

Wink-ing at Home Depot

It was only a matter of time before Home Depot jumped into the home automation ocean, and when it did it made quite a splash by partnering with Wink. Wink makes the mechanism for unifying your home automation devices, while Home Depot is working to be the provider for Wink-enabled devices from all manner of manufacturers; the two are working quite well together, it seems.

How Wink works

Wink has developed an API (application programming interface) that home auto-device manufacturers can incorporate into their devices. Once the API is part of a device, said device can be controlled via the Wink app, which runs on your iOS or Android smartphone. You can then control your home devices from anywhere in the world, so long as you have a connection to the Internet.

Will Apple take over the world (again)?

Apple is looking to be *the* company that bridges home automation devices for its users, and it has the brand recognition, resources, drive, talent, and business savvy to do just that. Since Apple is so deeply embedded into so many digital lives already, it only makes sense that the company would attempt to take this next step as a business. Of course, time will tell which of the companies in this chapter (or some other player yet to jump into the fray) becomes the company of choice in this area of home automation, but based on past experiences with other markets, don't bet against the Apple folks.

The whole thing basically works like this:

1. Go to your local Home Depot or visit www.homedepot.com.

2. Comb the store shelves or the website for products that feature the Wink app or Wink Hub logo (shown in Figure 14-1) on their packaging. A white logo (instead of blue) indicates that a Wink hub is required to use the product with the Wink app and other Wink-compatible devices.

3. Download the Wink app to your iPhone or Android smartphone. Open it and create a Wink account. (There is currently no support for the iPad or for Android tablets, but that will be alleviated soon. Check with Wink at www.winkapp.com for availability.)

4. If you purchased the Wink hub, install it per the instructions in the Wink app (download it before trying to set up your hub). You can get more information here: www.winkapp.com/faq#winkhub. Once your Wink hub is installed, it will communicate with the Wink Cloud. (Wink keeps up with your account and devices through the company's cloud computing network.)

Since the Wink app and hub work through the Wink Cloud, if your home's Internet connection goes down you will not be able to control your Wink-compatible devices via the Wink app. That doesn't mean your house is under some kind of Wink-induced lockdown; it simply means you have to revert to doing things the old-fashioned way until your Internet connection is restored.

5. Set up or install the Wink-compatible product you purchased from Home Depot.

6. Follow the super-simple (for most products, anyway) instructions found in the Wink app for adding the product to your list of Wink-controlled devices.

7. Sit back and relax while Wink makes your life simpler by a hundred fold.

Figure 14-1:
Wink-
compatible
products
sport one of
these logos
on their
packaging.

Images courtesy of Wink.

The Wink App logo has a light blue background with a white picture of a house, and indicates that the product will work directly with the Wink app with no need for a Wink hub. The Wink Hub logo has a white background with a light blue picture of a house, and indicates that the product must be used in conjunction with a Wink hub.

Home Depot's partnership with Wink

Your local Home Depot store or the Home Depot website (www.homedepot.com) are the best places to go to find products that are Wink-compatible. The advantage of going to the store is obviously the hands-on experience, but the advantage to the website is the capability to see all Wink-compatible products quickly and in one location.

For information about the Wink app or hub, skip Home Depot and go directly to Wink's website. The site has tons of information on how the app and hub work together and with compatible products, and the FAQ section is great for finding answers to your more technical questions. Visit www.winkapp.com for more info.

Wink supports a wide range of devices and manufacturers. The Wink hub currently works well with Z-Wave, ZigBee, Bluetooth LE, Wi-Fi, Lutron ClearConnect, and Kidde home automation communication protocols. However, not all protocols are supported (such as INSTEON), so do your due diligence.

Opting for Multi-Protocol Solutions

Perhaps you've been tinkering with home automation for a little while and you have a few devices that don't speak the same language (protocol). Or maybe you've found several items you'd like to use but are worried that you'll be swimming in a sea of apps since none of them seem to be compatible with one another. Whatever the case, in the following sections, I introduce you to some folks who are able to tie up all your loose home automation ends into neat bows of automation goodness.

Revolv-ing around a hub

Revolv is a company on a mission: to make any device you own work with and through its solution, which is the Revolv hub and its accompanying app. Since manufacturers of home automation equipment often use different types of communication protocols (ZigBee, INSTEON, and so forth), Revolv's approach to bridging the communication and interaction gap is to simply include all those protocols (along with their necessary hardware) into the Revolv hub. Once a device is connected to the hub, it can be controlled and paired with other devices using the Revolv app, which is supported by both iOS and Android devices.

Setting up a Revolv hub

The folks at Revolv have developed a nice product for creating unity among your home automation devices, and it's obvious they've put a lot of effort into their "one hub, one app" solution.

Out-of-the-box setup of the hub is simple and straightforward:

1. **Place the hub in a central location of your home to provide maximum wireless coverage for your devices.**

2. **Connect the hub to a power supply.**

3. **Download the Revolv app for your preferred device (smartphone or tablet) from the iOS or Android App Store.**

4. **Link the hub to your Wi-Fi.**

   This can be done through a really cool process involving your smartphone "flashing" (called "FlashLink" by Revolv) the security credentials for your wireless network into the Revolv hub using the LED flash on your smartphone, as shown in Figure 14-2.

5. **Use the Revolv app to automatically discover devices that have connected with the hub, or manually find them on your network.**

Figure 14-2:
Flashing wireless credentials into the Revolv hub with a smartphone makes the setup process that much simpler.

Image courtesy of Revolv.

You may now control your devices using the Revolv hub and app solution. Easy peasy, as my daughter says. I think Revolv is on to something here.

Updates and compatible devices

You can acquire the Revolv hub and app for a one-time price; it charges no monthly subscription fee to use the services (as some companies may charge), which is a very nice plus in my estimation. All updates to the supported protocols and the app are also free, and those are additional high marks for the Revolv solution.

Revolv has compiled quite a nice list of compatible devices, manufactured by the likes of:

- Belkin
- GE
- Honeywell
- INSTEON
- Leviton
- Nest
- Philips
- Sonos
- Trane

. . . and the list keeps growing! Visit www.revolv.com/devices for an up-to-the-minute listing of manufacturers and devices.

Of course, I recommend you check out www.revolv.com for more information, including a great video that shows how to set up a Revolv hub and demonstrating the "flashing" technique I describe earlier in this chapter.

Building your CastleOS

CastleOS is seeking to bring unity into the home automation space by doing things a bit differently than Apple or Revolv, mainly because it is a Microsoft Windows–based system. CastleOS can also use a Microsoft Kinect system, which allows you to deliver speech commands to your home automation devices. So if you're someone who is completely anti-Apple and gung ho, pro-Microsoft, CastleOS will be right up your alley! (That's intended as a joke, by the way.)

The aforementioned computing platform prejudices are in no way prerequisites for using CastleOS. The basic system software runs from a Windows-based computer, but the software that controls your home automation devices can run on any device that has a web browser. This means that if you have a Mac, a Linux-based computer, an iOS device, or an Android device, you can still use CastleOS for your home automation needs. I should also mention that if you don't own a Windows-based computer but still want to use CastleOS, the company does provide stand-alone mini-computers that run the CastleOS software.

How CastleOS works

CastleOS states that it is a "protocol-agnostic system" and its product is intended for use with "any and all home automation protocols," which is a very good thing for you and me. So, if you're someone who has a plethora of devices running the gamut of home automation protocols (or if you're still working on purchasing said plethora), CastleOS just might be a good bet for you.

The first part of the CastleOS puzzle is the Core Service, which acts as the central hub for controlling all the home automation devices in your house. The Core Service software is installed on a Windows-based computer and communicates with your home automation devices via your network.

Accessing the apps

The second piece that is needed to control your devices is one of the CastleOS remote access apps. Currently, CastleOS works with an HTML app (shown in Figure 14-3) and the Microsoft Kinect (for voice control); CastleOS is working on providing native iOS and Android apps as of this writing.

Any device that can run a web browser can access the HTML app:

- ✔ **Computers:** Any web browser will do to access the CastleOS HTML app.
- ✔ **iOS devices (iPad, iPhone, iPod):** Safari is the recommended browser, but other web browser apps can be tried if Safari isn't your cup of tea.
- ✔ **Android devices (smartphones and tablets):** Google's Chrome browser is recommended, since it is the native browser for the Android system.
- ✔ **Windows Mobile, BlackBerry, and others:** Use your browser of choice.

The Kinect app is where the coolness factor is kicked up a notch. Using your Kinect, you can tell CastleOS exactly what to do. If you're a fan of *Star Trek* you'll instantly pick up on the verbiage: "Computer, turn on the lights," "Computer, turn on the television," and so on. The Kinect relays your voice commands to the CastleOS Core Service software in an instant and executes them with authority!

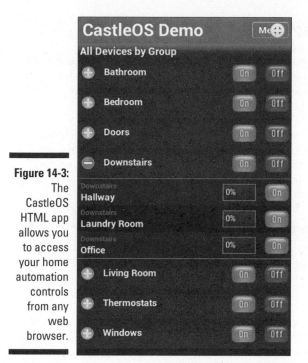

Figure 14-3:
The CastleOS HTML app allows you to access your home automation controls from any web browser.

The CastleOS team provides help on the Download section of the company's website for users of mobile devices to easily access the HTML app. Just visit www.castleos.com/Download.aspx for the lowdown.

CastleOS turns EPIC

Chris Cicchitelli is the brains behind CastleOS. His idea for home automation was so cool that Destination America's *EPIC* television program featured Chris and his family on the show! Mind you, the segment does show Chris doing a bit more than simply setting up the CastleOS software, such as installing wiring and all that jazz, but don't be put off by that. CastleOS is meant to be a simple do-it-yourself home automation control and unification solution, not a home wiring nightmare.

You can check out the video segment, as well as in-depth product information and support, at the CastleOS website: www.castleos.com.

Link (sys)ing with Staples Connect

Staples and Linksys have partnered together to create the Staples Connect brand of home automation unification. Connect is yet another app-hub combination, but it does distinguish itself from the competition in a few ways that you'll soon discover.

Staples has partnered with several home automation companies to make sure that their products work with the Connect system, and the Connect hub comes with several of the most common home automation protocols installed, so you have a wide range of products to choose from should you go with the Staples/Linksys solution.

How Staples Connect works

The Connect app talks to the Connect hub, which in turn talks to the Connect-compatible devices in your home. This is pretty standard, as you've seen so far with other companies in this chapter, but a couple of differences make Connect stand out:

- ✔ Connect uses a web app, along with iOS and Android apps, to control your devices. This affords more options for control of your devices than some of the other folks discussed so far. You can get the app at both the iOS and Android App Stores.

- ✔ The iOS and Android apps can run on the iPad and Android-enabled tablets, respectively, while others are currently limited to the iPhone and Android smartphones.

The Connect hub contains hardware and software needed to control devices running Wi-Fi, Z-Wave, and Lutron ClearConnect protocols. While this seems more limited than other options, plans to add support for INSTEON, ZigBee, and Bluetooth are in the works.

The Staples Connect system is as simple as any other on the market to put into action:

1. Head over to your local Staples store or visit the Staples Connect site to find compatible devices and to purchase the Connect hub.

2. Download the Staples Connect app from the Apple App Store or Android App Store, depending on your device.

3. Create an account by tapping the Sign Up button, as seen in Figure 14-4, or use your credentials to sign in with an existing account if you have one.

4. After you create and activate your account, you will receive a setup guide that walks you through simply and quickly adding devices to the

Connect hub. This guide is a great help, so bookmark it in your browser or create a PDF of the page and save it for future use.

5. Install the Connect hub to your existing Wi-Fi router and follow the instructions in your app or the setup guide for completing setup.

6. Add devices to your Connect hub as instructed, and start home automating!

A successful partnership

I'll be honest: I've always thought of Staples as a place to go to purchase office products and the like, not as a go-to store for my home needs. However, I must say that through its partnership with Linksys, Staples has done as good a job as anyone with its Connect initiative. I give especially high marks to the Staples Connect website (`www.staples.com/sbd/cre/marketing/staples-connect/`), which is a great place to learn not just more about Connect, but also about home automation in general. The site has some great articles and a nice FAQ that help home automation newbies hit the ground running. Kudos to Staples for educating the public about home automation!

Figure 14-4:
Tap the Sign Up button to create a new account, or sign in with an existing one.

Image courtesy of Staples.

The end-all, be-all in home automation?

You may be wondering why a product or service you've heard of or even used is nowhere to be found in this chapter. I believe that the companies I mention in this chapter are the best folks out there in the unification game. That's not to say others aren't doing a good job of bringing the home automation chaos into a more controlled state, though.

None of the products and services I mention is a catch-all for every little (and not-so-little)

home automation need. Some do a better job at supporting protocols, while others do a better job with their app interfaces. In short, there is no end-all, be-all company. The home automation game is still in its infancy, so there are bound to be bumps in the road along the way to home automation harmony.

That said, don't be surprised if one of them, or perhaps an unforeseen newcomer, does take up that "end-all, be-all" mantle in the near future.

Part V
The Part of Tens

Enjoy an additional Home Automation Part of Tens chapter at `www.dummies.com/extras/homeautomation`.

In this part . . .

- Find ten easy ways to begin automating your home without breaking the bank.

- Discover ten popular websites that focus on smart home automation.

- Learn about ten additional ways to automate your home.

Chapter 15

Ten Easy Ways to Begin Automating Your Home

In This Chapter

▶ Discovering how to quickly begin automating your life

▶ Starting automating with simple devices

▶ Finding ten easy-to-implement products

*U*p to this point, I've discussed the 411 on home automation in today's technical environment, and I've covered the gamut from the simplest of devices to install and set up to the more labor-intensive ones (even some that require professional installation). What I now want to do is wade you gently into the smart home automation pool.

Some folks like to take things easy when venturing into something new or different, especially when it comes to technology. I have family who were hesitant about getting cellular phones, and when they bought their first one it was just the most basic of devices: phone calls only, thank you very much, with the Internet button avoided like the plague. Now, those same folks have the latest and greatest in smartphones, and are even finding themselves frequently using Facebook and downloading apps at a rapid-fire rate. Sometimes all it takes is getting your feet a little wet to make you want to dive headlong into the deep.

If that description sounds like you, then this chapter is right up your alley. I want this to be your jumping-off point if you aren't sure where to begin or if you just want to get a feel for the technology. In this chapter, I go over some of the simplest surefire devices that you can use to start automating your home quickly and easily. Please keep in mind that I am in no way endorsing these devices over any others, with the exception, of course, that they are the simplest home automation devices that I've found when it comes to how quickly you can be up and running after you unbox them. Onward!

Wink

I speak a bit about Wink (and its relationship to Home Depot) in Chapter 14, but now I'd like to introduce you to some of the great products Wink offers.

The Wink platform allows you to use some home automation devices without need of the Wink hub (see Figure 15-1), while other devices require it. Whether a device needs the hub or not depends on how its manufacturer designed it. In some cases, it isn't a matter of whether the manufacturer wants the device to use the hub or not, but the hub may simply be a necessity based on the nature of the device.

The Wink hub connects to your Wi-Fi router so that it not only can connect Wink-enabled devices in your home to your smart device, but also so that you can control your smart devices when you're away.

A Wink-enabled device is one that incorporates the Wink software. Wink software allows the device to communicate with the Wink hub and Wink app on your smart device, as well as with other Wink-enabled devices. For example, a motion sensor from one company will work with a lighting system from another company to trigger the lighting based on movement within the home.

I first take a look at some of the Wink-enabled products that don't require the use of the Wink hub in order for you to control them with the Wink app on your iOS or Android smartphone or tablet.

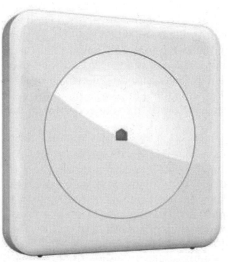

Figure 15-1:
The Wink hub connects Wink-enabled devices to your smartphone or tablet.

Image courtesy of Wink.

Why use the Wink app?

Your automated lighting comes with its own app, as does your front-door lock. Come to think of it, your motion sensors have their own apps, too. So why bother with the Wink app? I answer that with another question: "Why not use one app instead of three?" That's what the Wink app can do for you. As long as your devices are Wink-enabled, they will work within the Wink ecosystem, meaning you can control all the devices from one app, even though they may all be made by different manufacturers.

As I mention in Chapter 14, items that do not require the use of the Wink hub will have the light blue Wink logo with white lettering on their packages.

Philips Hue products

You meet the Philips Hue line of smart LED light bulbs back in Chapter 6, but that chapter mainly focuses on the A19 size bulbs, which replace standard 60-watt bulbs that you screw into an everyday lamp socket. That isn't all that Philips has to offer when it comes to automated lighting, though. However, I first want to tackle some reasons I think the Hue products belong in this chapter:

- They're great products. Hue products are not only simple to use and set up, which is a criterion for this chapter, but they also work exactly as advertised.

- Hue devices work nicely with other home automation platforms or on their own.

- What could be simpler than screwing in a light bulb?

Using standard A19 Hue bulbs is a great idea for your entire home, but Philips also has other Hue lighting devices that are worth checking into, and they're just as simple to set up as the A19 bulbs. Philips refers to these devices as Friends of Hue (FoH, for the cool kids in the audience).

The LivingColors Iris, shown in Figure 15-2, and the LivingColors Bloom are wonderfully stylish lamps that incorporate the Hue technology. All you have to do is plug them in and link them to the Hue bridge, and you can then control them using the Hue app or the Wink app.

Figure 15-2:
The Philips
LivingColors
Iris is a
really cool
lamp that
works with
your other
Hue lights,
as well as
the Wink
app.

Image courtesy of Koninklijke Philips N.V.

Another awesome Hue product is the popular Philips LightStrips (see Figure 15-3). LightStrips are strips of light (flexible plastic strips that contain LED lights) that you can bend and shape into whatever form you like, allowing you to place them in areas most lights just can't go. You can give your home an incredible new look by placing them under cabinets, behind beds, and other areas you normally wouldn't think of placing a light. And don't forget, you can change their colors to match your mood, decor, or whatever else strikes your fancy. They make really great night lights, too.

Figure 15-3:
Philips
LightStrips
let you take
lighting
into places
and mold it
into shapes
you've
never
dreamed of
before.

Image courtesy of Koninklijke Philips N.V.

You will need a Hue starter kit, which comes with the Hue bridge, in order to use the Iris, the Bloom, and the LightStrips with your Hue network. It's this bridge that connects your Hue devices to your W-Fi, and therefore the Internet and your smart devices.

The lights in the LivingColors Iris and Bloom do not use the same type of LEDs as the original Hue bulbs. Instead, they use RGB to create their colors, which can explain why the colors they generate may sometimes slightly differ from the original bulbs, even when choosing the same color from the color picker in the app.

Dropcam

Security is one of the major reasons folks are moving toward home automation, and webcams are a large part of the solution.

Dropcam is one of the leaders in the field of webcams for home automation, like the one shown in Figure 15-4, and its cameras work hand-in-hand with the Wink app. The original Dropcam, along with the Dropcam Pro, provide streaming video and audio so that you can see and hear what's going on in your home, even when you're a million miles away (as long as you have an Internet connection that far away, of course).

Figure 15-4:
Dropcam cameras give you crystal-clear video and audio of your home and its occupants, from anywhere you have an Internet connection.

Image courtesy of Dropcam, Inc.

Here are some of the features that come with Dropcam:

- The original Dropcam has a great 107-degree viewable area, while the Pro has an impressive 130-degree view. You'll be able to view most areas in any room of your home.

- Both cameras can zoom in so you can get a closer look. Dropcam has a 4X zoom, while the Pro sports up to 8X.

- Dropcams also act as a spy, detecting motion and sound in a room and sending you notifications upon detection.

- Dropcams contain a microphone and a speaker, allowing you to communicate with the folks in the room where the Dropcam is located. Wouldn't it be cool to tell Fido to get off the furniture when you are across the country?

- Night vision is built into the Dropcams, so even at night you'll get clear streaming video. Dropcam Pro may be the better of the two in terms of night vision clarity.

You can do much more with Dropcam cameras, and they're a cinch to set up:

1. Plug in your Dropcam's power cord.

2. Discover the Dropcam with your Dropcam app.

3. Begin watching and listening to the goings-on in the room where your Dropcam resides.

Visit `www.dropcam.com` to see all the cool ways you can use your Dropcam camera to stay in touch and to keep your home safe.

Nest Protect

You're probably familiar with the Nest thermostat, as is most of the free world, but what about the newest Nest product, the Nest Protect?

Nest Protect (see Figure 15-5) is a smart smoke and carbon monoxide detector, providing alerts to you on your iOS or Android device if there's a problem. Nest Protect will even talk to you in a remarkably human-sounding voice!

Nest Protect comes in two models: one battery-powered and the other wired. Both use a variety of methods to alert you to a potential problem:

- Voice alerts
- Alarms
- Notifications on your smartphone or tablet

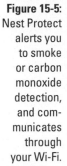

Figure 15-5:
Nest Protect
alerts you
to smoke
or carbon
monoxide
detection,
and com-
municates
through
your Wi-Fi.

Image courtesy of Nest Labs.

Voice alerts are very specific to the problem. You'll hear something like "Heads up, there's smoke in the dining room" and other warnings that tell you the nature of the problem and where it is.

Nest Protect also has a light ring around the Nest button, which helps identify the level of the threat based on the color of the light. A really neat feature of the light is that when the Nest Protect detects motion at night it can turn on the light ring to help illuminate your way. I think that's just a really thoughtful feature from the folks at Nest, demonstrating their attention to detail and functionality. Thumbs up, Nest!

Setting up your Nest Protect is simple, too:

1. Unbox the Nest Protect.

2. Download the Nest Mobile app from your iOS or Android App Store.

3. Open the app and create a Nest account, or sign in to your existing account.

4. Tap the icon for adding a smoke and CO alarm.

5. Scan the code on the back of your Nest Protect with your smartphone or tablet's camera.

6. Pull the blue tab all the way out of your Nest Protect.

7. Open your smartphone's or tablet's network settings and connect to the Nest Protect network.

8. Go back to the Nest app on your device and enter information for your home Wi-Fi when prompted. You'll want to have your Wi-Fi network's password handy.

9. Your Nest Protect will literally tell you when it's successfully connected to the Internet.

10. Tell your Nest Protect which room it is in; you do this through the Nest app.

11. Install your Nest Protect in the room, following the directions needed based on the model you have.

Now that the Nest is set up, you can use the Wink app to control it without having to revert back to the Nest app.

Hop on over to `https://store.nest.com/product/smoke-co-alarm/` to see videos of the Nest Protect in action.

Quirky Spotter

Quirky, Inc., is a company that helps inventors make their dreams come true. Denny Fong of Toronto, Canada, was the inventor of one of Quirky's niftiest devices, the Spotter, shown in Figure 15-6.

Figure 15-6: Quirky's Spotter is five sensors in one device, and it can remotely alert you to whatever's going on in your home.

Image courtesy of Quirky Incorporated.

The Spotter is a sensor. Okay, to be more accurate, it's a really smart sensor. Fine, you dragged it out of me: The Spotter is actually five sensors in one awesome and small package. Because Spotter is so small (it's not tiny, mind you), you can place it almost anywhere, and because its design is so streamlined, it won't be an eyesore. The Spotter uses sensors to detect:

- ✔ Sound
- ✔ Motion
- ✔ Humidity
- ✔ Light
- ✔ Temperature

These sensors will keep an eye on any area of the home in which you place them. If you really want to keep tabs on the place, get multiple sensors and place them all over.

You set up Spotter using the Wink app on your smartphone or tablet, and it's as easy as turning the Spotter on and holding your smart device close enough to detect it. Once your Spotter is activated, you can set up rules for it, such as alerting you when the clothes dryer is finished, or when a door is opened. The number of uses for Spotter are limited only by your imagination.

Spotter can be placed virtually anywhere, too, since it can be mounted in three different ways:

- ✔ Screws
- ✔ Adhesive backing
- ✔ Built-in magnet

I think Spotter is one of the more useful of what I consider to be "bare-bones-basic" home automation technologies. Check out more about Spotter at www.quirky.com/shop/609.

Quirky+GE Pivot Power Genius

Quirky's at it again, but this time with the help of GE, with the Pivot Power Genius (see Figure 15-7). The Pivot Power Genius is a power strip that does so much more than the traditional rectangular kind that we're all used to. Pivot Power Genius is a smart device, meaning you can control the power for each outlet on the strip, effectively allowing you to turn connected devices on or off from your smartphone or tablet.

Image courtesy of Quirky Incorporated.

Figure 15-7:
The Pivot
Power
Genius is a
smart — and
bendy —
power strip
for today's
automated
home.

While I love the capability to work with smart devices, my favorite feature may be its least technical: the fact that the power strip bends at each outlet. This allows you to accommodate various plug sizes and to also fit nontraditional spaces. With old-fashioned power strips, you have to place the large blocky plugs in the last outlet or you would end up covering another outlet, and sometimes the blocky plugs are so heavy they don't stay in the outlet because there's no support for them at the end of the strip. Pivot Power Genius corrects those issues, and looks pretty cool, too.

Go to `www.quirky.com/shop/633` to see a video showing how easy it is to set up the Pivot Power Genius using the Wink app on your smart device.

The next two devices I describe require the Wink hub be installed on your network to use them, but I don't consider that a bummer. The Wink hub opens the proverbial door for you to add so many other devices to your home automation system that it's worth the relatively low cost to purchase it.

Leviton Dimming Plug-In Lamp Module

Don't want to install new wiring to automate your lamps? Prefer to use your traditional bulbs as opposed to the smart LED variety but still want the ease and benefits of home automation? Do you have a Wink hub or are strongly considering getting one?

If you answered yes to those questions, Leviton has just what you need: the DZPD3 Dimming Plug-In Lamp Module, shown in Figure 15-8.

Image courtesy of Leviton Manufacturing Co., Inc.

This thing couldn't be any simpler:

1. Plug your lamp into the DZPD3.

2. Plug the DZPD3 into an electrical outlet.

3. Fire up the Wink app on your smartphone or tablet and discover the DZPD3. You now have full control over the dimmer using your Wink app.

Since your Wink hub is Z-Wave–compatible, your DZPD3 will work with it and the Wink app, allowing you to dim, turn on or off, or set up rules and scenes for your module. Buy multiple dimmers so that you can control the lights throughout your home.

Find the DZPD3 at Wink's product site: `www.wink.com/products/leviton-dzc-dimming-plug-in-lamp-module/`.

Quirky Tripper

How would you like to use your smartphone or tablet as a personal security guard? It won't be able to toss unwanted intruders out on their ears, but it can alert you to a problem so that you or someone else can handle it. How can such a magical wonder be?

The folks at Quirky are rather busy, and they show up in this chapter yet again with another fine product: the Tripper. Tripper is a good-looking, and surprisingly small, sensor that you place on any doors, cabinets, or windows that you want to keep up with. You can dream up countless ways to use Tripper, shown in Figure 15-9.

Image courtesy of Quirky Incorporated.

Figure 15-9: Quirky's Tripper alerts you when doors or windows are opened or closed.

✔ Place it on cabinets to alert you when the kids are trying to get snacks (or worse, into the cleaning supplies).

✔ Place one on your front and back doors to alert you when someone enters the home.

✔ Put a Tripper on windows so that you know when they're open and closed.

✔ Combine Tripper with your lighting system so that your lights come on when a door is opened.

✔ Tripper can be linked to your thermostat so that when a window is closed your thermostat will automatically begin cooling or heating, or when a window is opened your thermostat can shut off, saving you some serious coin on your electric bill.

Tripper works with your Wink hub and app to provide you with control and alerts no matter where you are, with the standard caveat that an Internet connection is required.

Uses for Tripper are almost endless: All you have to do is think of what you'll do with it. Quirky has done it again, in my humble opinion. Take a gander at the Tripper at www.quirky.com/shop/706.

WeMo

This isn't the first time I mention WeMo in this book, for sure, but since this chapter is about devices that are crazy-simple to start your home automation adventure, WeMo has to be included.

Belkin's WeMo line of affordable home automation products are some of the simplest to set up and use, and they're also just plain good devices. WeMo devices don't need a hub, either — even better! WeMo devices communicate with your iOS or Android smart device through your Wi-Fi network and the Internet, with nothing in between.

Time to meet a few of the WeMo devices that the home automation newbie would be wise to investigate before splurging on something else.

Insight Switch

Belkin's WeMo Insight Switch is much like other smart switches in the fact that it enables you to remotely turn on and off any devices that are plugged into it. But that's where similarities begin to fade.

Belkin also offers a WeMo Switch, which does much of what the Insight Switch does:

- ✔ Turns electronic appliances on and off.
- ✔ Uses the WeMo app on your smartphone or tablet to control and monitor devices.
- ✔ Can schedule times for devices to power on or off.
- ✔ Plugs into any standard 120-volt electrical outlet.

However, the Insight Switch, shown in Figure 15-10, also gives you *insight* (clever of me, don't you think?) into how much power your devices are using, which makes it kind of like a technical tattletale, but when it's your dollars going to the power company you'll be glad to overlook the tattling part. Insight Switch does more than just tattle, though:

- ✔ Insight monitors usage of devices, such as the amount of time a device has been on.
- ✔ Insight provides an estimate of the power costs for devices plugged into it.
- ✔ Insight can send you an email detailing power consumption for devices you're using with it.

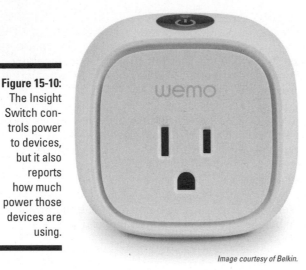

Image courtesy of Belkin.

Figure 15-10: The Insight Switch controls power to devices, but it also reports how much power those devices are using.

Visit `www.belkin.com/us/F7C029/p/P-F7C029/` (sorry for the weird URL, but that's how Belkin rolls) to learn more about the Insight Switch and ways you can use it in your home automation environment.

The WeMo Insight Switch can use IFTTT (IF This Then That) recipes to customize your automated lighting experience. Scroll to the bottom of the aforementioned website for the Insight Switch to see more information about using it with IFTTT.

NetCam

Belkin's NetCam Wi-Fi–capable web camera is also part of the WeMo universe of home automation products. There are actually two models of NetCam cameras, but I want to point you to the NetCam HD+ Wi-Fi Camera with Glass Lens and Night Vision.

Yes, that is the actual name of the camera. Don't fret, though; I just call it the NetCam from here on.

As you can see in Figure 15-11, the NetCam is one cool-looking device, and you can place it just about anywhere; you can even mount it on a wall.

Figure 15-11:
NetCam
keeps an
eye on your
home for
you, and
even lets
you peek
in on the
action from
anywhere
in the world.

Image courtesy of Belkin.

Belkin has packed a lot of good stuff into this little camera:

- ✔ Night vision helps you clearly see who's sneaking snacks from the fridge.

- ✔ The built-in microphone and speaker enable you to justly scold the scoundrel you caught sneaking a snack in the middle of the night, and even hear his whimpering retort.

- ✔ Motion sensors help you know when activity is taking place, such as someone skulking around in said kitchen.

- ✔ A wide viewing angle ensures you'll see as much of your room as you need.

- ✔ Use the WeMo app to control your NetCam.

In addition to those great features, you can subscribe to Belkin's Cloud+ Premium Services, which lets you store your streaming video in the cloud. This allows you to view the video at your leisure.

Setting up the NetCam is almost laughably (in a good way) easy:

1. Install the NetCam app on your iOS or Android smart device.

2. Plug your NetCam into an electrical outlet.

3. Flip up the switch on the back of NetCam.

4. Join the NetCam network by going to the network settings on your iOS or Android smart device.

5. Open the NetCam app and follow along with the instructions for adding your NetCam to your network.

6. Create a Belkin account so you can register your NetCam. You'll be able to use this account to view your NetCam's video on other devices, too.

7. Flip the switch on the back of your NetCam downward, and now you're done with set up.

Keep your Wi-Fi network's password close at hand if you don't know it. You need it in Step 5 of the setup process.

Once setup is complete, you can begin immediately viewing streaming video from your NetCam on your smartphone or tablet. Just a heads-up for parents: Your kids will grow to hate NetCam because they won't be able to get away with nearly as much stuff as they used to. You, however, will love it.

Thanks (the most sarcastic kind you can imagine) to Belkin for giving me another odd URL to pass along to you to discover more about NetCam: www.belkin.com/us/F7D7606/p/P-F7D7606/.

LED Lighting

Way back in Chapter 6, I introduce you to the WeMo way of automating your home's lighting using Belkin's LED Lighting Starter Set. I'm not going to bore you with the details since they are discussed in the aforementioned chapter, but I do want to remind you about it in this chapter.

I also want to clue you into something else, though: A little company called Osram Sylvania likes WeMo's LED lighting so much that it has decided to partner with Belkin on making home automation lighting even better. To kick off the partnership, Sylvania has released a WeMo-compatible bulb, the Ultra iQ LED BR30 smart light bulb. (Why can't these home automation folks come up with better names for this stuff?) The Ultra iQ LED BR30, shown in Figure 15-12, is intended for recessed lighting needs, so Sylvania and Belkin are beginning to fill in gaps in the WeMo line of lighting products. Ultra iQ bulbs are long-lasting: up to 50 years of life (based on using them for 3 hours a day)! There is much more automated lighting goodness to come from this partnership, but for now, the Ultra iQ LED BR30 is the only fruit borne of it.

Figure 15-12:
Belkin and
Sylvania are
teaming up
to make
home
automation
lighting
even better,
starting with
the Ultra
iQ LED BR30
bulb.

Image courtesy of Belkin.

The Ultra iQ LED BR30 works with the WeMo app and the WeMo Link, just as Belkin's own WeMo smart bulbs do:

- Control your Ultra iQ bulb remotely.
- Set a schedule for your Ultra iQ to turn on or off.
- Pair the Ultra iQ bulbs with your other WeMo lights to create lighting scenes.

If you already have a WeMo Link and are using WeMo bulbs, give the Ultra iQ a look if you also have recessed lighting that you'd like to control from the WeMo app. As ever, I leave you with an ever-annoyingly vague URL for this WeMo-compatible product: www.belkin.com/us/72627-Belkin/ p/P-72627/.

Chapter 16

Ten Great Websites for Home Automation

In This Chapter

▶ Discovering the best sites on the web for home automation

▶ Finding out what each site offers

▶ Shopping for home automation products online

*I*n this day of everything-is-connected-ness, most of us frequently hit the Internet when we want to learn more about a certain topic, find the best shopping bargains, get quick tips on performing a task, catch the latest news, find out how the latest movies fared with the critics, and so on. It's no different with home automation, to be certain. The web is packed with information on home automation topics, covering anything from task how-to's to buying the latest products at the best prices.

In this chapter, I introduce you to ten of my favorite home automation sites on the web. Some of them are great places to shop, others are chock-full of info for getting things done, and still others are a mix of these and more. I can attest to having become well acquainted with each of these sites, and they are the ten best that I've found as of this writing for covering the ever-broadening topic of home automation.

By the way, these sites are discussed in no particular order. I'm not playing favorites here: just giving you lots of great information.

Smarthome

The folks at Smarthome have been doing the home automation thing since 1992, so I'd say they know a thing or two about the subject. Their website, `www.smarthome.com`, has been a home automation staple on the Internet since 1995.

Smarthome.com, shown in Figure 16-1, offers a huge range of home automation devices covering the following and more:

✔ Lighting controls

✔ Security

✔ Home theater

✔ Thermostats and energy controls

✔ Pet care

Figure 16-1: Smarthome. com offers a huge range of products, focusing mainly on INSTEON technologies.

Smarthome.com also provides other products for making life within your home "smarter," such as:

✔ Smart clothing

✔ Personal safety products

✔ Weather stations

✔ Items for your automobile

Smarthome.com really wants to be your one-stop online shop for all things home automation; its range of product choices is impressive. However, there is one potential sticking point: Smarthome.com is owned by SmartLabs,

Inc., which manufactures its own line of home automation products. The potential sticking point I mention has nothing to do with SmartLabs, which is a fine company, but with its reliance on INSTEON as its home automation communication protocol of choice. Don't get me wrong — INSTEON is great. But if you are someone who doesn't already incorporate INSTEON devices into your home automation environment or you simply have an aversion to them in general, then Smarthome.com may not be the best place on the web for you.

CNET

If you're a tech-savvy person, CNET may already be a site that you check out on a frequent basis. Being someone who fancies himself in the tech-savvy category, I often pay CNET a visit, but I must confess my surprise at just how much CNET knows about home automation. Everyone knows that CNET is a great place to go for reviews on software and computing, smartphones, and other tech devices, but it's only been relatively recent that most folks have started thinking of their homes as part of their tech lives. Since our homes are becoming as technical as seemingly everything else in the known universe, CNET is on board with a great site for product reviews: www.cnet.com/topics/smart-home.

A visit to CNET's Smart Home site is prescribed for anyone who wants the lowdown on the latest and greatest home automation devices. My favorite part of the site is the list of best home automation devices, in which it ranks the top-of-the-line products in several categories, including (but not limited to):

- ✔ Smart hubs
- ✔ Smart thermostats
- ✔ Security monitoring
- ✔ Locks

You can access this list by clicking the Best Smart Home Devices tab on the site, shown in Figure 16-2.

CNET excels (in my humble opinion) in its video reviews. The video reviews are great because they give you a sense of seeing the product in action — an almost hands-on approach to investigating a product.

Figure 16-2:
CNET's
list of Best
Smart Home
Devices is a
must-read.

CEA

The stated mission of the Consumer Electronics Association (CEA) is to grow the consumer electronics market, and since home automation definitely fits within the consumer electronics spectrum CEA is very much interested in its comings and goings.

CEA deals with both the companies that produce electronics devices and the folks who consume them (I bet you that's how it came up with its name). Since this is the case, you can trust the CEA to look out for the interests of both parties. As consumers, you're mainly interested in what CEA can do for you in that respect.

A visit to www.ce.org (note there's no "a" in the URL) will present you with a huge amount of information. You can easily navigate to the home automation content by holding your mouse pointer over the Consumer Info tab on the home page and selecting Home Systems from the list of items (shown in Figure 16-3).

CEA's Home Systems web page provides several great videos for helping you gain an understanding of home automation systems and what you can do to enhance your home.

A couple of other areas of interest on the Home Systems web page are the Want It? and Got It? sections.

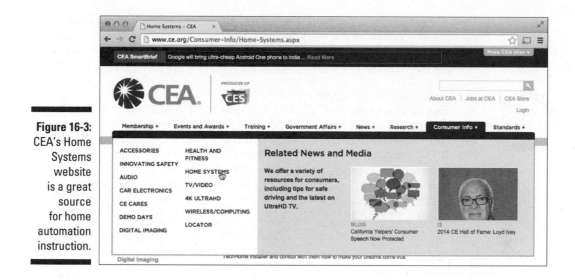

The Want It? section lists several articles that deal with home automation technologies that you may be interested in. Each article explains how each technology works and how to get started.

The Got It? section sports articles that discuss devices you already have and how to get the most use out of them.

SmartThings

Smart Things, found at www.smartthings.com, is one of the better-known companies working in the "Internet of Things" space, and it is a major player in the home automation arena. Its website is also quite a place for home automation junkies to hang out and learn a thing or ten about making things "just work."

The site offers a multitude of fare:

- You can download the SmartThings app, which is quite nice for running your home automation environment.
- Shop the entire lineup of SmartThings products, including the popular Home Starter Kits.
- Share your experiences with SmartThings devices and gain knowledge from other SmartThings aficionados in the Community section.
- Download SmartThings developers tools and documentation, if you're of the geeky persuasion.

My favorite section is the blog. The SmartThings blog is jam-packed with information on how to use your SmartThings devices, understanding technologies that will make your foray into home automation more productive (such as learning about wireless network repeaters and range), and more.

The blog also touts SmartThings' affection for IFTTT. IFTTT is pronounced "ift" (like "gift" without the "g"), and it stands for If This Then That. IFTTT uses commands called *recipes* that enable you to make connections between web apps. SmartThings has a channel on the IFTTT website that boasts of 180+ IFTTT recipes that will tie your SmartThings devices together with other web applications seamlessly. Check out the channel, shown in Figure 16-4, at `https://ifttt.com/recipes/search?q=smartthings&ac=false`.

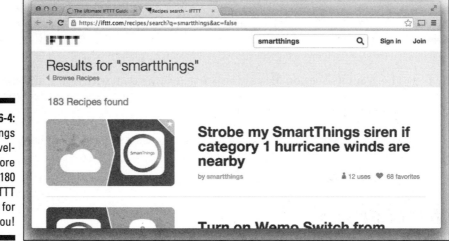

Figure 16-4: SmartThings has developed more than 180 IFTTT recipes for you!

Amazon

At first blush, Amazon might seem out of place in this chapter: "What do those book guys know about home automation, anyway?" Well, actually, Amazon knows quite a bit about the topic, thank you very much, and it has quite a nice site dedicated to home automation and relevant products. I'll even go so far as to say that Amazon probably does the topic as much justice as anyone else on the web.

First of all, it's Amazon, so the product selection is out of this world when it comes to shopping for home automation devices. Amazon doesn't just carry devices for one company; it carries devices for all of them! And the prices at Amazon are just plain tough to beat, as you probably already know.

Secondly, Amazon does a great job of educating its customers when it comes to learning not only the technologies behind home automation, but also understanding what options are available when it comes to specific home automation tasks. The Home Automation Resources & Buying Guides section is a great place to go for comparing solutions and devices. The Communication Protocols guide, shown in Figure 16-5, is by itself worth the price of admission (if there were one, that is).

Figure 16-5: Amazon's Communication Protocols guide is just one of many great home automation buying guides.

Amazon lists more than 3,000 home automation products, so be sure to leave some breadcrumbs on the trail if you decide to go venturing into the vast forest of home automation goodness. You'll find items covering the gamut of home automation, and Amazon has done a great job of organizing them into the following categories:

- Energy & Lighting
- Monitoring & Security

✔ Entertainment

✔ Wearable Tech (there's some really cool stuff in there!)

✔ Network Accessories

There's also a Shop & Learn category that offers a wonderful Solution Center, Home Automation Guide, New and Innovative devices, and much more to further immerse you into your smart home experience.

Amazon is a massive website, and giving you the URL to the Home Automation section would be a grueling ordeal for both you and me, dear reader. To get to the Home Automation section of Amazon's site:

1. **Go to www.amazon.com in your favorite web browser.**

2. **Click the Shop By Department button in the upper-left corner of the page and select Full Store Directory.**

3. **Browse the directory page for the Home, Garden & Tools section and click the Home Automation link.**

It may seem like a lot of work to get there, but it'll be worth your while, I promise.

Home Controls

Home Controls is a company that's been in the home automation business for a long time: 25 years, to be exact! These folks know more than a thing or two about the subject, and they're more than willing to share their knowledge with you (and sell you some home automation goodies at the same time).

When I say Home Controls likes home automation, I'm not kidding. Allow me to quote a couple of lines from its website in case you need convincing: "Would you even consider throwing out your TV remote in favor of getting up to change the channel or volume? Not us! You'd have to pry our remotes away from us, kicking and screaming." Now, that's dedication to the automation and convenience lifestyle, folks.

The Home Controls site offers some great features:

✔ An up-to-date blog that informs customers and seekers alike about the latest and greatest products offered by this fine company

✔ Links to Home Controls' Facebook and Twitter pages (this company is all about connecting with its customers)

✔ Option to subscribe to the Home Controls e-newsletter, which will keep you knowledgeable when it comes to home automation technologies and tips

✔ Capability to view or download its entire catalog of home automation products

✔ A Home Health Tech Store section that offers great products that make life easier for people who have special needs, such as folks who live with impairments

Home Controls also offers *Inside A Smart Home*, which gives the layout of a typical smart home and all the wonder it can behold. It's a really neat document that lists major areas of home automation, labels, and locations in the home that are affected by them, and gives an explanation of how technologies can benefit you. This nifty diagram (you can see part of it in Figure 16-6) makes the concept of home automation and what one can accomplish with it a visible reality.

Visit Home Controls at www.homecontrols.com for more info.

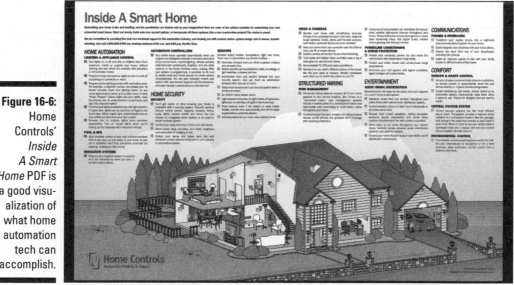

Figure 16-6:
Home Controls' *Inside A Smart Home* PDF is a good visualization of what home automation tech can accomplish.

Z-Wave.com

I discuss home automation protocols in Chapter 1, but there are also sites that are dedicated to informing the public and developers alike on the merits of specific protocols. Z-Wave.com is one such site, and as its name implies, it is solely dedicated to all things Z-Wave.

Z-Wave is a popular protocol, as evidenced by the number of companies that are implementing its technology into their home automation products. Companies such as ADT, Ingersoll Rand, Bosch, Honeywell, LG Electronics, Verizon, and literally scads (and yes, I do literally mean *scads*) of others are all on the Z-Wave bandwagon. Z-Wave.com provides a link to the Z-Wave Alliance website, which is `www.z-wavealliance.org`; the Z-Wave Alliance is *the* place where all the companies that use Z-Wave hang out, discuss their wares, and the like. According to the Z-Wave Alliance itself, it is "comprised of industry leaders throughout the globe that are dedicated to the development and extension of Z-Wave." You can see a list of those scads of companies that participate in the Alliance by checking the Members section of the site.

Z-Wave.com is a great jumping-off point for people interested in learning more about the protocol, products it supports, and how you can incorporate it into your home automation environment. The site explains what Z-Wave is and how it works, and offers product videos to help you determine the best fits for your home.

If you're bent toward the more technical side of Z-Wave, and may even want to discover how to develop products using the protocol, I recommend clicking the Z-Wave Developers link in the upper right of the Z-Wave.com home page to visit the Z-Wave site for developers (shown in Figure 16-7). The Developers site offers tons for the Z-Wave nerd and other interested parties:

- A technology comparison to other home automation protocols
- Access to the Z-Wave Developers Kit
- Explanations of the Z-Wave technology: How and where it works
- Details on the Z-Wave market and how to position products within it
- The latest news and information about Z-Wave events

And now for potentially the most obvious part of this entire chapter: You access Z-Wave.com by visiting — wait for it — `www.z-wave.com`.

Figure 16-7:
The Z-Wave
Developers
site is a
veritable
cornucopia
of Z-Wave
technical
and
marketing
information.

ZigBee Alliance

Oh, it's on now! I discuss Z-Wave.com in the preceding section, so it's only fair that I throw the ZigBee protocol a bone, too, right?

ZigBee Alliance is certainly aimed at those interested in the more technical aspects of home automation, and is focused with laserlike precision on the implementation of the ZigBee protocols' standards.

Go to `www.zigbee.org` (shown in Figure 16-8) and check out the links on the left side of the page. These links provide a mountain of information about ZigBee, including the following:

- Alliance membership
- White papers that discuss ZigBee tech in great detail
- The vast market for ZigBee-compatible devices
- A massive list of products that incorporate the technology
- How to become a certified ZigBee developer
- The scoop on the latest ZigBee news and events

ZigBee standards cover much more than just simple home automation. ZigBee standards have been developed for many other markets, too, such as commercial building systems, remote controls, health care monitoring, and more.

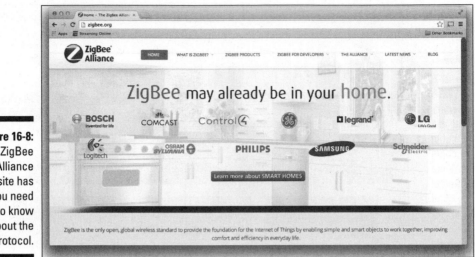

Figure 16-8:
The ZigBee
Alliance
website has
all you need
to know
about the
protocol.

Lowes

The big-box home stores for do-it-yourselfers have finally gotten into the home automation games for themselves, and this has resulted in them offering some great products and home automation information on their respective websites.

I kick it off with Lowes, which is as good a place as any to start. Lowes has just recently launched Iris, which is the company's proprietary Home Management System. Iris is Lowes' offering to help DIY home automators control their homes with a smart hub and app from anywhere they may happen to be. Lowes does offer some non-Iris-related products, but the majority of them are centered around it.

Aside from learning about Iris and how it works to join your home automation tasks under one controlling app and hub, there's not much in the way of basic home automation technology explanations or tips. However, I do still recommend the site, especially if you're someone who has an affinity for Lowes and will be going with Iris for your home automation needs. To learn more about Iris, visit the site (shown in Figure 16-9) at `www.lowes.com/Iris`.

Figure 16-9:
Iris is Lowes' Home Management System, incorporating a smart hub and app to control your devices.

Home Depot

In the interest of full disclosure, I admit that I prefer Lowes to Home Depot (just barely, though) when it comes to a bricks-and-mortar store where I can purchase my home project needs and speak with knowledgeable associates if I have questions. But when it comes to the approach to home automation, I'm leaning toward Home Depot, both in its own implementation of home management technology (Wink, discussed in Chapter 14) and in its home automation product offerings.

The Home Depot site offers a great selection of items that fit within the Wink family of home automation products, and they cover the gamut of features you use in your home:

- ✔ Energy management
- ✔ Entertainment
- ✔ Lighting
- ✔ Security and locks
- ✔ Motion sensors
- ✔ Thermostats

And more!

To access Home Depot's home automation site, follow these steps:

1. **Type www.homedepot.com into your favorite web browser.**

2. **Move your mouse pointer over Electrical under the Shop by Department heading on the left side of the page.**

3. **Click Home Automation within the pop-up menu that displays, as you see in Figure 16-10.**

From here, you can browse the Home Depot selection of home automation products. ***Hint:*** Scroll down the page to find the Home Automation Education section, which has some good information to complement the knowledge you're already gaining from this tome.

Don't be confused that the Home Depot site labels devices as Wink-compatible. This doesn't mean they won't work with other home automation devices or smart hubs; most of them certainly will, such as the Philips Hue light bulbs, the Schlage Touchscreen Deadbolt, and more.

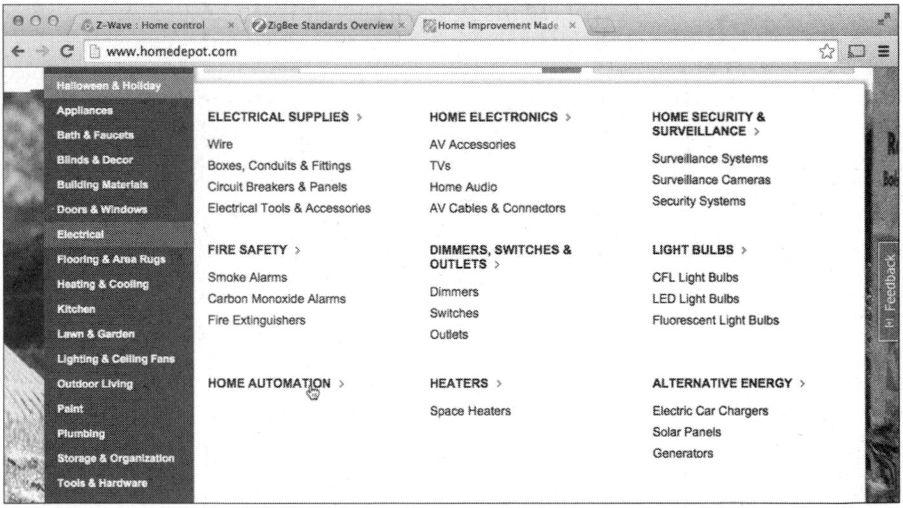

Figure 16-10:
Home Depot's Home Automation section can be accessed through the Electrical department of the website.

One more place to visit: *Consumer Reports*

We all know *Consumer Reports* magazine as the good folks who do product testing for us so that we don't have to, but did you know they've broadened their scope to cover home automation products as well? They not only review products and give them a thorough run-through, but they also provide unbiased opinions on which devices and solutions are worth your time and money — and those that are better left on the store shelves. Get the lowdown at the website, www.consumerreports.org.

Chapter 17

Ten Other Options for Automating Your Life

In This Chapter

▶ Cleaning your gutters automagically

▶ Remotely feeding and cleaning up after your pets

▶ Never touching your toilet's handle again

▶ Tackling other tasks with home automation devices

*B*y this point, you have discovered all about how home automation works and how you can control it via your smartphone, tablet, and computer. Life is great, your home is whirring away without a care, and you know all the tasks you need to keep scratching your home automation itches.

Or do you know them all (home automation tasks, that is)? Might there be some other home automation gems that didn't fit so neatly into the earlier categories and chapters up? Could you be missing out on the one, super-cool home automation trick that could keep you from ever going back to the days without automatic ovens? Will I ever stop asking questions and get on with this chapter?

The answer to the first question is no, but to the rest I resound with a hearty "yes!"

The devices you're about to discover do indeed exist, and they are actually quite helpful, no matter how odd one or two of them may seem.

Cleaning Your Home's Gutters

Ah, yes, it's "that time of the year" again: The gutters on your house are choked with leaves, pine straw, and goodness knows what else, so it's time to grab the ladder and get to work. Here's how it typically goes:

1. Place a ladder close enough to reach a section of your home's gutters.

2. Climb said ladder.

3. Clean gunk out of the gutter.

4. Climb down said ladder.

5. Reposition the ladder.

6. Repeat Steps 1 to 5, ad nauseam, until the grim task is complete.

Surely — *surely* — there must be another way, right? You bet there is, friend: Clean those gutters *automagically*!

iRobot is known for making mundane household chores something that robots can do for us, saving us time as well as our backs. They've done it again with yet another great (and dare I say, cool) tool: the Looj. The Looj, shown in Figure 17-1, is a robotic gutter cleaner that does the vast majority of the work for you. Sure, you still have to climb the ladder to place the Looj in your gutter, but after that you can sit back and sip a glass of iced tea while Looj does all the grungy toiling.

The Looj senses the debris in your gutter and knows how best to go about using its auger to churn the junk right out. It even comes with a remote control, built into its detachable handle, that you can use to tell it when to get to work and when to stop, or to even allow you to manually control its actions. Other great features include:

- A 50-foot operating range between the Looj and its remote control, meaning much fewer ladder moves

- Interchangeable auger flaps that are customized to the type of cleaning you need to do

- Capability to clean a 30-feet section of gutter in an average of 5 minutes

Check out the Looj by visiting `www.irobot.com/us/learn/home/looj.aspx`. You'll find tons of information there, including a great video that shows you just how the Looj works its gutter-cleaning magic.

Figure 17-1:
Looj in,
trash out:
Who knew?

Image courtesy of iRobot Corporation.

The Looj fits into most K-style gutters (the most common type) with ease. However, if you want to be sure it will work in your gutters, iRobot has provided a PDF template that you can print and use to determine if the Looj will fit. That's mighty fine pre-sales customer service, in my humble opinion.

Making a Robot Part of Your Family

Remember Rosie the Robot from *The Jetsons*? Most of us used to wonder how awesome it would be to have R2D2 and C3PO be our pals, right? *Lost in Space*'s Will Robinson was always under the watchful eye of his friend, Robot (who could even sing and play a guitar). For decades, the prospect of having a robot not just be a tool but be part of your family has been a dream of geeks the world over. Heck, let's don't kid ourselves: Most of us, geek or not, think that a truly interactive robot that works within our family dynamic would be pretty awesome to own. That day is coming sooner than some of us thought.

Allow me to introduce JIBO (see Figure 17-2).

JIBO (pronounced *JEE-bow*) is the brainchild of famed MIT robotics pioneer, Dr. Cynthia Breazeal. JIBO's going to work his way into your family's heart. JIBO is being hailed as the world's first family robot, and once you meet him you'll know why. JIBO can do all sorts of things with and for you:

✔ Built-in cameras allow JIBO to recognize members of the family and interact with them individually. For example, JIBO can recognize you and remind you of tasks that you have scheduled, then moments later can recognize your child and tell him or her a story.

- The cameras also allow JIBO to act as an avatar for video calls; it feels as though you're in the room with those you're communicating with.

- You can carry on a conversation with JIBO from anywhere in the room.

- JIBO learns how to interact with you as he gets to know you.

- JIBO expresses himself naturally and with emotive cues.

- The JIBOAlive Toolkit allows you to customize JIBO even more, making your JIBO truly your own.

- The JIBOAlive SDK allows developers to create new and innovative content for JIBO.

Figure 17-2:
Your family's new best friend, JIBO.

Image courtesy of JIBO.

And this is only the tip of the JIBO iceberg. JIBO's potential to be the first truly interactive family robot is through the roof, as evidenced by the introduction video that you can view at www.myjibo.com. The video is truly the best way of demonstrating just how innovative JIBO is and how it can affect your daily life.

As of this writing, the only downside to JIBO that I can find is that you can only pre-order him for now. JIBO is such a potentially game-changing experience in the realm of robotic interaction that I just had to share the news now, even before you can purchase one. (Please check www.myjibo.com for news on shipping dates.) JIBO could truly revolutionize the home and will be a wonderful addition to any home that employs automation.

Feeding Pets While You're Away

You're going to be away from home for the day or two (or more), but you can't take Fido or Fluffy with you. What to do when it comes to feeding your furry companion? Well, you could just tear open the pet food bag and leave it on the kitchen floor for him, or ask your neighbor's completely unreliable teenager to "watch after" your pawed pal. If neither of those sounds like a viable option, consider the SmartFeeder from Petnet, shown in Figure 17-3.

The SmartFeeder is true to its name: This device feeds your pets according to the schedules you set and with the amounts of food you determine. There's no worrying that beloved companions will either starve or engorge themselves.

Figure 17-3:
Petnet's SmartFeeder will keep your pet's tummy full, but not too full.

Image courtesy of Petnet.

The SmartFeeder app, seen in Figure 17-4, plugs you into the device from anywhere and allows you the ultimate in pet-feeding convenience:

✔ The Dashboard can be accessed from your smartphone, tablet, or computer's web browser.

✔ Set completely customizable feeding times and portion amounts from anywhere at any time.

✔ Be notified of your pet's feeding activities, including when feedings are scheduled, when they've completed, and how much food remains in the feeder.

✔ You can actually monitor your pet's caloric intake and compare it to other animals of similar breeds and ages!

You likely have tons of questions about a device like this (no, it won't supply water; they're developing a separate device for that), and Petnet has the answers to your questions in the Support section of its website. Visit Petnet at www.petnet.io to learn more about this really great product.

Do you have more than one pet? Each SmartFeeder device will work with only one pet at a time, so you'll need multiple feeders. The good news is that they can all be controlled via one app.

Figure 17-4:
The
SmartFeeder
Dashboard
app allows
you full
feeding
control and
a mountain
of dietary
info for your
pets.

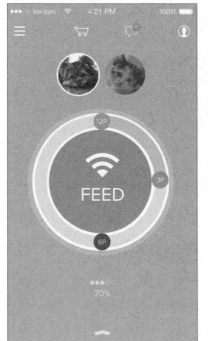

Image courtesy of Petnet.

Cleaning Up Kitty Litter

Of course, I just had to follow up the automatic pet feeder with the obvious device: an automatic kitty litter cleaner. Makes sense, no? These devices don't use app or web technology, but they do automate (quite well) what used to be one of the most unpleasant tasks of a cat lover's life.

Using standard litter

There are automatic kitty litter machines, and then there is the Litter-Robot II from Automated Pet Care Products, Inc. This is the crème-de-la-crème of automatic kitty litter cleaners that use standard clumping kitty litter. And while it won't connect with your iPhone or Android device so you can monitor your kitty's business (does anyone actually *want* to do that?), it will keep the rest of your home from smelling like a sewer — *bonus*! — without ever having to gets your hands messy. The Litter-Robot II, shown in Figure 17-5, doesn't rake your kitty's "stuff" away; instead, it sifts it, which means it gets all the litter and leaves nothing to chance. The only thing you have to do is empty the discard drawer of the machine into your wastebasket. Done.

Cat lovers, head on over to www.litter-robot.com to check out this great product.

Figure 17-5:
The Litter-Robot II automatically takes care of your kitty's business so that you don't have to.

Image courtesy of Automated Pet Care Products, Inc.

A kitty toilet? Why, yes, indeed!

Tired of dealing with litter altogether? Wish you never had to buy another bag of the stuff again? Wouldn't it be great if your cat could not only use the toilet, but that she could even flush it?

The CatGenie is your answer! CatGenie is a self-flushing, self-washing kitty litter box that utilizes reusable litter. You can set the thing to automatic and it acts as your kitty's own customized toilet. No kidding!

What makes CatGenie different is that you connect to a water supply in your home. It will actually use water and a sanitizing solution to flush your cat's business away. There's a great video on the CatGenie website, www.catgenie.com, in the Newsroom section, that shows you how the CatGenie can be set up with its own water lines or you can have it flush directly into a human litter box (also known as your toilet).

This warning isn't anything more than a heads-up, so don't be alarmed. Although you may no longer need to buy kitty litter, you will need a steady supply of the sanitizing solution the CatGenie uses to clean itself. According to the CatGenie's creator, PetNovations, the cost of the solution is actually less than what you'd spend on litter in a year.

Cleaning Your Pool the Robotic Way

The fine folks at iRobot are about to make another appearance in this chapter; they're just too good at what they do to keep them out. This time, instead of helping with your gutters, they effortlessly clean your pool for you.

Anyone who's ever owned a swimming pool knows the horrible feeling that comes when you realize it's time to clean it. The time, the chemicals, the effort, and the money spent almost make you wish you just had a robot to do it all for you.

iRobot to the rescue! iRobot's Mirra is the perfect robotic solution to cleaning your pool, and all you have to do is drop it in and it will get to work. No more scrubbing the sides of your pool with a brush, or scraping the surface with a net to clean out debris, hair and other yuckiness. With Mirra, all you need to do is empty the canisters that collect the stuff it gets out of your favorite swimming hole.

Mirra, shown in Figure 17-6, uses the following technology to keep your pool spotless and ready to entertain:

- ✔ iRobot's iAdapt Nautiq technology allows Mirra to determine all on its own how to best clean your pool, regardless of its size or shape.

- ✔ Mirra is equipped with all it needs to work in any in-ground pool, regardless of its surface type.

- ✔ Mirra's floating power cord won't get tangled; built-in sensors determine Mirra's orientation in the pool.

- ✔ Mirra filters more than 70 gallons of water per minute.

- ✔ Large cleaning canisters are available for purchase if you need something for heavier cleanup jobs.

- ✔ This little gem can even climb steps!

You can find out more about Mirra, and watch a really interesting video on its use, by checking out www.irobot.com/us/learn/home/mirra.aspx.

Figure 17-6:
Mirra is the
perfect pool
cleaner
for the
automated
home.

Image courtesy of iRobot Corporation.

Waking Up to a Fresh Cup of Joe

Any truly dedicated coffee drinker worth his or her weight in coffee beans knows you can automatically create your own brews with a programmable coffeemaker. You had to know that at some point you'd be able to use your smartphone or tablet to handle the task, too, right?

Mr. Coffee (of course; who else?) is bringing the app-controlled coffeemaker to your kitchen with its Smart Optimal Brew Coffeemaker Enabled with Wemo. And yes, that's the real name of this coffeemaker (I just stick to calling it the Smart Brew for the sake of saving you reading time and sparing a couple of trees in the printing of this book).

The Smart Brew can do exactly what you'd expect: automatically brew your coffee on your schedule, which you set from anywhere in the world using the Wemo app on your smartphone or tablet. Figure 17-7 shows a person doing just that, as a matter of fact.

The Wemo app, coupled with your Smart Brew coffeemaker, allows you to do some neat tricks with your coffeemaker you've never been able to do remotely before:

- ✔ Check the Smart Brew's status and even turn it off.
- ✔ Receive notifications when the Smart Brew needs to remind you of a scheduled or finished brew.
- ✔ Create brewing schedules for up to one week, and adjust the schedule as needed.

Figure 17-7: Set up coffee brewing schedules to fit your daily needs using the Wemo app.

Image courtesy of Belkin.

Starting Your Vehicle Remotely

I think by now it's pretty obvious that most things in or around your home can be remotely controlled in some fashion. How about automobiles? They're kind of like second homes, aren't they? Many of you probably spend as much or more of your waking hours in your automobiles as you do in your homes anyway. And besides, since you park your automobiles on the property, they're more or less an extension of your home. If you can start your coffee automatically with an app, heat the house with an app, check foods on the grill with an app, and pretty much everything else with an app, why not start your car with an app?

If this sounds like something that might be up your alley, Viper has the right tool for you: SmartStart.

SmartStart is a system that will connect your car to the cloud, allowing you to start your car and even track its movements from anywhere using the SmartStart app (see Figure 17-8). With the SmartStart system, you can:

- Lock and unlock your automobile.
- Remotely start your automobile.
- Arm or disarm your alarm system.
- Instigate your automobile's panic alarm.
- Open the trunk remotely.
- Control multiple vehicles from a single app.
- Allow multiple users to control a single vehicle.
- Use keyless entry into your automobile.

Sure, your vehicle probably comes with some of these features built in to its remote, but those functions will only work if you're in a certain proximity to the vehicle. With SmartStart, you can be anywhere in the world and use these features, as long as you and your automobile are within range of a cell tower. This system has a bounty of advantages:

- If you're locked out of your vehicle somehow, another authorized user can unlock it for you using his or her SmartStart app.
- Your automobile can be toasty in the winter or frosty in the summer before you even walk out of the grocery store.
- You can keep tabs on where your kids of driving age are on a Friday or Saturday night.
- Find your car easily in a crowded parking lot (the value of this will be more than obvious come Christmastime, I promise).

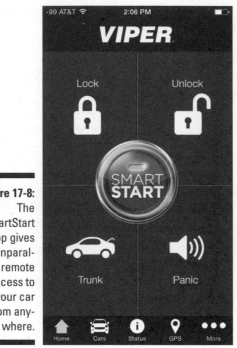

Figure 17-8:
The SmartStart app gives you unparalleled remote access to your car from anywhere.

The list can go on and on, but you get the drift. For much more information, visit www.viper.com/SmartStart. Check out all the systems the company offers, and even customize a system to your needs.

I must make you aware that Viper charges a monthly fee for service (you'll need to find the plan that suits your personal needs), which is understandable, since Viper is using its servers and must access cellular networks to offer you the SmartStart services.

Extend your SmartStart's features with Viper's SmartStart GPS, which allows you to locate your car anywhere, set speed limit alerts, be notified when the vehicle is located in certain areas, and more.

Flushing Your Troubles Away Automatically

An automated home just wouldn't be complete without one essential thing, and I think you know what I'm talking about.

Automatically flushing toilets! Yes, I went there (if you'll pardon the pun).

Being the mature folks that we are, I'm sure we can navigate this topic with some modicum of decorum. Let's just dive right in!

Surely, it's everyone's dream to be able to go to the restroom without having to worry about actually flushing the toilet, correct? I can't imagine how such an invention wouldn't rank right up there with fire, the wheel, and life in general. I don't know about you, but my life's so hectic I just don't want to waste the time necessary to push that little handle down on the side of the toilet every time I use it. What a hassle!

Okay, all kidding aside, while at first the idea of an automatic flushing toilet may sound a little silly, in truth it is a very good idea. Here are a few reasons why an automatically flushing toilet is something worth considering:

✔ Sanitary reasons are reason enough alone, if you ask moi.

✔ Anyone with children in the home (regardless of their ages) knows that more often than not the simple job of flushing is often ignored or forgotten altogether.

✔ Anyone with a man in the home (regardless of his age) knows that more often than not the simple job of flushing is often ignored or forgotten altogether.

Now that I've gotten the utmost attention of the moms and wives in the audience, I'd like to introduce you to Rubbermaid's Auto Flush Tank. The Auto Flush Tank (the sensor for which is shown in Figure 17-9) is easy to install on almost any toilet that uses a standard water tank. Some features of the Auto Flush Tank include:

✔ Battery life of up to 3 years or 100,000 flushes (that's a lot of flushes, ladies and gentlemen).

✔ Operates in one of three user-settable modes:

- *Object detection, meaning it will automatically detect when a person is moving away and it will flush.*

- *Object detection with extended delay, meaning it will wait a few seconds before flushing once it detects someone has moved away (so as to avoid any surprises, if you know what I'm saying).*

- *Wave only, meaning that the toilet will only flush when someone waves a hand in front of the sensor, which is placed on the wall behind the toilet.*

Figure 17-9:
The Auto Flush Tank's sensor mounts on the wall behind a toilet for optimal user detection.

To find out more about this "one giant leap for mankind," visit www.rubbermaidcommercial.com and enter *autoflush tank* (no space between "auto" and "flush") in the search field in the upper-right corner of the page. The page for the Auto Flush Tank will appear automatically. By the way, don't be thrown off that this is considered a commercial product by Rubbermaid; it works perfectly fine in a home.

I recommend searching for "Rubbermaid Auto Flush Tank" on www.amazon.com. Amazon does sell the product, you can read the sterling reviews, and the price can't be beat.

Pulling the Shades from Across the Room

We've all seen sci-fi movies where the windows dim or shades close at the clap of a hand or when a simple voice command is given, only to go home and look at the shades and blinds in our homes and wonder, "Why can't *you* do that?" You'll be thrilled to know that they actually can!

Hunter Douglas is a well-known company to anyone who's shopped for window blinds and shades, and they're the good people I want to bring to your attention in this part of the chapter. Hunter Douglas has developed a system that will adjust your shades or blinds to your liking with the use of an app on your iOS or Android devices. This app is called Platinum, and it works in conjunction with the Platinum App Bridge and Platinum Repeaters, along with an impressive line of motorized Hunter Douglas shades and blinds.

The Platinum App Bridge acts as the communication hub between your iOS or Android devices and the motorized blinds or shades. The Platinum Repeaters enhance the signal strength of the Bridge throughout the home (Hunter Douglas recommends at least one Repeater for each room you want to control shades or blinds in). The app, shown in Figure 17-10, allows you full control of all the motorized Hunter Douglas blinds and shades in your home.

Here are some of the advantages to using the Platinum app to automatically control your blinds and shades:

- ✔ Lowering your blinds when it's hot outside helps keep your home cooler when you're away. In the same line of thought, raising your blinds in the daytime when it's cold out helps keep your home warmer. Can you say "energy bill savings"? I knew you could!

- ✔ Set up different scenes so that shades raise and lower automatically to your specification at given times.

- ✔ You can raise or lower your blinds from anywhere in the world; no need to be in the home or even near it for the app to work.

Figure 17-10: Hunter Douglas's Platinum app can control your motorized blinds and shades without you ever leaving the couch.

Image courtesy of Hunter Douglas.

Please check out www.hunterdouglas.com/platinum-app-info to find out more about the app:

- ✔ Find answers to commonly asked questions in the handy FAQ section.
- ✔ Discover the lines of blinds and shades that are supported.
- ✔ Locate a Hunter Douglas dealer near you.

The app is rather large at almost 100MB, so don't be alarmed if it takes a few minutes to download to your iOS or Android device. Actual time depends on your Internet connection speed, of course.

Controlling Your Home's Humidity

Your home's humidity is no trifling matter, as anyone with gas heating or who lives in a really dry climate can attest to. If you're like me, allergies can be severely affected, depending on how humid the air is. Humidifiers are a necessary commodity in some households; wouldn't it be nice if you could automate those darned things?

Holmes has developed a humidifier that you can control, and you can do it from your iOS or Android device, no less! The Holmes Whole House Smart Humidifier Enabled by Wemo (there's good old Wemo again) allows you to control your home's humidity like never before. The Wemo app is all you need to run the show (once you've acquired the humidifier, of course), and it does a dandy of a job:

- ✔ Get notifications when water levels in the humidifier reach low levels.
- ✔ Check on the filter life level so you know when it needs to be changed. You can even order new filters from the app.
- ✔ Adjust the humidity levels in your home from anywhere, and I do mean *anywhere*.
- ✔ Set the humidifier's schedule to operate only when you want it to.
- ✔ Create preset humidity levels that the humidifier will work to maintain.

Go to www.holmesproducts.com/humidifiers/HCM3888C-U.html to gather more information about this truly helpful product, shown in Figure 17-11. The site includes three videos that can give you great insight into how the product works and how it can better manage the humidity in your home.

Figure 17-11:
The Holmes Smart Humidifier makes it super-easy to maintain humidity levels in your entire home.

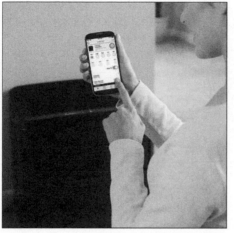

Image courtesy of Belkin.

Index

• *Number* •

8-track players, 166

• *A* •

AcuRite Weather Environment System
  5-in-1 weather sensor, 200–202
  app and website, 200
  barometric pressure, 202
  forecast, 201
  hygrometer, 201
  Internet Bridge, 200–201
  outdoor humidity, 202
  outdoor temperature, 202
  rain data, 202
  rain gauge, 201
  thermometer, 201
  weather station display, 200
  website, 202
  wind chill, 202
  wind direction vane, 201
  wind speed and direction, 202
  wind speed anemometer, 201
ADT Pulse system
  alerts, 117
  light control, 117
  live camera feeds, 117–118
  monitoring, 117
  Pulse app, 117
  Pulse Voice, 117
  Pulse web portal, 117
  remote alarming, 117
  remote disarming, 117
  thermostat control, 117
  touchscreen, 117
  website, 117
air-conditioner, Quirky Aros, 39
Alarm.com
  battery backup, 116
  Image Sensor, 116

integrating systems, 116
  interface, 116
  system control, 116
  website, 116
  wireless cellular technology, 116
alarms, using for home security, 111
Allen, Christopher, 145
Amazon, 168, 290–292
Ambrogio Remote app, using with LawnBott
      mowers, 216
Android
  app, 232
  versus iOS, 231
  smartphones, 231–232
  support for, 32
  versions, 231
Android apps
  keeping up to date, 247
  using with Nexus Player, 182
  using with tablets, 237
Android OS versions, keeping
      up to date, 237
Android tablets
  Google/HTC Nexus 9, 238
  LG G Pad, 238
  Nvidia Shield, 238
  Samsung Galaxy Tab S, 238
  Sony Xperia Z3 Tablet Compact, 238
Apple, home automation
      goals, 255
Apple TV, 166
  1080p HD video, 176
  accessing content, 176–177
  connecting to television, 177
  controlling, 177
  interface, 176
  iTunes account, 176
  mirroring content, 177–178
  Remote app, 177–178
  sharing content, 177
  streaming content, 177
  viewing content, 177

Apple TV *(continued)*
  watching movies, 177
  on wireless networks, 25
Apple's HomeKit, 42. *See also* Homekit
apps. *See also* websites
  AcuRite Weather Environment
    System, 200
  Ambrogio Remote, 216
  Android, 232
  Apple's HomeKit, 42
  August locks, 123
  Blumoo home entertainment, 173
  Bose SoundTouch speakers, 186
  Brillion, 13, 143–145
  CastleOS, 42
  Creek Watch, 164
  Driblet water monitoring, 161–162
  home entertainment, 167
  HTML, 260–261
  hue, 94–95
  Husqvarna My Automower app, 213
  IBM's Creek Watch app, 164
  iDevices Connected App, 147–148, 150
  INSTEON, 42, 102
  keeping up to date, 245–248
  Kevo deadbolt, 129–130
  Kinect, 260
  laundry, 82–83
  Lennox thermostats, 68
  Lockitron, 128
  Lyric thermostats, 57
  My Smart Appliances, 143
  Nest Mobile, 60
  Netatmo JUNE device, 197–198
  Netatmo Weather Station, 195
  Nexia's Home Intelligence app, 72
  number of, 41–43
  PetNet SmartFeeder, 305–306
  Piper home security, 133
  Platinum App Bridge, 315
  Pulse, 117
  Rachio Iro sprinkler system, 223
  Remote for Apple TV, 177
  Revolv, 42
  Robomow, 211
  Roku, 180–181
  single solutions, 42
  Smart Access Range, 141
  SmartThings, 105

  SoundTouch speakers, 186
  streaming media content, 176–177
  system-specific, 32
  Trane thermostats, 71–72
  using, 14, 31
  using with smart locks, 14
  Wally sensors, 159–160
  weather on Smart ThinQ
    Refrigerator, 139
  WeMo, 108
  WeMo Switch, 62
  Wink, 39, 42, 256, 269
APX Alarm company, 118
aquarium cleaning, automating, 76,
    87–88
ARCHOS Weather Station
  air quality, 198
  atmospheric pressure, 198
  comparing to Netatmo, 199
  features, 197
  humidity, 198
  indoor module, 198–199
  noise level, 198
  outdoor module, 198
  soil module, 199–200
  temperature, 198
  website, 199
August
  app, 123
  partnership with HomeKit, 253
August locks, comparing to Lockitron,
    127, 129
August Smart Lock, 123–125
  account setup, 124
  encryption, 124
  installation, 124
  replacing deadlock with, 124
  seeing in retail setting, 124
  using with Bluetooth, 124
  website, 123, 125
Auto Flush Tank
  battery life, 313
  illustration, 314
  user-settable modes, 313
automating
  aquarium cleaning, 76
  damp mopping, 76
  dust mopping, 76
  floor scrubbing, 76

grill cleaning, 76
vacuuming, 76
automation goals
  apps, 41–43
  committed versus tinkering, 39–40
  manufacturers, 38–39, 47
  multiple users, 40
  pacing, 38
automation software
  Home Control Assistant, 241–242
  HomeSeer, 241
  HouseBot, 241
automobile automation, SmartStart, 311–312

• B •

bacteria, removing from floors, 80
bandwidth, explained, 24
beginning automation. See also home automation
  Dropcam, 271–272
  Insight Switch, 279–280
  LED Lighting, 282–283
  Levitron Dimming Plug-In Lamp Module, 276–277
  Nest Protect, 272–274
  NetCam, 280–282
  Philips hue products, 269–271
  Quirky Spotter, 274–275
  Quirky Tripper, 277
  Quirky+GE Pivot Power Genius, 275–276
  WeMo, 279–283
  Wink platform, 268
Belkin home security
  motion sensors, 114
  Switch + Motion website, 115
  webcams, 114
  WeMo Motion, 115
Belkin products. See also WeMo products
  Cloud+ Premium Services, 281
  NetCam, 280–282
  WeMo Insight Switch, 279–280
Belkin thermostats, WeMo Switch, 61–63
blinds, automating, 314–316
Blumoo home entertainment
  app, 173
  base station, 172–173

benefits, 173
Bluetooth, 172
connecting speaker, 173
macros, 173
product support, 173
virtual remotes, 173
website, 173
Bosch Indego robotic mower
  cutting slopes, 219
  illustration, 219
  perimeter wire, 219
  PIN code, 219
  safety features, 219
  self-charging, 219
  website, 220
  yaw sensor, 219
Bose sound systems, 168, 185–186
BotVac 70e, 85
Braava mopper
  damp cloth, 81
  dry cloth, 81
  GPS system, 81
  interface, 81
Breazeal, Cynthia, 303
Brillion app, 13
  controlling oven with, 143–145
  website, 144
Broadcom, partnership with HomeKit, 253
browsers, 239–240

• C •

cameras, using for home security, 112.
  See also Dropcam webcam
candies, gauging temperature in, 152
car automation, SmartStart, 311–312
carbon monoxide detectors, 120, 272–274
cassette tapes, 166
CastleOS
  accessing apps, 260–261
  Core Service, 260
  EPIC television program, 261
  functionality, 260
  HTML app, 260–261
  Kinect app, 260
  platform unity, 259–260
  website, 42, 261
CatGenie kitty toilet, 308

CDs, 166
CEA (Consumer Electronics Association)
    website, 288–289
Chamberlain, partnership with HomeKit, 253
Cheat Sheet, 4
Chrome browser, using with Chromecast,
    183–184
Chromebooks, 244
Chromecast
  features of, 168
  footprint, 182
  illustration, 183
  popularity of, 182
  price, 182
  setting up, 183
  on wireless networks, 25
Cicchitelli, Chris, 261
cleaning automation, 76–77
  Grillbot, 85–87
  gutters, 302–303
  iRobot, 77–82
  LG, 82
  Neato Robotics, 84–85
  RoboMap, 82–84
  RoboSnail, 87–88
CNET website, 287–288
coffee brewing, automating, 310
ColorTouch thermostats
  compatibility, 74
  interface, 73
  language settings, 74
  passcode, 74
  SkyPort technology, 74
  touchscreen, 74
  uploading items to, 74
ComfortLink II
  XL950 thermostats, 70–73
  Zoning System, 73
computers
  Chromebooks, 244
  Macs and OS X, 239–240
  PCs and Linux, 242–244
  PCs and Windows, 240–241
  Windows tablets, 241–242
Connected App, using with iDevices,
    147–148, 150
connectivity
  losing, 26
  providing, 25

Consumer Reports website, 299
Control4 website, 10
convection wall oven, 143
convenience of home automation, 11–13
cooking automation. *See* kitchen automation
Cree, partnership with HomeKit, 253
Crestron website, 10
Crock-Pot Smart Slow Cooker
  capacity, 138
  cooking time, 138
  cord storage, 138
  features, 138
  handles, 138
  illustration, 138
  temperature, 138
  website, 138
Cyber Rain
  Cloud app, 221
  comparing to Rachio Iro sprinkler
      system, 223
  receiving problem alerts, 221
  saving money, 220
  using, 220–221
  website, 222

• D •

damp mopping, automating, 76
deadbolt, locking and unlocking, 123–125.
    See also Yale products
devices. *See also* networked devices
  adding cautiously, 27–30
  testing on networks, 26
dimmers
  INSTEON products, 99–100
  plug-in lamp modules, 48
  remote control switches, 47
Dimming Plug-In Lamp Module,
    276–277
dishwasher automation, 142–143
Driblet
  app, 161–162
  smart meter, 160–161
  software, 161
  water monitoring, 160–162
Dropcam webcam. *See also* cameras
  illustration, 271
  microphone, 272
  motion detection, 272

night vision, 272
speaker, 272
viewable area, 272
website, 272
zooming in, 272
dual-band technology, 98, 101
dust mopping, automating, 76

• E •

ebooks, buying, 166
ecobee3 thermostats
cloud icon, 65
cooling indicator, 65
features, 64
full menu, 65
heating indicator, 65
incompatibility with, 64
installing, 64–66
interface, 63, 65
learning model, 64
Quick Changes button, 65
remote sensors, 66–67
setting up, 64–66
slider, 65
temperature display, 65
touchscreen, 64
web interface, 66
website, 64, 67
wiring adjustments, 64
Edison, Thomas, 90
Egg Minder by Quirky, 153–154
electrical devices, controlling with
        WeMo Switch, 108
electrical work, requiring, 33–35
entertainment. *See* home entertainment

• F •

firewalls, using, 29
floor cleaners, Scooba, 79–80.
        See also mopping
floor scrubbing, automating, 76
Fong, Denny, 274
Food Channel recipes, 139
Friendly Machines, 208
fuel, monetary savings, 16
future technology, 22

• G •

gas, monetary savings, 16
GE (General Electric)
Brillion-enabled devices, 143
convection wall oven, 143
GE oven temperature, controlling, 13
geofencing
hue bulbs, 94
Lyric thermostats, 57
glass-break detectors, 120
Google Cast extension
downloading, 183–184
installing, 183–184
Google Chromecast
features of, 168
footprint, 182
illustration, 183
popularity of, 182
price, 182
setting up, 183
on wireless networks, 25
Google Nexus Player, 181–182
Google Play, 166
Google TV, 181
Google/HTC Nexus 9 tablet, 238
Google's Chromecast, 168
grill cleaning. *See also* iGrill
automating, 76
Grillbot, 85–86
Grillbot
features, 85–86
illustration, 86
using, 86–87
website, 86
gutters, cleaning, 302–303

• H •

Haier, partnership with HomeKit, 253
hard floors, scrubbing with
        Scooba, 80
Harmony Ultimate One remote
button functions, 174
channels, 174
charging station, 174
compatibility, 174
device control, 174

Harmony Ultimate One remote *(continued)*
  illustration, 174
  setting up, 175
  touchscreen, 174
heating, monetary savings, 15
Holmes humidifier, 316–317
home automation. *See also* beginning
    automation
  convenience, 11–13
  defined, 8
  going large, 47
  old-fashioned way, 8–10
  self-installing systems, 10
  starting small, 47
  universal products, 46–47
Home Control Assistant, 241–242
Home Controls website, 292–293
Home Depot automation
  partnership with Wink, 257
  website, 297–298
  Wink app, 256
  Wink partnership, 255
home entertainment
  8-track players, 166
  Apple, 176–178
  apps, 167
  Blumoo, 172–173
  Bose, 185–186
  cassette tapes, 166
  CDs, 166
  on computers, 167
  dedicated apps, 167
  devices, 168
  digital delivery, 166
  ebooks, 166
  Google, 181–184
  Logitech, 173–175
  media services, 166
  online stores, 166
  purchasing, 166
  Roku, 178–181
  Roomie, 168–172
  social media sites, 168
  Sonos, 186–188
  Sony Walkman, 166
  streaming media, 166
  subscription services, 168
  technology, 167–168
  on television, 167

  vinyl records, 166
  website, 10
  Wi-Fi networks, 168
  Wi-Fi-enabled systems, 168
home networking protocols.
    See protocols
home security. *See also* security
  alarms, 111
  apps, 14
  cameras, 112
  lighting, 14
  locks, 111
  monetary savings, 15–16
  motion detectors, 14, 112
  scenarios, 111
  smart locks, 14
  Wi-fi cameras, 14
home security products
  ADT, 117–118
  Alarm.com, 115–117
  August, 123–125
  Belkin, 114–115
  Kwikset, 129–132
  Lockitron, 126–129
  Piper, 132–134
  Schlage, 120–122
  SmartThings, 112–114
  Vivint, 118–120
  Yale, 125–126
home temperatures. *See also* thermostats;
    weather stations
  controlling, 39
  keeping level, 15
  knowing, 192
  preferences for, 52
  saving money, 52–53
  setting remotely, 52–53
HomeKit
  Annoying Company scene, 255
  Away from Home scene, 254
  command sets, 254
  Date Night scene, 254
  developer's site, 255
  Morning scene, 254
  Nighttime scene, 254
  requirements, 252–253
  scenes, 254
  tasks, 254
  using, 255

HomeKit partners
  August, 253
  Broadcom, 253
  Chamberlain, 253
  Cree, 253
  Haier, 253
  Honeywell, 253
  iDevices, 253
  iHome, 253
  Kwikset, 253
  Marvell, 253
  Netatmo, 253
  Osram Sylvania, 253
  Philips, 253
  Schlage, 253
  Skybell, 253
  Texas Instruments, 253
  Withings, 253
HomeSeer automation software, 241
Honda Miimo mower
  blades, 218
  cutting patterns, 219
  illustration, 218
  quietness, 218
  safety, 218
  self-charging, 218
  waterproof feature, 218
  website, 219
Honeywell, partnership with HomeKit, 253
Honeywell thermostats
  Lyric installation, 55–56
  Lyric setup and use, 56–57
  round model, 54–55
  website, 55, 57
  Wi-Fi compatible, 57
HouseBot automation software, 241
HTC One M8 smartphone, 232
HTML app, using with CastleOS, 260–261
hub, including in starter kit, 47. *See also*
    Revolv hubs
hue app
  features, 94
  interface, 95
  setting up, 95
hue products
  A19 starter pack, 93
  bulbs, 93–94
  color customization, 94
  geofencing, 94

LED lighting, 93
Lighting Recipes, 94
matching colors, 94
schedules, 94
website, 97
hue tap
  features, 97
  illustration, 96
  lack of batteries, 97
  portability, 97
  use of kinetic energy, 97
Hulu, 166
humidity, controlling in home, 316–317
Hunter Douglas Platinum system,
    314–316
Husqvarna
  reputation, 211
  robotic mowers, 212
  websites, 214
Husqvarna Automower
  boundary wire, 213
  built-in settings panel, 213
  cutting height, 213
  energy saving, 212
  guide wire, 213
  inclines, 213
  My Automower app, 213
  safety features, 213
  secured PIN, 213
  weatherproof feature, 212
Hwang, Rafael, 153

● **/** ●

IBM's Creek Watch app, 164
iComfort thermostats
  installing, 69
  interface, 70
iDevices
  Connected App, 147–148, 150
  iGrill, 145
  iGrill 2, 145–147
  iGrill mini, 147–149
  Kitchen Thermometer, 149–150
  Kitchen Thermometer mini, 151
  partnership with HomeKit, 253
  Pro Candy Probe, 152
  thermometers, 151

iDevices community, sharing
    dishes with, 150
IFTT (IF This Then That) recipes, 280, 290
iGrill, 145. *See also* grill cleaning
    smoking food with, 148
    website, 148
iGrill 2
    features, 147
    illustration, 146
    using, 146–147
iGrill mini
    iDevices Connected App, 147
    illustration, 149
    LED light, 147
    meat temperatures, 147
iHarmony zoning, using with iComfort
    thermostat, 70
iHome, partnership with HomeKit, 253
iMacs, 240
Indego robotic mower
    cutting slopes, 219
    illustration, 219
    perimeter wire, 219
    PIN code, 219
    safety features, 219
    self-charging, 219
    website, 220
    yaw sensor, 219
Indigo Domotics website, 240
Insight Switch
    features, 279–280
    IFTT (IF This Then That) recipes, 280
    illustration, 280
installing
    August Smart Lock, 124
    ecobee3 thermostats, 64–66
    Google Cast extension, 183–184
    iComfort thermostat, 69
    Lockitron, 127–128
    Lyric thermostats, 55–58
    Nest thermostats, 58–59
    Trane thermostats, 71–72
INSTEON app, 42, 102
INSTEON hub
    accessing, 101
    dual-band technology, 101
    features, 101
    illustration, 101

incident alerts, 101
purchasing, 101
storage of settings, 101
website, 102
INSTEON Hub Starter Kit, 47–48
INSTEON LED bulbs, 98–99.
        See also LED bulbs
color temperature, 99
cost, 99
dimming feature, 99
hours lasting, 99
sockets, 98
using with motion sensors, 99
website, 99
INSTEON products
    2474DWH dimmer, 99
    2477D dimmer, 100
    2477DH dimmer, 99
    2477S dimmer, 99
    dual-band technology, 98
    energy monitoring, 97
    Leak Sensor, 162–163
    motion sensors, 97
    remote controls, 97
    security, 97
    smoke detection, 97
    sprinkler controls, 97
    SwitchLinc dimmers, 99
    thermostats, 97
    water leak sensor, 162–163
    Wi-Fi cameras, 97
INSTEON protocol, 20–21
Internet connectivity
    losing, 26
    providing, 25
intrusions, monitoring networks for, 30
iOS
    versus Android, 231
    smartphones, 228–231
    support for, 32
    tablets, 236–237
iOS 8, 231
iOS apps, keeping up to date, 245–246
iPad models
    Air, 236
    configurations, 237
    mini, 237
iPhones, 229–230

Iris Smart Kit, 48
iRobot cleaning automation
  Braava, 81–82
  DryDock Charging and Drying Stand, 80
  introduction of, 77
  Looj gutter cleaner, 302–303
  Mirra pool cleaner, 308–309
  NorthStar Navigation System, 81–82
  Roomba, 77–79
  Scooba floor cleaner, 79–80
  Virtual Wall, 79
  website, 82
iTunes, 166

• J •

JIBO robot, 303–304
John Deere TANGO E5, 217

• K •

Kevo deadbolt
  app, 129–130
  colored light ring, 130
  features, 130
  gaining access to, 129
  Inside-Outside technology, 130
  key fobs, 129
  lock with key fob, 131
  physical key, 129
  sharing ekeys, 129
  smart lock, 131
  SmartKey technology, 130
  support site, 130
  unlocking doors, 131
  user access, 130
Keychain passwords, using, 110
Kindle, 166
Kinect app, using with CastleOS, 260
kitchen automation
  benefits, 136–137
  conveniences, 145
  Crock-Pot Smart Slow Cooker,
      137–141
  GE Brillion technology, 143–145
  iDevices, 145–152
  Quirky Egg Minder, 153–154
  Smart ThinQ Refrigerator, 139–140

Whirlpool's 6th Sense Live
      Technology, 141–143
Kitchen Thermometers, 149–151
kits, WeMo Switch + Motion, 11
kitty litter
  cleaning up, 307
  self-cleaning box, 40
kitty toilet, 308
Kwikset
  Kevo deadbolt, 129–132
  partnership with HomeKit, 253
  website, 132

• L •

lamp module, 276–277. *See also*
      lighting technologies
laptops, on wireless networks, 24
laundry app, 82–83
lawn automation. *See also* robotic
      mowers worldwide
  benefits, 207
  Husqvarna, 211–214
  LawnBott, 214–216
  low maintenance, 207
  mowing, 207
  Robomow, 208–211
  saving money, 207
  tasks, 207
  watering, 207
lawn watering
  Cyber Rain, 220–222
  Rachio, 222–223
LawnBott models
  LB75DX, 214
  LB85EL, 214
  LB200EL, 214
  LB300EL, 214
  Lb02200 Spyder, 214–215
LawnBott mowers
  Ambrogio Remote app, 216
  battery life, 214
  EL models, 216
  GPS unit, 214
  perimeter wire, 215
  rain sensor, 214
  safety, 216
  securing with PIN, 214

LawnBott mowers (continued)
  SMS support, 216
  software updates, 214
  yard slopes, 214
Leak Sensor, availability of, 162
LED bulbs. See also INSTEON LED bulbs;
      TCP Connected lighting; WeMo's LED
      Lighting Starter Set
  in starter kits, 47
  using, 15–16
LED Lighting, 93, 282–283
Lennox thermostats
  app, 68
  features, 68–69
  iComfort alert, 68
  iComfort installation, 69
  iComfort model, 67–70
  iHarmony Zoning System, 70
  interface, 67
  Nuvango covers, 69
  One-Touch Away mode, 68
  remote control, 68
  touchscreen, 67–69
  using with HVAC units, 69
  Weather-on-Demand, 68
  website, 70
Leviton devices, 276–277
LG G Pad tablet, 238
LG G3 smartphone, 232
LG products
  Smart Laundry app, 82–83
  Smart ThinQ appliances, 82
  Smart ThinQ Range, 140–141
  Smart ThinQ Refrigerator,
      139–141
lighting, controlling, 14–15
lighting automation
  benefits, 91
  dimming, 91
  remote control, 91
  security features, 91
lighting devices, controlling with WeMo
      Switch, 108
Lighting Recipes
  Concentrate, 94
  Energize, 94
  Reading, 94
  using with hue app, 94

lighting technologies. See also lamp module
  Belkin, 107–108
  INSTEON, 97–102
  Morning settings, 92
  motion sensors, 92
  Party settings, 92
  Philips, 92–97
  presets, 92
  scheduling, 91
  Sleep settings, 92
  SmartThings, 104–106
  TCP, 102–104
  the Lighting University website, 94
Linksys, partnership with Staples, 262–263
Linux, support for, 32
Linux home automation software
  Minerva, 242
  Pytomation, 242
Litter-Robot II, 307–308
Lockitron
  app download, 128
  batteries, 128
  comparing to August, 127, 129
  features, 126–128
  illustration, 127–128
  installing, 127–128
  receiving notifications, 128
  SMS text messages, 128
  website, 129
locks. See also Yale products
  August Smart Lock, 123–125
  Schlage electronic, 122
locks, using for home security, 111
Logitech Harmony universal remotes
  IR only, 174
  website, 175
Lombard, Stuart, 63
Looj gutter cleaner, using, 302–303
Lowes website, 296–297
Lyric thermostats
  app download, 56–57
  configuring, 56
  connecting, 56
  creating account for, 56
  Geofencing feature, 57
  installing, 55–56
  instructions for installation, 56–57
  setting up, 56–57

temperature adjustment, 57
tools for installation, 56
using, 56–57
website, 56

• M •

Mac models
  mini, 240
  Pro, 240
MacBook models
  Air, 240
  Pro, 240
Macs. *See also* OS X
  iMacs, 240
  Indigo Domotics, 240
Marvell, partnership with
    HomeKit, 253
media services, subscribing to, 166
Miimo mower
  blades, 218
  cutting patterns, 219
  illustration, 218
  quietness, 218
  safety, 218
  self-charging, 218
  waterproof feature, 218
  website, 219
Minerva home automation
    software, 242
mini remotes, 48
Mirra pool cleaner, 308–309
monetary savings
  fuel, 16
  heating, 15
  LED bulbs, 15–16
  lighting, 15
  water leak detection, 15
mopping. *See also* floor cleaners
  floors with RoboMop, 82–84
  hard floors with Braava, 81–82
motion detectors, 14, 112, 119
motion sensor, Smart Home Security kit, 112
movies, watching on Apple TV, 177
mowing lawns. *See* lawn automation; robotic
    mowers worldwide
music systems, making wireless, 187
My Smart Appliances app, 143

• N •

NASA photo, 90
Neato Robotics. *See also* robots
  BotVac series, 85
  Boundary Markers, 85
  lasers, 84
  scanning and mapping rooms, 84
  size of items cleaned, 85
  vacuums, 84
  website, 85
  XV series, 85
needs assessment
  existing systems, 45
  home size, 43
  network issues, 45
  outlets and switches, 44
  Wi-Fi concerns, 44–45
  yard maintenance, 43–44
Nest Protect
  carbon monoxide detector,
    272–274
  smoke detector, 272
Nest thermostats
  account setup, 60
  competition with, 63
  features, 56, 59–60
  installing, 58–59
  Leaf logo, 60
  Learning model, 59–60
  Learning type, 56
  Mobile app, 60
  website, 59
Netatmo products
  JUNE device, 196–198
  partnership with HomeKit, 253
  Urban Weather Station, 193–195
  Weather Map website, 196
Netatmo Weather Station
  app, 195
  comparing to ARCHOS, 199
  green indicator, 195
  indoor module, 194–195
  outdoor module, 194
  red indicator, 195
  starter kit, 193
  website, 195
  yellow indicator, 195

NetCam
  features, 280
  illustration, 281
  microphone, 281
  motion sensors, 281
  night vision, 281
  setting up, 281–282
  speaker, 281
  using with WeMo app, 281
  viewing angle, 281
  viewing streaming video, 282
  website, 282
Netflix, 166, 168
network issues, 45. *See also* wireless networks
  recognizing, 25–26
  resolving, 27
network range, limitation of, 26
network speed, testing, 26
networked devices, securing, 28–29.
    See also devices
Nexia's Home Intelligence app, 72
Nexus Player, 181–182
Nokia smartphones, 234
NorthStar Navigation System, 81–82
Nuvango covers, using with Lennox
    thermostats, 69
Nvidia Shield tablet, 238

• O •

OnePlus One smartphone, 232
on/off modules, including in starter kits, 47
operating systems
  Android, 32
  iOS, 32
  Linux, 32
  OS X, 32
  Windows, 32
OS X. *See also* Macs
  browsers, 239
  keeping apps up to date, 247–248
  support for, 32
Osram Sylvania, partnership with
    HomeKit, 253
oven
  controlling with Brillion app, 143–145
  convection wall, 143
  temperature control, 13

• P •

Pandora, 168
panic pendants, 120
passwords, uses for, 110
PCs and Linux, 242–244
PCs and Windows
  browsers, 240
  Home Control Assistant, 241
  HomeSeer, 241
  HouseBot, 241
PCS Powerline Control Systems, 19
pet care products, 307
pet-feeding automation, 305–306
PetNet SmartFeeder, 305–306
Philips
  lighting products website, 94
  partnership with HomeKit, 253
Philips Hue products
  A19 bulbs, 269
  LightStrips, 270
  LivingColors Bloom, 269, 271
  LivingColors Iris, 269–271
  starter kit, 271
Pioneer sound systems, 168
Piper home security
  affordability, 134
  app, 133
  built-in camera, 133
  built-in siren, 133
  HD-quality video, 133
  intrusion, 133
  lack of monthly fees, 134
  multicolored LED, 133
  receiving notifications, 133
  upgrading functionality, 133
  website, 134
Pivot Power Genius power strip, 40–41
platform unity
  achieving, 251
  HomeKit, 252–255
  lack of, 250
  multi-protocol solutions, 257–263
  Revolv hubs, 257–259
  single path approach, 251–257
  Staples Connect, 262–263
Platinum App Bridge, 315
pliers, having, 31

plug-in lamp dimmer modules, 48
pool cleanup, automating, 308–309
power requirements, 33
power strip, Pivot Power Genius, 40–41,
    275–276
preparation, importance of, 23
privacy functions. *See* home security
Pro Candy Probe, 152
protocols. *See also* security protocols
  defined, 17
  INSTEON, 20–21
  UPB (Universal Powerline Bus) protocol,
    18–19
  Wi-Fi, 21–22
  X10, 18
  ZigBee, 20, 39
  Z-Wave, 19
Pulse app, 117
Pytomation home automation software, 242

• *Q* •

Quirky products
  Aros air-conditioner, 39
  Egg Minder, 153–154
  Pivot Power Genius power strip, 40–41
  Tripper sensor, 277–278
Quirky Spotter
  humidity detection, 275
  illustration, 274
  light detection, 275
  motion detection, 275
  placement, 275
  sensors, Quirky+GE Pivot Power Genius
  setting up, 275
  sound detection, 275
  temperature detection, 275
  website, 275
Quirky+GE Pivot Power Genius,
    275–276

• *R* •

Rachio Iro sprinkler system, 222
  comparing to Cyber Rain, 223
  website, 223
range automation. *See* Smart
    ThinQ Range

Real Living locks, 125–126
refrigerator automation
  Smart ThinQ, 139–142
  Whirlpool's 6th Sense Live
    Technology, 142
Remote app, using with Apple TV, 177–178
remote control dimmer switches, 47
Retina 5K, 241
Revolv app, 42
Revolv hubs. *See also* hub
  Belkin devices, 259
  compatible devices, 259
  features, 257–258
  GE devices, 259
  Honeywell devices, 259
  INSTEON devices, 259
  Leviton devices, 259
  Nest devices, 259
  Philips devices, 259
  setting up, 258–259
  Sonos devices, 259
  Trane devices, 259
  updates, 259
RoboMop
  interface, 83
  using, 84
  website, 84
Robomow
  app, 211
  automatic shut off, 211
  Child Lock, 211
  choosing, 209
  cutting lawn in rain, 211
  dual mowers, 208
  illustration, 209
  introduction of, 208
  keeping in yard, 210–211
  programming PIN for, 211
  quietness, 211
  return to charging station, 211
  Robomap tool, 210
  safety features, 211
  websites, 208
  yard measurement, 209–210
Robomow models
  RC306, 208
  RM510, 208
  RS612, 208

Robomow models *(continued)*
  RS622, 208
  RS630, 208–209
RoboSnail aquarium cleaner
  features, 88
  illustration, 87
  website, 88
robotic mowers worldwide. *See also* lawn
    automation
  Bosch, 219–220
  Honda, 218–219
  John Deere, 217
robots, JIBO, 303–304. *See also* Neato
    Robotics
Roker, Al, 191
Roku media player, 166
  1080p HD, 180
  app, 180–181
  built-in Wi-Fi, 180
  channels, 180
  features, 179
  illustration, 179
  introduction of, 178
  remote, 180
  Streaming Stick, 179–180
  traveling with, 179
  versions, 179
  website, 180
  wireless networks, 25–26
Roomba robotic vacuums
  alert, 79
  charging station, 78
  Clean button, 78
  comparing to Scooba, 79
  features, 78–79
  indicator light, 79
  interface, 78
  number of units sold, 78
  programming, 79
  smart unit, 78
  spot cleaning, 79
  using Virtual Wall with, 79
  website, 77, 79
Roomie home entertainment
  Acer support, 171
  Apple support, 171
  Denon support, 171
  Google support, 171
  INSTEON support, 171
  iOS-only device, 172
  IP Compatibility, 169
  IR (Infrared) Compatibility, 169–170
  JVC support, 171
  LG support, 171
  Lutron support, 171
  Nest support, 171
  Onkyo support, 171
  Panasonic support, 171
  Philips support, 171
  Pioneer support, 171
  product support, 171
  Roku support, 171
  Samsung support, 171
  Serial Compatibility, 169
  Sharp support, 171
  Sonos support, 171
  Sony support, 171
  Tivo support, 171
  virtual remote, 170
  website, 172
  Yamaha support, 171
round thermostats, 54–55
routers. *See* wireless routers
Rubbermaid's Auto Flush Tank
  battery life, 313
  illustration, 314
  user-settable modes, 313

• S •

Samsung Galaxy
  smartphones, 232–233
  Tab S tablet, 238
Savant website, 10
Schlage
  Connect line, 120–121
  electronic locks, 122
  partnership with HomeKit, 253
  Touch line, 121–122
  website, 122
Scooba floor cleaner
  bacteria removal, 80
  comparing to Roomba, 79
  fluid tank, 79
  linoleum, 80
  marble, 80

scrubbing feature, 79
sealed hardwoods, 80
slate, 80
squeegee feature, 80
stone, 80
sweeping feature, 79
tile, 80
using, 79–80
water usage, 79
website, 80
Scott, Willard, 191
screwdriver, having, 31
securing networked devices
    firewalls, 29
    protocols, 29
security. *See* home security
security features, using, 29
security protocols, enabling, 29. *See also*
        protocols
sensors, Quirky Tripper, 277–278
shades, automating, 314–316
signal quality, considering, 26, 45
Skybell, partnership with HomeKit, 253
SkyPort technology, using with
        ColorTouch, 74
slow cooker
    capacity, 138
    cooking time, 138
    cord storage, 138
    features, 138
    handles, 138
    illustration, 138
    temperature, 138
    website, 138
Smart Brew coffeemaker, 310
Smart Home Security kit
    hub, 112
    moisture sensor, 112
    motion sensor, 112
    SmartPower Outlet, 113
    SmartSense Open/Closed Sensor, 113
    SmartSense Presence Sensor, 113
smart locks, using apps with, 14
smart outlet, WeMo Switch, 46–47
smart thermostats
    Belkin, 61–63
    benefits, 52–53
    ecobee, 63–67

Honeywell, 54–57
introduction of, 63
Lennox, 67–70
Nest, 58–60
saving time, 53
Trane, 70–73
Venstar, 73–74
Smart ThinQ Range
    boiling times, 140
    capacity, 140
    convection heating, 140
    cooking times, 140
    illustration, 141
    infrared grilling, 140
    Smart Access Range app, 141
Smart ThinQ Refrigerator
    Food Channel recipes, 139
    food expiration dates, 139
    food inventory, 139
    sending recipes to range, 139
    touchscreen, 139–140
    weather app, 139
Smart ThinQ technology, washer
        and dryer, 82
Smarter Home Security
    FortrezZ Siren Strobe Alarm, 114
    SmartPower Outlet, 114
    SmartSense Motion Sensor, 114
    SmartSense Open/Closed Sensors, 114
Smartest Home Security kit
    Jasco Pluggable Light Dimmer Outlet, 114
    SmartSense Moisture Sensor, 114
    SmartSense Motion Sensors, 114
    SmartSense Presence Sensor, 114
SmartFeeder, 305–306
Smarthome website, 285–287
SmartKey technology, 130
smartphones
    Android, 231–232
    explained, 229
    iOS, 228–231
    Nokia, 234
    Windows Phone, 232–235
    on wireless networks, 24
SmartStart car automation, 311–312
SmartThings, 48
    Aeon Labs Minimote, 106
    app, 105

SmartThings *(continued)*
  Hub, 104–105
  IFTT (IF This Then That) recipes, 290
  Jasco Pluggable Light Dimmer Outlet, 106
  lighting automation kit, 105–106
  Mobile app, 106
  partnerships, 105
  SmartPower Outlet, 106
  starter kit, 48
  website, 114, 289–290
smoke detection, 120, 272
smoking food with iGrill, 148
SNUPI Technologies, Wally product,
    158–159
software. *See* apps; automation software
Sonos HiFi wireless speakers, 186–188
  CONNECT:AMP, 187
  connecting, 188
  controlling, 188
  illustrations, 187
  PLAY:1, 186
  PLAY:3, 186
  PLAY:5, 187
  PLAYBAR, 187
  SUB subwoofer, 186
  website, 188
Sony Walkman, 166
Sony Xperia
  smartphone, 232
  Z3 Tablet Compact, 238
sound system manufacturers, 168
SoundTouch speakers
  app, 186
  connecting, 185–186
  station presets, 186
  streaming music, 185
speakers. *See* Bose sound systems; Sonos
    HiFi wireless speakers; SoundTouch
    speakers
sprinkler controls
  connecting to Internet, 220–221
  Rachio, 222
Staples, partnership with Linksys, 262–263
Staples Connect platform unity
  Android app, 262
  features, 262
  functionality, 262
  iOS app, 262

web app, 262
website, 263
starter kits
  hub, 47
  INSTEON, 48
  Iris Smart Kit, 48
  LED bulbs, 47
  mini remotes, 48
  on/off modules, 47
  plug-in lamp dimmer modules, 48
  remote control dimmer switches, 47
  SmartThings, 48
  Viper Starter Kit, 48
  wireless motion sensors, 47
streaming media, 166
  video, 176–178
  on wireless networks, 25
sweeping floors with Scooba, 79
swimming pools, automating cleanup of,
    308–309

● T ●

tablets
  Android, 237–238
  features, 235–236
  iOS, 236–237
  Windows, 241–243
  on wireless networks, 24
TCP Connected lighting. *See also* LED bulbs
  compatibility with Wink system, 104
  LED bulbs, 102–103
  starter kit, 103
  system setup, 104
  website, 104
technology overview, 16–17
television. *See* Apple TV; Google TV
temperatures. *See* home temperatures;
    thermostats
testing, network speed, 26
Texas Instruments, partnership with
    HomeKit, 253
thermometer. *See* Kitchen Thermometers
thermostats. *See also* home
    temperatures
  bimetallic strips, 54
  bulbs, 54
  manual type, 52–53

mechanical, 54
operating remotely, 15
programming, 53
technology, 53–54
wax pellets, 54
for weather stations, 192
toilet flushing, automating, 312–314
tools
pliers, 31
screwdriver, 31
voltmeter, 31
wire cutters, 31
Trane thermostats
ComfortLink II XL950, 70–71
ComfortLink zoning, 72–73
Nexia's Home Intelligence app, 72
self-installation, 71–72
third-party apps, 71–72
website, 71
Tripper sensor. *See* Quirky Tripper sensor

• U •

Ubuntu Linux distribution, 242–243
Ultimate One. *See* Harmony Ultimate One
remote
unity. *See* platform unity
universal products, using, 46–47
UPB (Universal Powerline Bus) protocol,
18–19

• V •

vacuuming. *See* Roomba robotic
vacuums
vehicles, starting remotely, 311–312
Venstar thermostats
ColorTouch model, 73–74
website, 74
vinyl records, 166
Viper products
SmartStart, 311–312
Starter Kit, 48
Virtual Wall, using with Roomba, 79
Vivint's Smart Home Security
package
carbon monoxide detectors, 120

control from touchscreen, 119
door/window sensors, 119
glass-break detectors, 120
key fob, 119
monitoring, 117
motion detectors, 119
nonemergency alerts, 119
panic pendants, 120
smoke detection, 120
text alerts, 119
touchscreen, 119
wireless system, 118
yard sign, 119
voltmeter, having, 31

• W •

Wally app, 159–160
Wally water monitoring
batteries for sensors, 158–159
hub, 158
sensors, 158
website, 159
WallyHome
Ethernet cable, 159
hub, 159
power cord, 159
sensors, 159
water
brushing teeth with, 156
drinking daily, 156
washing items with, 156
water conditions, tracking, 164
water damage, expense of, 156
water leak
detecting, 15–16, 156
sensor by INSTEON, 162–163
water monitoring
Driblet, 160–162
INSTEON products, 162–163
methods of, 157
reasons for, 156–157
Wally, 158–160
water usage, monitoring, 156–157
watering crops, 156
weather app, checking on Smart ThinQ
Refrigerator, 139

weather stations. *See also* home
    temperatures
  AcuRite, 199–202
  ARCHOS, 197–199
  Netatmo, 193–197
  thermostat, 192
Weather Underground website, 202–203
web pages, using to control devices, 32
webcams, Dropcam, 271–272
websites. *See also* apps
  AcuRite Weather Environment System, 202
  ADT Pulse system, 117
  Alarm.com, 116
  Amazon, 290–292
  ARCHOS Weather Station, 199
  August Smart Lock, 123, 125
  Belkin Insight Switch, 280
  Belkin Switch + Motion, 115
  Blumoo home entertainment, 173
  Bosch Indego robotic mower, 220
  Bose SoundTouch speakers, 186
  Brillion initiative, 144
  CastleOS, 261
  CEA (Consumer Electronics Association),
    288–289
  CNET, 287–288
  ComfortLink II Zoning System, 73
  Consumer Reports, 299
  Control4, 10
  Crestron, 10
  Crock-Pot Smart Slow Cooker, 138
  Cyber Rain, 222
  Driblet water monitoring, 162
  Dropcam webcam, 272
  ecobee3 thermostats, 64, 67
  Egg Minder by Quirky, 154
  GE network security, 144
  Google Cast extension, 183
  Grillbot, 86
  Holmes humidifier, 317
  Home Controls, 292–293
  Home Depot, 256, 297–298
  Home Entertainment, 10
  HomeKit developers, 255
  Honda Miimo mower, 219
  Honeywell thermostats, 55, 57
  hue products, 97
  Hunter Douglas Platinum system, 316

Husqvarna Automower, 214
iGrill devices, 148
iGrill products, 148
Indigo Domotics, 240
INSTEON dimmers, 100
INSTEON hub, 102
INSTEON Hub Starter Kit, 47–48
INSTEON LED bulbs, 99
INSTEON starter kits, 48
iOS 8, 231
iPhones, 231
Iris Smart Kit, 48
iRobot cleaning automation, 82
JIBO robot, 304
John Deere TANGO E5, 217
Kevo deadbolt, 130
Kwikset, 132
Lennox thermostats, 70
LG Smart ThinQ appliances, 82
the Lighting University, 94
Litter-Robot II, 307
Lockitron, 129
Logitech Harmony universal remotes, 175
Looj gutter cleaner, 303
Lowes, 296–297
Lyric thermostats, 56
Minerva home automation software, 242
Neato Robotics, 85
Nest Protect, 274
Netatmo Weather Map, 196
Netatmo Weather Station, 195
NetCam, 282
Piper home security, 134
power strip, 276
Pro Candy Probe, 152
Pytomation home automation
  software, 242
Quirky Spotter, 275
Quirky Tripper sensor, 278
Quirky+GE Pivot Power Genius, 276
Rachio Iro sprinkler system, 223
Revolv hubs, 259
RoboMop, 84
Robomow, 208–209
RoboSnail aquarium cleaner, 88
Roomba cleaning automation, 77, 79
Roomie home entertainment, 172
Savant, 10

Schlage, 122
Scooba floor cleaner, 80
Smarthome, 285–287
SmartThings products, 106, 114, 289–290
SmartThings starter kit, 48
Sonos HiFi wireless speakers, 188
SoundTouch speakers, 186
Staples Connect platform unity, 263
TCP products, 104
Trane thermostats, 71
Venstar thermostats, 74
Viper SmartStart, 312
Viper Starter Kit, 48
Wally products, 159
Weather Underground, 202–203
WeMo products, 108
WeMo Switch, 63
Whirlpool smart appliances, 143
Wi-Fi Alliance, 22
Windows Phones, 234
X10 protocol, 18
Yale locks, 126
ZigBee Alliance, 295–296
ZigBee protocol, 20
Z-Wave Alliance, 19
Z-Wave.com, 294–295
WeMo app, using, 108
WeMo Motion, illustration, 115
WeMo products. *See also* Belkin products
    Insight Switch, 279–280
    LED Lighting Starter Set, 282–283
    NetCam, 280–282
    smart bulbs, 283
    website, 108
WeMo Switch, 279
    app, 62
    connecting to devices, 61
    controlling lighting devices, 108
    features, 108
    illustration, 115
    interface, 62
    + Motion, 11
    plugging in, 61
    setting up, 61–62
    smart outlet, 46–47
    website, 63
WeMo's LED Lighting Starter Set, 107–108.
    See also LED bulbs

Whirlpool products, app for, app for, 143
Whirlpool's 6th Sense Live Technology
    smart dishwasher, 142–143
    smart side-by-side refrigerator, 142
Wi-Fi cameras, using, 14
Wi-Fi networks, unauthorized use of, 27.
    See also wireless networks
Wi-Fi protocol, 21–22, 24
Wi-Fi signals, blocking, 45
Windows and PCs
    browsers, 240
    Home Control Assistant, 241
    HomeSeer, 241
    HouseBot, 241
    support for, 32
Windows apps, keeping up to date, 248
Windows Phones, 232–235
Windows tablets, 241–243
Wink app
    compatible products, 256
    downloading, 39
    logo, 257
    partnership with Home Depot, 257
    using, 269
    using with Home Depot automation, 256
Wink hub and app, 31–32, 268
Wink system, compatibility with TCP, 104
wire cutter, having, 31
wireless motion sensors, 47
wireless networks. *See also* network issues;
    Wi-Fi networks
    Apple TV on, 25
    bandwidth, 24
    Chromecast on, 25
    laptops on, 24
    monitoring for intrusions, 30
    Roku devices on, 25–26
    smartphones on, 24
    streaming media on, 25
    tablets on, 24
    unauthorized use of, 27, 30
wireless range extender
    purchasing, 27
    using, 28
wireless routers
    getting multiple, 27
    identifying devices on, 30
    relocating, 27

wireless routers *(continued)*
  upgrading, 27
  using, 25, 45
wiring, getting done, 33–35
Withings, partnership with HomeKit, 253

X10 protocol, 18

Yale products. *See also* deadbolt; locks
  Real Living locks, 125–126
  Touchscreen Lever Lock, 125

yard, measuring for Robomow, 209–210
YouTube, 168

• Z •

ZigBee Alliance website, 295–296
ZigBee protocol, 20, 39
Z-Wave protocol, 19
Z-Wave.com website, 294–295

About the Author

Dwight Spivey (Mobile, Alabama) has been a technical author and editor for nearly a decade, but has been a bona fide technophile for close to three of them. He's the author *of How to Do Everything Pages, Keynote & Numbers* (McGraw-Hill, 2014), *OS X Mavericks Portable Genius* (Wiley, 2013), and many more books covering the tech gamut. His technology experience is extensive, consisting of OS X, iOS, Android, Linux, and Windows operating systems in general; desktop publishing software; laser printers and drivers; color and color management; and networking. His love of tech led him to discover the smart home and the wizardry behind what makes them tick, and *Home Automation For Dummies* was the fruit borne thereof.

Dedication

For Granddaddy, Grandmama, Dad, Aunt Faye, Uncle Preston, Uncle Winston, Uncle Frank, Uncle Larry, and Uncle Kenneth.

Author's Acknowledgments

Many sincere thanks to my agent, Carole Jelen of Waterside, and Wiley's own Aaron Black for steering me to this project.

The crew behind this book was so truly critical to its completion, and I want you all to know how grateful I am for your professionalism, dedication, hard work, and patience in working with me. Thank you to the following wonderful people, from the bottom of my heart: Katie Mohr, Senior Acquisitions Editor; Lynn Northrup, Project Editor; Earl Boysen, Technical Editor; Sheree Montgomery, Project Coordinator; and Debbye Butler, Copy Editor.

Finally, I must thank my wife, Cindy, and our four blessings from God, Victoria, Devyn, Emi, and Reid, for being so patient with me. Through late nights, early mornings, and many absences during this project, they've been my rock and my reason. I love you guys.

We're proud of this book; please send us your comments at http://dummies.custhelp.com. For other comments, please contact our Customer Care Department within the U.S. at 877-762-2974, outside the U.S. at 317-572-3993, or fax 317-572-4002.

Some of the people who helped bring this book to market include the following:

Publisher's Acknowledgments

Acquisitions and Editorial

Senior Acquisitions Editor: Katie Mohr

Project Editor: Lynn Northrup

Copy Editor: Debbye Butler

Technical Editor: Earl Boysen

Editorial Assistant: Claire Brock

Sr. Editorial Assistant: Cherie Case

Project Coordinator: Sheree Montgomery

Cover Image: © iStock.com/AAA-pictures

pple & Mac

ad For Dummies,
th Edition
78-1-118-72306-7

hone For Dummies,
th Edition
78-1-118-69083-3

Macs All-in-One
or Dummies, 4th Edition
78-1-118-82210-4

S X Mavericks
or Dummies
78-1-118-69188-5

logging & Social Media

acebook For Dummies,
th Edition
78-1-118-63312-0

ocial Media Engagement
or Dummies
78-1-118-53019-1

WordPress For Dummies,
th Edition
78-1-118-79161-5

usiness

tock Investing
or Dummies, 4th Edition
78-1-118-37678-2

nvesting For Dummies,
th Edition
78-0-470-90545-6

Personal Finance
For Dummies, 7th Edition
978-1-118-11785-9

QuickBooks 2014
For Dummies
978-1-118-72005-9

Small Business Marketing
Kit For Dummies,
3rd Edition
978-1-118-31183-7

Careers

Job Interviews
For Dummies, 4th Edition
978-1-118-11290-8

Job Searching with Social
Media For Dummies,
2nd Edition
978-1-118-67856-5

Personal Branding
For Dummies
978-1-118-11792-7

Resumes For Dummies,
6th Edition
978-0-470-87361-8

Starting an Etsy Business
For Dummies, 2nd Edition
978-1-118-59024-9

Diet & Nutrition

Belly Fat Diet For Dummies
978-1-118-34585-6

Mediterranean Diet
For Dummies
978-1-118-71525-3

Nutrition For Dummies,
5th Edition
978-0-470-93231-5

Digital Photography

Digital SLR Photography
All-in-One For Dummies,
2nd Edition
978-1-118-59082-9

Digital SLR Video &
Filmmaking For Dummies
978-1-118-36598-4

Photoshop Elements 12
For Dummies
978-1-118-72714-0

Gardening

Herb Gardening
For Dummies, 2nd Edition
978-0-470-61778-6

Gardening with Free-Range
Chickens For Dummies
978-1-118-54754-0

Health

Boosting Your Immunity
For Dummies
978-1-118-40200-9

Diabetes For Dummies,
4th Edition
978-1-118-29447-5

Living Paleo For Dummies
978-1-118-29405-5

Big Data

Big Data For Dummies
978-1-118-50422-2

Data Visualization
For Dummies
978-1-118-50289-1

Hadoop For Dummies
978-1-118-60755-8

Language &
Foreign Language

500 Spanish Verbs
For Dummies
978-1-118-02382-2

English Grammar
For Dummies, 2nd Edition
978-0-470-54664-2

French All-in-One
For Dummies
978-1-118-22815-9

German Essentials
For Dummies
978-1-118-18422-6

Italian For Dummies,
2nd Edition
978-1-118-00465-4

Available in print and e-book formats.

Available wherever books are sold. **For more information or to order direct visit www.dummies.com**

Math & Science

Algebra I For Dummies,
2nd Edition
978-0-470-55964-2

Anatomy and Physiology
For Dummies, 2nd Edition
978-0-470-92326-9

Astronomy For Dummies,
3rd Edition
978-1-118-37697-3

Biology For Dummies,
2nd Edition
978-0-470-59875-7

Chemistry For Dummies,
2nd Edition
978-1-118-00730-3

1001 Algebra II Practice
Problems For Dummies
978-1-118-44662-1

Microsoft Office

Excel 2013 For Dummies
978-1-118-51012-4

Office 2013 All-in-One
For Dummies
978-1-118-51636-2

PowerPoint 2013
For Dummies
978-1-118-50253-2

Word 2013 For Dummies
978-1-118-49123-2

Music

Blues Harmonica
For Dummies
978-1-118-25269-7

Guitar For Dummies,
3rd Edition
978-1-118-11554-1

iPod & iTunes
For Dummies, 10th Edition
978-1-118-50864-0

Programming

Beginning Programming
with C For Dummies
978-1-118-73763-7

Excel VBA Programming
For Dummies, 3rd Edition
978-1-118-49037-2

Java For Dummies,
6th Edition
978-1-118-40780-6

Religion & Inspiration

The Bible For Dummies
978-0-7645-5296-0

Buddhism For Dummies,
2nd Edition
978-1-118-02379-2

Catholicism For Dummies,
2nd Edition
978-1-118-07778-8

Self-Help & Relationships

Beating Sugar Addiction
For Dummies
978-1-118-54645-1

Meditation For Dummies,
3rd Edition
978-1-118-29144-3

Seniors

Laptops For Seniors
For Dummies, 3rd Edition
978-1-118-71105-7

Computers For Seniors
For Dummies, 3rd Edition
978-1-118-11553-4

iPad For Seniors
For Dummies, 6th Edition
978-1-118-72826-0

Social Security
For Dummies
978-1-118-20573-0

Smartphones & Tablets

Android Phones
For Dummies, 2nd Edition
978-1-118-72030-1

Nexus Tablets
For Dummies
978-1-118-77243-0

Samsung Galaxy S 4
For Dummies
978-1-118-64222-1

Samsung Galaxy Tabs
For Dummies
978-1-118-77294-2

Test Prep

ACT For Dummies,
5th Edition
978-1-118-01259-8

ASVAB For Dummies,
3rd Edition
978-0-470-63760-9

GRE For Dummies,
7th Edition
978-0-470-88921-3

Officer Candidate Tests
For Dummies
978-0-470-59876-4

Physician's Assistant Exam
For Dummies
978-1-118-11556-5

Series 7 Exam For Dummies
978-0-470-09932-2

Windows 8

Windows 8.1 All-in-One
For Dummies
978-1-118-82087-2

Windows 8.1 For Dummies
978-1-118-82121-3

Windows 8.1 For Dummies
Book + DVD Bundle
978-1-118-82107-7

_e_ Available in print and e-book formats.

Available wherever books are sold. **For more information or to order direct visit www.dummies.com**

Take Dummies with you everywhere you go!

Whether you are excited about e-books, want more from the web, must have your mobile apps, or are swept up in social media, Dummies makes everything easier.

Leverage the Power

For Dummies is the global leader in the reference category and one of the most trusted and highly regarded brands in the world. No longer just focused on books, customers now have access to the For Dummies content they need in the format they want. Let us help you develop a solution that will fit your brand and help you connect with your customers.

Advertising & Sponsorships

Connect with an engaged audience on a powerful multimedia site, and position your message alongside expert how-to content.

Targeted ads • Video • Email marketing • Microsites • Sweepstakes sponsorship

21 Million Monthly Page Views & 13 Million Unique Visitors

# of For Dummies

Custom Publishing

Reach a global audience in any language by creating a solution that will differentiate you from competitors, amplify your message, and encourage customers to make a buying decision.

Apps • Books • eBooks • Video • Audio • Webinars

Brand Licensing & Content

Leverage the strength of the world's most popular reference brand to reach new audiences and channels of distribution.

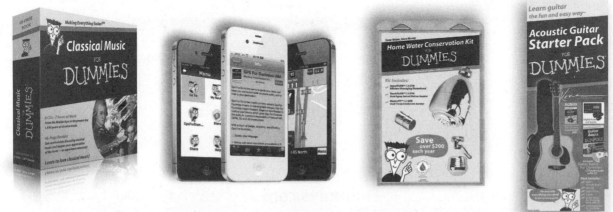

For more information, visit www.Dummies.com/biz

FOR
DUMMIES
A Wiley Brand

Dummies products make life easier!

- DIY
- Consumer Electronics
- Crafts

- Software
- Cookware
- Hobbies

- Videos
- Music
- Games
- and More!

For more information, go to **Dummies.com** and search the store by category.

FOR
DUMMIES
A Wiley Brand